M.W.Fifer
Healer·Prophet·Fool

to my friend
Jim Henderson

Gerd Asche

Gerd Asche

Order this book online at www.trafford.com
or email orders@trafford.com

Most Trafford titles are also available at major online book retailers.

Note for Librarians: A cataloguing record for this book is available from Library
and Archives Canada at www.collectionscanada.ca/amicus/index-e.html

Printed in Victoria, BC, Canada.

ISBN: 978-1-4251-7769-0 (soft)
ISBN: 978-1-4251-7770-6 (ebook)

*Our mission is to efficiently provide the world's finest, most comprehensive
book publishing service, enabling every author to experience success.
To find out how to publish your book, your way, and have it available
worldwide, visit us online at www.trafford.com/10510*

Trafford rev. 10/7/2009

www.trafford.com

North America & international
toll-free: 1 888 232 4444 (USA & Canada)
phone: 250 383 6864 ♦ fax: 812 355 4082

To my wife,
Doctor Ursula Asche,
who
made it all possible.

ACKNOWLEDGEMENTS

The epic of Doctor Fifer's odyssey and the imprint of his struggle on the infant Colony of British Columbia are the sum of extensive research, incurring numerous debts from generous contributors and their agencies. Members of our communities of Hope and Yale, British Columbia, among them the late Augustine (Gus) Milliken, noted historian and archaeologist, have added the anecdotal spiciness of local folklore. My thanks go to Frances Thomas of Hope, British Columbia, for her enthusiastic help in deciphering near-illegible historical manuscripts into hard copy, and to Bruce Mason, curator of the Yale Museum, who has clarified details in the history of Yale and introduced me to the technique of safe, retort-less, gold extraction. Lawren Grace, I.C.T., of Hope, British Columbia, has created the book design and given a great deal of good advice. To John Gonzales, Senior Librarian (ret.) of the California State Library in Sacramento, I have contracted my debt for recovering the protagonist's track, vanished due to the name change from Pfeiffer to Fifer, and for facilitating access to the early 19th century California newspapers, mediated through the Fraser Valley Regional interlibrary loan. The assistance of the professional staffs of the Provincial Archives in Victoria, the map vault of the Surveyor General for British Columbia in Victoria, the Special Collection of the University of British Columbia in Vancouver, the Hudson's Bay Archives in Winnipeg, Manitoba, the Redpath Library of McGill University in Montreal, the Bancroft Library of the University of California, Berkeley, the Presidio Army Museum, San Francisco, the National Archives in Washington, D. C., and the Newspaper Museum of the British Library in Colindale, London, are appreciated. I express my gratitude to the editors of the Journals of the British Columbia Medical Association and the Canadian Medical Association, for publishing earlier selections of the monograph. Particularly, and not least, I am indebted to writer Joan Bridgeman of Hope, British Columbia, whose literary talents and keen interest in the history of our province have made this project a reality.

Yale, British Columbia

July 2008

1

Yale, British Columbia, August 7, 1861

Knock! Knock! Knock! KNOCK!

"Ah Chung!"

The voice calling my name is as brusque as the knock. I do not answer. I know who it is. Mr. Tennent, the magistrate's clerk. I know what he wants. 'You unLerStan?' his words mock me as the Eviction Notice atop the shingle on the door mocks the good name of the doctor, my master.

My master, Doctor Fifer, is dead, murdered, leaving me, his Chinaman, his "boy", his servant-cum-assistant, alone in his abandoned house, hiding from men who were his friends.

Knock! Knock! Knock! KNOCK!

The sound of destiny, of my ill fortune. The order being re-tacked to the door says I must be cleared out by the end of the month. That was seven days ago. Seven long nights. I stand motionless, holding my breath, my heart pounding, waiting, listening, until I am certain that the unwelcome intruder has gone.

It has been a long day, stooped over, packing; I step from the empty house and stretch my legs, my back. The fresh air is a welcome embrace. The sun has dipped behind Mount Lincoln but its light still guides my feet to the path along the water which the doctor and I walked every evening. The almighty Fraser River can be malicious. With its brown waters rushing, its current deceptive, its undertow is dangerous, ready to take a man in an instant, even at this low-water season; it is another river of tears.

I lean into the warm August wind as it pushes up river, its breath sucking the juices from the scored salmon weighing down the Indian drying racks. It is as if the Lord of the Winds has flung his burlap bag over his shoulder and is walking away from me in anger, blowing sharp sand in my face. He pulls my queue like a drunken miner and lifts my frock coat up to my waist.

Now, with the doctor dead, I walk alone, along the river pathway, over to the graveyard. At twilight, I visit him here, in this cemetery on this newly-cleared slope, the resting place of my only friend, my protector.

I sit here, on this patch of dry grass by the fresh grave, to be with him in spirit, the way that we took tea before bedtime, when I would tell him of my day's progress.

But wait! Footsteps, interrupting our evening ritual. Someone is approaching. Trouble? Danger? What if a White man were to discover me, a lone Chinaman, a heathen, here in the shadows in a Christian cemetery? I must be cautious, until I can determine who comes.

Reverend Crickmer. A friend. What can he be wanting here, alone? "Good evening, Reverend Crickmer."

"Ah Chung! I didn't see you there, behind that stump. I did not expect to meet anyone; How are you doing? I hear that Mr. Tennent is giving you trouble about vacating the house?"

"I am managing. Thank you, Reverend Crickmer. I cannot change destiny, sir." Indeed, the coins I cast this morning counsel 'Perseverance at the foot of the Golden Mountain, above journey before good fortune,' but I know not to speak of divination to the reverend. "I am busy packing; soon my duties will be completed and I will be free to go." But to go where? To do what? This too I do not mention.

"This is a terrible business," the reverend responds. "I saw the advertisement in the *Victoria Colonist* last week. 'To the Medical Profession.

TO BE SOLD BY PUBLIC AUCTION, at YALE, British Columbia, by order of the Mortgagees, on the 31ˢᵗ May next, (unless previously disposed of by private contract,) the House in Front Street, Yale, Store Fixings, Stock in Trade, Furniture, and Effects of THE LATE DR. FIFER' An 'eligible opportunity', 'a lucrative business,' 'a thriving locality' it concludes. I cannot believe it.

"I cannot believe that he is gone, Ah Chung. I remember as if it were yesterday, rather than last month. The day after the American celebration it was. The fifth of July. I was calling at the post for parish mail, for a letter from the bishop in London, long due. The place was busy. It was shortly after six, when you burst through the door, with a loud, out-of-breath 'Murder! My master is shot! Doctor Fifer is dead! What can I do?'

I heard you cry out these words, Ah Chung. My heart wanted to stop. All I could think to do was dash home, to Mrs. Crickmer, to tell her the news. She saw me walking in, my face devoid of all colour, and as she rushed to me all I could utter was: 'Oh, Sophia, an incomprehensible crime! Our friend! Fifer! Murdered! Shot to death by a patient!' Sophia, Mrs. Crickmer, could only gasp: 'Oh, Dear Lord, no!' We fell into each other's arms and I held her there, for fear she might faint. All we could do was comfort each other.

"And she, my beloved wife, said something that struck me, and I remember her words as if she said them here tonight. 'Isn't it strange?' Mrs. Crickmer exclaimed. 'I saw the doctor passing by the house at three o'clock this afternoon. I could not help noticing his unusual appearance; how he hung his head in a peculiar fashion and swung his arms. He looked so sad. I cannot imagine him dead. Dear Lord, may his soul rest in peace.' Mrs. Crickmer had sensed in the poor man's unusual deportment some vague premonition that he was walking straight to his doom."

So involved is Reverend Crickmer in reliving the events of that fateful day that he only now notices the effect of his story upon me, the listener and the victim's right-hand man. "Oh, Ah Chung. I am sorry. You must miss him more than all of us."

"Yes, I do miss him, sir. We were like a family; the doctor called it "a symbiotic experience," living in close relationship, each benefiting from the association. Were it not for Doctor Fifer, I would be a nameless Celestial, languishing in the federal penitentiary at San Quentin, California, doing hard labour, perhaps long dead. Since the day Dr. Fifer, when he was the prison doctor, rescued me from unjust incarceration, I have served him with gratitude, as his Chinaman and medical assistant. I stood by him in the hard times in San Francisco when, to avoid persecution, he changed from Doctor Pfeiffer to Doctor Fifer—an ineffective measure—-and I accompanied him on the flight north to Yale in the British Territories." I refrain from saying how I truly feel–that his murder has left me alone, without friend or protector.

"With respect, sir, your wife's, Mrs. Crickmer's, notion is correct. Dr. Fifer was troubled by bad omens and bad luck. He gave up the notion of being invulnerable when he received word of the death of a good friend, a fellow doctor, in San Francisco, shortly after Christmas, and more recently, of the suicide of another friend, also a doctor, haunted by the actions of the Vigilance Committee. Finally, the suicide of Doctor Sponeyk, after his arrival from Strasburg, Germany, gave him melancholy forebodings. And something about Lady Franklin's visit disturbed him, her search, as the devoted wife, longing for any trace of her lost husband, and the lack of support from the government in her search. When the news arrived of the bombings in Charleston, the impending war between the States shocked him too. 'To think that democracy should come to this! Are these signs the harbingers of an apocalypse?' the doctor wondered. Then, there were professional disappointments. He had discovered that the drug aconite, extracted from the roots of wolfsbane, relieved his patient Robert Wall's sexual difficulties; instead of a thank you and paying the fee, the lad turned against him. Rumours of Wall's threatening to kill him reached Dr. Fifer some weeks ago. 'Too much darkness, Ah Chung; it does not bode well,' he had tried to tell me. I should have done something, but what?"

The parson nods, understanding my despair. "We had all heard the rumours, Ah Chung. But what could anyone have done? The doctor was well respected here; he has been our friend ever since our arrival from England more than a year ago."

By 'our friend' I know the parson speaks for himself and his wife. Indeed, Dr. Fifer was both friend and landlord, having converted his first office building into an accommodation suitable for the Anglican minister and his wife.

"He was everyone's friend, Ah Chung. Who could imagine anyone wanting to harm him? I know you are aware of the doctor's contributions to the civic activities of our community. We had just begun to work on the Great Exhibition Committee, to ensure that Yale and the Colony of British Columbia are suitably represented in London next year. He volunteered to be the chairman. At the first meeting, I took the cleric's liberty to open with an invocation, asking the Lord's blessing upon our committee's work. And the doctor said, 'Thank you, Reverend. That was most appropriate for our first meeting.' Another committee member, Mr. Allard, as you know, a French-speaker and an irreverent Papist, only laughed. He knew that the doctor was a good Methodist, and that he meant by 'first' that my prayers are inappropriate for subsequent meetings. That's just the kind of person Dr. Fifer was, showing respect to every member, but favouring none. 'We are grateful to have God's representative on board,' the doctor confided to me after we adjourned."

The reverend is smiling at the memory of his friend's gentle rebuke. I do not try to explain to him how Dr. Fifer felt about the separation of church and state and his opposition to favouring any one established church in the colony.

"Dr. Fifer came to Yale to get away from the world of violent conflicts, not to enrich himself monetarily but to practice medicine and surgery in peace."

The Reverend's words and intonation remind me of the eulogy he delivered at Dr. Fifer's funeral. As a public speaker, he likes to memorize his sermons, and takes every opportunity to practice his elocution. "Although Doctor Fifer was an American citizen and a veteran of the Mexican War, he keenly proved his loyalty to the new country." Reverend Crickmer's voice has lost its shakiness and now rings with the firmness of conviction.

"Full of enthusiasm, he took on the duties as chairman of the Yale Town Council, the first mayor in the Fraser Valley, a *primus inter pares* among the many Americans here. The government in Victoria and Governor Douglas himself, usually not pro-American, were impressed by his initiatives."

"We had all heard of Robert Wall's ravings, Ah Chung. Who could have guessed that a madman could carry out such threats?"

"Irrational. The doctor had called him 'irrational', sir."

"Exactly. A pathological condition in a patient. An illness. I concur." Doctor Fifer, after surviving the dangers of two oceans, the conflict with Mexico, the Indian war with Yosemite, the grave prognosis of typhoid fever's rose-coloured rash, the persecution by McGowan's Law and Order Party, and the arduous journey from San Francisco to New Caledonia, surviving those perils, the doctor had ideas of his own divine immortality. That's why he did not take any action. "It is a matter of medical treatment, Ah Chung, certainly not a matter for the law, he insisted. What, but what, could anyone have done?"

Perhaps. Perhaps. Too late now.

"After the murderer was captured, this Robert Wall, it became my duty to attend to the young man's spiritual salvation. I feel I can confide in you, Ah Chung, as you will not unclose a confidence. During my jail visits, while I was preparing the prisoner Wall for life after death, he made a confession. It is my professional opinion that he must have committed the ghastly deed in a state of mental insanity, as if the will to carry out the act were not his own. This gives me grounds to believe that the prisoner does not deserve to die. I cannot accept that extinguishing a young life is consistent with our Lord's message of love and mercy. 'A new law I give unto you.' Was that not what He said?"

I look at Reverend Crickmer as if to say, you, a White preacher, are asking me, a Chinaman, here, in the darkness of the cemetery? But he continues as if I am his equal, and what he says overwhelms me.

"As a minister of the Church, I decided to write to the Governor, whom I met under happier circumstances. Perhaps Governor Douglas will remember me favourably. I outlined the case in detail and begged for commutation of the sentence to anything but death. I also chose, to avoid false hopes and to prevent more suffering in case it is denied, I chose not to speak to anyone of this appeal, until I mention it to you here, on this grave."

"Oh, now I understand, sir, your walking alone at this hour, at this place. It is unusual to see you here. I feared you were unwell, or perhaps that Mrs. Crickmer is unwell. You are anxious to receive the reply."

"Mrs. Crickmer is well, thank you, Ah Chung, but you are correct, I could not sit patiently and wait. Time is running out—the execution is set for eight o'clock." The mystery behind the parson's amble is revealed; he has received no reply to his appeal. In a state of extreme concern for his charge, Reverend Crickmer is seeking a physical outlet from the mental strain. He walks the trail along the riverbank, through to the graveyard, keeping in full sight of the river, his keen eyes on the water to spot any steamer or canoe on its way carrying the mail to Yale. He would have walked on to Gordon Creek, on to Emory's Bar, had he not come upon my lone figure here by the grave. The opportunity to share his burden seems to relieve the anxiety. We sit quietly, watching the lights of the Lands and Fleming steam sawmill come on across the river at Sawmill Point. The sparks from the burner give an orange glow to the sky. They are operating

13

day and night to produce 2 x 12 planks for the flumes supplying water to the miners' rockers and sluice boxes. They also cut boards to build houses, to knock together simple furniture for the miners' comfort and, upon request, supply one-inch knot-free pine boards for coffins.

It is a quiet night. There is something haunting about the hour, in this place some people think of as spooky. The wind whines mournfully through the tops of giant cedar. It is not difficult to see how the Indians imagine spirits inhabiting this place.

Sitting in silence, Reverend Crickmer and myself, we are watching every ripple of the river flowing by. I shudder as my eyes catch movement in the darkness below. The outline of a canoe emerges. But the boat is not carrying mail from Victoria. It has come from across the river and is loaded with bulky freight.

As the three paddlers pull up to shore, we can see their cargo: heavy timbers, a pile of loose boards, and a man-sized box. The man in charge, about my own age, recognizes my companion.

"Reverend Crickmer!" He is a little overbearing when he extends his burly hand. "I'm Jehil Hoadley Hale, resident of Yale, carpenter by trade and gold digger by choice." Hale's two Indian helpers carry the load up the bank, placing the pine box to one side, and begin erecting a weird-looking structure over my master's resting place.

"Yes, Reverend," Mr. Hale responds to the minister's inquiring expression about the wooden contraption looming above us. "Judge Begbie's special order, appeasing the townspeople of Yale, to build the scaffold smack on top of Doctor Fifer's grave. An uncanny place; it makes me feel uneasy; your presence, sir, is heartening.

"To tell you the truth, Reverend, I hail from San Francisco. The good doctor knew me there as 'Jehil with the slivers' or 'here comes Slivers again'." He was a wizard getting foreign bodies out from under my fingernails, painlessly snipping a wedge out of the nail, then using sharp tweezers and gently extracting the culprit. A real wizard he was, with those steady hands. We have lost a good man who did a lot for the community. His death was plain cold-blooded murder.

"You may be surprised to learn, Reverend, that the house in which you now live was my first building project in the new territory. After I completed the construction, Doctor Fifer bought the place, cash on the spot. He requested that I convert the house into a medical office with a storefront for his drugs. When he and his assistant Ah Chung moved to the larger building on the corner of Victoria and Fraser Streets, I reverted the doctor's old offices to a residence; I put up a partition dividing the store into a hallway and a decent-sized withdrawing room; two upstairs rooms became bedrooms, and another small room which had been the doctor's office, overlooking the river, served as the new dining area to accommodate you and your family. Although I tried to make the alteration merit its new spiritual occupant, there was no space in the back of the house for a kitchen. That's why, when you first arrived, your good wife had to do the cooking outside in the summer kitchen."

"In wet weather, my good wife used her parapluie to stay dry and keep the fire alive; we managed, thank you." Preferring to reserve a degree of social distance, the reverend reverts to Hale's past: "Tell me, Mr. Hale, the California gold rush has been long over, for ten years at least. What have you been doing since your arrival here in Yale?"

"Well, Reverend," Mr. Hale lowers his voice, "I had become known in San Francisco for the quality of my craft as gallows-builder. In the end, I had to escape the vengeance of the victims' relatives and fled to British North America. The New Caledonia gold discovery was an opportunity to disappear from the scene and get the ghastly experience out of my mind. Here in Yale, with the number of Law and Order boatmen around at Hill's Bar, I kept quiet about my past. I did not want it known that I had contracted with the Vigilance Committee to build the gibbets that hanged their buddies. I no longer fear for my personal safety, but I cannot escape the guilt which haunts me, over my contribution to what went so wrong in California. I have not had a good night's sleep since."

I had known that this Mr. Hoadley Hale was an educated man, able to read and write and do the ciphers; now, by his own admission, I learn that he possesses a conscience also.

"At the beginning," Mr. Hale continues, "I saw my work as a noble contribution to support justice and keep peace in the city. As with most businessmen, Doctor Fifer here too", and he gently nudges the grave mound with his boot, "I was under pressure to join the Vigilance Committee. We were ten thousand strong. By the time I had second thoughts about the movement, it was too late; membership is for life."

"Mr. Hale, I must admit, for me, a minister of the Church of England, hailing from the Old Country, these American-style circumstances and controversies are difficult to understand. Even Mrs. Crickmer has wondered whether our dear friend does not lie here because of his membership in that execrable vigilance committee. Do you think she may be right?"

Carpenter Hale tucks up his breeches and slumps down irreverently on the long box. "Ay, I've wondered that myself, sir, knowing the history as I do. It is possible that the infamous Ned McGowan is implicated. This man has an extensive criminal record in the States and after his arrival here, he caused nothing but trouble for Governor Douglas. Ned was an accessory in the murder of the San Francisco newspaper publisher James King of William. Ned McGowan, with an interest in the opposing *San Francisco Herald*, planted a story about a certain Casey who did time at Sing Sing, the notorious prison, and King promptly printed it in *his* paper. The disclosure turned Casey white with rage; he furiously sought out the paper's editor and shot him. The weapon, a derringer pistol, was provided by McGowan. It is certainly possible that McGowan's long finger may have pulled another trigger here in Yale."

Reverend Crickmer slaps a mosquito on his cheek and misses. "My wife has the same idea about McGowan. I cautioned her against unjustified conclusions, 'You have no proof, Sophia Crickmer, that McGowan played a part,' I warned her, but she came up with strong arguments. 'Although we know that McGowan sold his claims and is no longer in British Columbia, he may correspond by Wells Fargo mail with his best friend, Martin Gallagher, who is still around. The inquest revealed that the murderer Robert Wall was emotionally unstable, a poor Catholic Belfast boy under the influence of the papist McHagan who incited him to commit the murder and provided him with a pistol. Was the Irish McHagan a remote tool in the hands of the Irish Gallagher and McGowan?' Her assumptions go on and on."

The discussion between carpenter and parson has reached the crux of the matter. Feeling confident enough to join their conversation, I add, "Yes, Reverend, Mrs. Crickmer mentioned her suspicions to me herself, one afternoon when we met at the Hudson's Bay store and she invited me back to a cup of tea." I choose not to repeat how she told me about the warm spot she had for my master, calling him a nice man; how she had commented that not even her husband Burton ever paid such compliments on her china cups of English tea with cream and sugar. "There are more possibilities, Ah Chung," Mrs. Crickmer said to me that day. "A woman's eyes can see what men might miss. There is another motive. It's the deadly sin of envy, Jealousy. There is talk of McGowan's animosity, his uncontrolled jealousy against our doctor, and his scheming and his sweltering rage to retaliate."

"Lucy Allard, the daughter of the Hudson's Bay clerk, told me that McGowan spent some money buying her a dress that she didn't like and never wore. She put it on for me; it was gaudy and much too big; however, her accepting the gift may have given McGowan the one-sided impression of a bond. He wanted to take her out to a ball; she didn't go, of course. One evening, when the doctor was visiting with the Allards, enjoying their good, dark brandy, McGowan walked in and saw the doctor talking to Lucy. Thinking that he had surprised the two (he may well have), he turned pale but kept control in the presence of the girl. In icy, pretended courtesy, he complimented the doctor out the door, and the indoor formality turned into a vicious beating *al fresco*. All seems allowed in love and in war. It's the American way, they say. That's what Mrs. Crickmer said to me."

"Yes, I heard that story too, Ah Chung," Mr. Hale confirms, "There must be more to this crime than a madman acting alone. I agree with Mrs. Crickmer that there is the possibility of a jaundiced eye over a young woman's favours."

"Mrs. Crickmer has also heard the gossip of planned interference with the execution of Robert Wall," Reverend Crickmer adds. "A posse is supposed to 'spring' the culprit. The rumour has had sufficient substance to cause Magistrate Sanders to call for a number of Yale citizens to come forward to be sworn in as auxiliary police for the execution tomorrow morning. 'By whose clandestine machinations other than McGowan's has this action come about?' my dear wife keeps asking."

"I can not contradict your good wife's intelligent reasoning," Mr. Hale says, confirming my own feelings, and the two leave it at that.

Reverend Crickmer is an inquisitive person; he continues probing into Hale's past. "This is all before my time on this continent, in this New World," he says, "Tell us more, Mr. Hale, of those evil times before you came to Yale. Go on, please, sir."

"Well, Reverend, ye' see, it happened like this: My career turned when Mr. Coleman, the head of the San Francisco Vigilance Committee, designated me to construct some device, a derrick, to hang two convicted murderers side by side and simultaneously. I had built gallows before that, but this was my first short order, and my first for a double hanging." Hale's voice becomes subdued and confidential, sounding guilty; I can barely hear what he is saying. "The newspaperman who called himself Mr. King of William, the victim of Casey's vicious assault with a gun, had been clinging to life for days. When King died, the Vigilance Committee decided that immediate hanging of the murderer Casey would set an excellent judicial example. Since a double hanging would enhance the Committee's reputation for efficiency and prompt action, another prisoner, Cora, who had killed a US marshal, was to be the second man to be executed. There was no time to build a proper gallows; instead, I fixed two beams jutting out from the upper floor of the Committee headquarters.

"To my horror, I received orders to stand by as a trouble-shooter during the execution. I felt very uneasy watching the official hangman, Mr. Nixon, push the two blindfolded men off the windowsill; Casey first, and then Cora were thus suspended. The drop was insufficient to snap the necks; they strangled slowly as the crowd watched and cheered. Ever since then, they's called us 'the Stranglers'.

"Another double execution was to convey the same message to all criminals in town. The two men sentenced to be hanged at the same time were Joseph Hetherington for killing a Dr. Randall, who owed him money, and Philander Brace, a New York clergyman's son, twenty-one years of age, who was suspected of murdering three men. The Committee executive allowed me two days to erect the full-scale gallows in the centre of the street. The difficulty in the construction was to build a reliable double trap-door mechanism, releasing both platforms at the same time. I worked on the project day and night, experimenting with heavier weights serving as substitute for the condemned, until I was satisfied that the controls would not let me down. It turned out to be an elaborate construction, quite successful in its mechanical performance."

In the near darkness, at this gravesite, I actually welcome the carpenter's chatter describing the mechanical workings during hanging. It is a distraction. Both Mr. Crickmer and I are suspended between attending to the macabre reality while still clinging to the anticipation of a hoped-for letter of commutation of Robert Wall's death sentence. Yet, if the appeal for Wall's life is denied, the stage must be set for a flawless, humane ending, when we must rely on the smooth function of this death machine.

Mr. Hale continues: "There are several ways to accomplish the task of execution; I chose the one most reliable method: In the final phase, a large weight, attached below the trap on which the prisoner stands, once released by a sliding bolt, will pull the platform down and out of the way. The release action is initiated by another weight, connected by rope and pulley to the bolt that holds the trapdoor closed. This weight is held in suspension by a small cord that passes directly under a sharp razor. Stepping on the razor cuts the cord. The stone weight falls, withdraws the bolt, and the weighted trap drops down.

"Although the mechanism was reliable, the Committee had requested me to stand by during the execution. From within ten feet of the scaffold, I could hear every word that was said. When the drop fell successfully, there was a shudder, like an electric current running through the crowd. My own heart seemed to stop. For a long time the scene haunted me with guilt and shame.

"We could all see the writing on the wall: We the People who make the law must be prepared to enforce it; however well-intended, this kind of justice could not last. The protesting voices challenging our authority became louder. The criminals on the loose found umbrage in the so-called Law and Order Party and clamoured for an end of the 'Stranglers' regime of the Vigilance Committee. Voluntary exodus seemed the simplest solution for me."

Hoadley Hale has been sitting on the pine box in front of us; now he stands, stretches, leaning one arm against the grisly derrick rearing directly above. His Indians have assembled the ready parts as quickly as a child completes a favourite puzzle. Mr. Hale continues giving us details of his craft, stories of other botched executions.

"I've seen hangings in the south where the terminal writhing, prolonged through slow strangulation, gave the crowd a spectacle. Nobody seemed to care about reliability, whether the apparatus functioned properly or not. A defective contraption is cruel; it means a slow death. Having it work properly is an act of mercy. I always took pride in my work, despite the bad press from the opposition newspaper, although the opposing Law and Order Party's methods of killing were equally inhumane, or equally humane.

"Mr. Nugent, editor of the *San Francisco Herald,* claiming righteousness a prerogative of the Law and Order movement, castigated the Vigilance Committee's executions. "The Vigilance Committee should do some research, check out the latest new and improved methods of hanging," Nugent sniped. "Learn new scientific points," he demanded, "to be more humane and Christian-like." He was right in pointing out what went wrong, that the fall should be sufficient to break the necks except that the noose did not slip properly and caught around the chin, causing a slow and painful death. "Geez, sorry Reverend, but those boys convulsed and danced for five minutes; I could hear the rasp, their stifled gasping for breath."

By now, the carpenter feels enough at ease in our presence to recall the accusation as if the hateful editorial had been printed to name and blame him personally. Addressing the parson, Mr. Hale admits: "To tell you the truth, sir, I've been out of this business for more than ten years now. I'm not altogether comfortable about this here structure. I have heard that you are mechanically inclined. Would you give me peace of my mind by going over the mechanism with me to see if the drop'll function properly?"

What can Reverend Crickmer say? I know he is good at making things work. Did he not bring back to life my master's timepiece after it stopped for days? He would have become an engineer, I heard him tell the doctor, had not his dear mother insisted on a spiritual career. He can not say No to the carpenter's request; he feels a moral obligation to contribute to the accurate function of the fateful device.

Deep into the night, I watch Reverend Crickmer, servant of the Christian God, help the carpenter, while I, Ah Chung, Chinaman and servant to the victim in the grave below us, stand by with axle grease,

21

beef tallow, and brown soap. Preacher and carpenter, side by side, painful though the duty is, test again and again, with heavy stones, the wooden trigger mechanism that draws the bolt from beneath the drop, until they are certain it will function without fault.

The Indians having completed their carpentry, have retreated to the canoe from which they have been watching as the two men, in shirtsleeves, test the mechanism. As I am facing the direction of the town, I notice the outline of another man along the path towards this eerie place of tryst. He is soberly dressed in a long black coat. He interrupts Mr. Hale and Reverend Crickmer by offering his hand and proclaiming in an unctuous voice: "The paths of glory, gentlemen, the paths of glory. Ebenezer Strathscore, at your service." A lump forms in my throat as his purpose, at this specific location, dawns on me.

Reverend Crickmer responds with his name and Hale's, and then mine: "Ah Chung, Dr. Fifer's, the victim's, Chinaman." He continues: "Yes, sir, this is the place. The place of rest, soon to be the place of departure. Which would be your purpose, Mr. Strathscore?" The parson is unaware why the apparition with the shriveled face of an embalmed Egyptian has chosen to visit this spot.

Strathscore responds, evasively.

"We left New Westminster by special canoe three days ago. Paddling hard against the fast current, the crew took advantage of the river's eddies and stayed close to the shore, barely avoiding a collision with the upper deck of a monstrous hull of a ship, partly submerged in the sand just below Cornisah Bar."

"Aye, sir. The wreck of the fateful explosion when the boiler of the *Yale* blew, near Hope, on Easter Sunday last. With the loss of many lives, five whites and uncounted Indians and Chinamen," Mr. Hale offers. He does not mention the loss of investment, another of the tragedies over which Dr. Fifer was mulling. Gone is the vision of improved transportation to Yale; the explosion destroyed his dream of expanding his office into a hospital with the latest modern sanitary conveniences, a model for the young colony. I mention nothing. It is possible that neither of these men is aware that many investors lost all they had.

Strathscore continues. "On our second day, it became too dark to continue up river; the crew pulled in at Hope, fifteen miles short of our destination. I had a letter of introduction to the Hope magistrate, Mr. Peter O'Reilly, who provided perfectly suitable accommodation for the night. After breakfast, he dispatched me with a note to the Yale Magistrate, Captain Sanders, who has quartered me in a room of the courthouse."

Mr. Strathscore, it seems, prefers privacy to physical comfort. Despite the August heat, he has remained indoors during daylight, out of sight to the public. To Mr. Hale's inquiry he replies: "It concerns me not, that the building holds another resident, chained to the wall of the death cell." Without exactly stating his business, but recognizing both the reverend and the gallows-maker as co-workers in the venture, Strathscore continues his account. "At the jail, I viewed my charge through the gaps between the boards making up the cell walls. I estimate the body weight to be about fourteen stone. From a table of numbers, I extrapolated the required height of the 'drop' to be between four and five feet, taking into account the total body weight from which, of course, the weight of the head must be subtracted."

I watch Reverend Crickmer digesting everyone of these details, I see him cringe as Strathscore's *raison d' être* begins to dawn on him.

And Ebenezer Strathscore continues. "Assessment of the object's state of musculature is a mandatory measure. Six weeks of incarceration will weaken the muscles of the neck and require a reduction in drop. If during the fall the momentum of the body exceeds the strength of the muscle mass there can be the embarrassing accident of dividing the head from the body."

Strathscore has studied the mechanics and the anatomical

23

aspect of sudden deceleration at the neck, causing, what he calls, "*acute flexion-abduction* at the level of the first and second cervical vertebrae." He predicts the desired result of "dislocation of the *odontoid* process, destruction of the spinal cord and instant death. The heart may continue for a minute or two but usually ceases immediately from the systemic shock."

"Should this mechanism fail, the rope, if applied correctly, will serve as a back-up. It will push the culprit's tongue against the hard palate and posterior pharynx, inevitably bringing about asphyxia. The process actually is one of throttling, or choking to death, a deviation from the desired humane quick end. It occurs mostly to neophytes in the trade. I have always condemned this back-up procedure that would come into play in botched executions."

I notice Reverend Crickmer turn pale again, listening to the ghastly details while still hoping for the Governor's reprieve. Every word emerging from the hangman's mouth tears a shred off the silver lining for his charge's life in the death cell.

Mr. Strathscore drones on; he rarely has such an opportunity to promulgate his craft. "Three fail-safe actions would effectively suspend body function: obstructing respiration would be enhanced by interference with blood supply to the brain; in the third place, the nerve plexus comprised of the *vagus* and *glossopharyngeal* nerves would be disconnected.

"Correct placement of the noose is the quintessential factor; it determines how many minutes the condemned person lives after the drop. Placing the rope between the lower jaw and the *hyoid* bone, just above the Adam's apple, would allow two minutes. A finger's breadth lower, across the larynx, directly on the Adam's apple, would mean one and one-half minute. The shortest time to extinguish the culprit, only a few seconds, is by constriction at the level of the *cricoid* bone, below the Adam's apple. In my experience, it is best to position the noose's brass ring under the left jaw, below the mastoid bone, to prevent the loop from catching over the chin. This misfortune and the resulting catastrophe of a bungled dispatch has occurred to executioners who have relied on placing the ring behind the left ear. Improper placement during dressing the noose could occur when the features of the neck are obscured by the object's hood.

"At earlier executions when the prisoner's arms and legs were kept free, the criminals would sometimes reach up and grasp the rope with their hand, or their feet would catch the edge of the trapdoor, prolonging the act. On these occasions the executioner had to climb below and put all his weight onto their legs. This hindrance of judicial consummation has been overcome by placing a wide leather belt around the waist to pinion elbows and hands and by binding the legs with a single strap below the knees. Correct location of the prisoner on the trapdoor is also critical. Even one inch off centre could cause the body to swing and cushion the effect of the drop."

Strathscore steps forward, mounting the platform, and marks the spot with a chalk where, in the morning, he will place his charge, plumb below the rope's point of suspension.

"But it is still a nasty business, is it not, Reverend? It has brought out the philosopher in me. I easily pocket my twenty-pound note but I would prefer to be a philanthropist, a humanitarian. I postulate that the punishment of a criminal should be useful. When a man is hanged, he is good for nothing. Yet, it seems I'm fighting a losing battle against capital punishment; the best I can do at this point in time is humanize the execution by pioneering my modification, the 'long drop,' to spare the condemned the agony of choking and strangulation. I always bring my own bag of tools. A coil of rope, one end spliced with a shiny one-inch brass eye through which passes the other end, forming a running noose; a tight leather washer keeps it from sliding open. It is going to work reliably, having been well stretched on previous applications."

It seems, once the flood of words has begun, there is no damming Strathscore. "In my spare time, I have taken up playing the violoncello; the salubrious sound of the instrument calms the tempestuous mind. My favorites are Bach's suites, a magical and biblical music, narrating stories in a comprehensible language, from the archaic to the refined, about the immeasurable dimensions and variations of the human experiment, *quia absurdum est.*"

He recounts buying the yellowed sheets at a London used-book shop some thirty years ago. Playing Bach has taught him humility and compassion, he says, transforming him into a paragon of an abolitionist. If he can convince the powers that be to abolish the death penalty, it may provide the redemption he seeks.

"How absurd it is," Reverend Crickmer agrees, and then falls deathly quiet. I know he is thinking of his own unanswered letter.

Mr. Hale, however, unaware of our suspense, takes up the conversation. Awed by the little man's knowledge, he gives the conversation a profane twist: "Do you know about Mandrake root, the plant allegedly growing where the hanged man ejaculates?"

Strathscore is only too happy to expostulate. "Genesis mentions the mandrake and Leah's conceiving six sons and one daughter. Thomas Newton's *Herbal to the Bible* describes the mandrake, *mandragora officinarum*, as 'a creature, having life, engendered under the earth of some person put to death for murder'. However, in my own experience, such mystic theory of the origin of the mandragora root is bunk. On the gibbet, the last thing on a person's mind is ejaculation.

"I've come tonight to measure the height of the drop," Strathscore concludes, getting at last to the task at hand. He asks me to hold the lantern while he uses a tape measure. He expresses satisfaction; the space below the trapdoor is better than six feet.

I know my place as a Celestial; listening attentively and speaking only when spoken to helps me remain unobtrusive. Yet, it pleases me that I have been able to follow the discourse on human anatomy and physiology. The time I spent as a medical assistant to Doctor Fifer, when I learned about the human skeleton in English, has been useful. I cannot deny a certain respect for Mr. Strathscore's movement to abolish the death penalty. I am gratified to hear of efforts to humanize this despicable method of disposing of peoples' lives.

As a child in China, I was forced once to attend an execution. The condemned man was held to sit on a crossbar, losing his body parts one by one. First the axe took one arm off at the shoulder and then chopped the other; next, one leg and then the other was hacked off at the knee. Still conscious, the bleeding victim, without limbs, was held there for the beheading. It seems to me that, in this new world, with the guillotine and the long drop, capital punishment is easier to take. It is not for me to judge whether, in this year of the rooster, these improvements reflect the pioneer spirit and the quest for knowledge. Perhaps, in this year the Christians call "the Year of Our Lord 1861," these improvements are a result of the influence of the age of enlightenment. Perhaps they merely reflect the desire for greater efficiency under the cloak of being more humane. Perhaps hanging is more humane than the alternatives—transportation to Australia, Van Diemen's Land, the Fee Jees, or incarceration. Dr. Fifer told me that Vancouver's Island had been considered as another penal colony, until complaints from the adjacent American territories quashed the idea. No one wants criminals in their midst or at their borders. Yet what are the alternatives?

The newspaper correspondents in San Francisco and Victoria miss no opportunity to print a detailed description of a public hanging or the tragic circumstances surrounding a departure by suicide. From San Francisco we read: "A regrettable accident. At the American theatre recently, Mlle. Duret, in the character of 'Jack Shephard,' while enacting the hanging scene, accidentally got the rope uncomfortably tight about her neck, and was much alarmed. Her nerves were so much shocked that it was some time before she could retire to her dressing room." Such sensational news reports I would gladly forgo, but I do miss our evenings together, with Dr. Fifer reading the stories aloud as I prepare the tea.

I cannot stay here much longer. Mr. Strathscore and Mr. Hale are going on and on. The Indians are nodding off in the canoe. I stretch my legs and, pushing myself up, I rest my palm above Dr. Fifer's heart and grip a fistful of gravel dirt, earth, roots, and pebbles. Reverend Crickmer, taking my movements as my intent to leave, stands also.

"Yes, Ah Chung; let us depart. My 'busy housewife plies her 'evening care.'" We take our leave, choosing the high trail back into the townsite. Darkness feels total, but our feet are familiar with the path. Far below, in the river, I see the movement of stars. It is more than twinkling; it is more than the current rocking starry reflections. I look up and, in my vertigo, the sky is falling, I am falling.

"Steady there, man," Reverend Crickmer reaches for my elbow. He looks up too and sighs, "Yes. The Perseids."

And then I remember Dr. Fifer's explanation: 'The Perseids fall every August; it is an illusion, Ah Chung. The turning of the earth makes the stars seem to fall. Hundreds of stars. They fell last year. They will fall next year.' He meant to be reassuring, telling me not to fear. But all I could think of was the falling star that followed us as we embarked from San Francisco to Fort Victoria. 'We should not go, Dr. Fifer,' I warned. 'Nonsense, Ah Chung. This is the new world. We must leave those superstitions of the past behind us.'

If only we had been able to. To leave the past behind.

I am lost in my memories. We walk past the dark courthouse where Robert Wall is lodged, shackled, ignorant of the appeal for his life. Reverend Crickmer is troubled by the uncertainty of the decision from Victoria, suffering under Strathscore's presumption of Wall's impending execution. In the conflict, the Reverend returns to the hangman's musical discussion. "Bach," he snorts. "I can almost imagine Bach on the violoncello, soothing the condemned man's soul. I think not. Berlioz, perhaps. *Symphonie phantastique.* The story of a poet who, unhappy in love, takes an overdose of opium and dreams of his own passions and desires, of his beloved, her murder, and his own death. The fourth movement, entitled 'March to the

Scaffold,' depicts the protagonist's dream of his own execution for having killed his faithless beloved."

The Reverend Crickmer chats on while I barely listen. His words have brought me back to my day's duties, packing up the doctor's house. On the wall of his office, his favourite needlework sampler, its stitches reading: "*De medico, profeta, y loco, todos tenemos un poco.*" The prophet. The mad man. "We each have within us a bit of the healer, a bit of the foreteller, and a bit of the fool." He liked that expression. Written in Spanish, it reminded him, he said, of his early experience in California, during the Mexican War. That's the word he used, when I pointed out the ominous nature of the comet, the bad fortune it bode, as we departed from San Francisco. "Don't be the Madman, Ah Chung. Don't be the Fool."

2

Move up, you fool! Move up!" Sailors were yelling down at draymen reining nervous horses. Pacific Wharf in San Francisco's harbour had been abuzz since daybreak. Fresh-water hoses were rolled out. Food wholesalers were delivering vegetables and sides of beef and buffalo. Horses and cattle were corralled beside us. We took care to avoid the droppings of hundreds of cackling Leghorn chickens stacked in coops above our heads. On and on it went.

Although there was still much cargo waiting to be loaded, the Commodore was already sitting low in the water and listing every time a new wagon load was emptied on to the deck. Indeed, in the official investigation which followed, a witness testified that "the ship was overloaded; there were on deck a hundred and fifty tons of freight that should have been in the hold of the ship."

It is only three years ago that we had decided to leave San Francisco, in June, 1858, and yet it seems like another lifetime. We stood, two of more than one thousand impatient passengers waiting to board, in a line which snaked from the roped-off gangplank all down Pacific Wharf and up the street, circling the building where a bespectacled man at a wicket was still selling more tickets. We had been standing on the boardwalk for hours, with nothing further to say to each other or to those standing next to us, when I heard my mother tongue. One of my countrymen, walking along the wharf, approached me and, in Guangzhou accent, offered to sell me food.

Dr. Fifer handed over some coins and the vendor wrapped chunks of cooked pork in a cone of newspaper and handed it to me. "*Um goy,*" I said, bowing our thanks, and we devoured the treat in no time.

As I searched for some place to toss the greasy paper, Dr. Fifer snatched it from my hands, shook it open, and, as was his habit, began to read aloud to me:

"FROM OUR VICTORIA CORRESPONDENT IN THE BRITISH TERRITORIES—April 25, 1858 promised to be a fine spring Sunday. From his elevated pulpit in his imposing Christ Church, Reverend Cridge could see Fort Victoria's inner harbour below. Was it by divine intuition that he had selected the Book of St. John for his sermon?

Jesus then lifted up his eyes, and saw a great company come unto him.

He saith: 'Whence shall we buy bread that these may eat?'

One of his disciples saith unto him. 'There is a lad here, which hath five barley loaves, and two small fishes: but what are they among so many?'

At the conclusion of the homily, the collection plate was passed, the last hymn was sung, and the benediction pronounced. The congregation rose to leave. Standing outside in groups in the warming spring sun, they chatted. As the fading sounds of the reed organ drifted through the open door of the church, their peaceful Sunday mood was shattered by an unexpected apparition."

The doctor elbowed me. "Are you with me, Ah Chung? Am I allaying your foolish fears? There's a harbour, and a fort; that means stores, food and shopping; and there's a community, and a church. Civilization, or at least what passes for such, here in the new world. See, your idea that we are heading into uncharted territory is false. You don't have to worry."

I nodded and tried to smile. Dr. Fifer liked to read these things to me, articles in all sorts of newspapers, and I liked to listen. Nothing I could say would deter his enthusiasm about our new venture. He continued reading from the article about the church service:

"Before their very eyes, a big American side-wheeler, loaded to the railing with roistering men, pulled into the small harbour below. The vessel dropped anchors and began to disgorge its freight of passengers. There were at least 450 of them, almost the equivalent of the town's population. The foreigners were high-booted men in red flannel shirts, armed with revolvers and Bowie knives. At first their appearance created fear among the Victorian residents. Soon their conduct showed that they were not the fire-eaters they had appeared to be, and the local people became reconciled to their presence when they began to spend their quarter eagles, which were very acceptable.

"These passengers were gold seekers who had arrived too late in California to make their fortunes and wanted to try their luck in the new fields. Moreover, they brought dollars, dollars, and dollars!"

"Well, Ah Chung. We are not gold seekers. Not that kind of gold, anyway. But we will have come from California to try our luck, and the British colonists are prepared to welcome us as long as we have dollars, dollars, dollars."

The doctor was jovial that day, at the thought of our imminent departure. Our choice to leave. "Choosing to leave, Ah Chung, is not the same as running away," he had chided me the day before as I packed. I must never say we were running away. The doctor was a proud man.

Dr. Fifer read on:

"The problem was how to supply this goodly multitude with provisions, and that was a puzzler. However, with a dint of scraping and gathering together from their country larders, and raising the prices, the Victorians succeeded in getting them all fed. Soon they rejoiced in the increase in trading possibilities. C.A. Bayley, owner of the only hotel, the 'Hotel by the Bay,' at the corner of Government and Yates Streets and operator of a general store, a restaurant, a lodging house, and a butcher shop, reported: 'I took in the situation, immediately bought up all the bread in town, and had to feed over 250 men who would not wait for the meat to be cooked but were satisfied with the appearance of it having been subject to the cooking stove.'"

"Nothing to worry about, Ah Chung. It is a miracle, like the story of the Loaves and Fishes. We shall not starve in a land of such bounty." Now I knew he was joshing with me; I had never feared that we might starve.

Other men in the queue were listening in as the doctor continued reading aloud:

"The scene was beyond description, an invasion of sorts, in the way it overwhelmed the village. Hundreds of tents were pitched everywhere, wherever a man could claim a patch of rock or mud. The miners started building boats with or without pitch to travel the distance of ninety miles to the mainland and then to ascend the Fraser River. Many hundreds were lost crossing the Gulf of Georgia or being assailed by the Natives; but the impetus was gold and to be there first."

"Well, we will not 'be there first', Ah Chung. But when we arrive, we will already have patients in need of our services, and they will be able to pay."

Dr. Fifer was always good at finding the bright spots, like the miners finding gold in the gravel.

As we continued standing in line with our baggage, a man dressed in preacher clothes, possibly from the mission around the corner, walked past, handing out flyers with English writing. Dr. Fifer took one of the leaflets and glanced down at it. He declined to read it to me; his eyes avoided my own. But a man in mechanic's overalls ahead of us in the line began to read aloud, knowing many of those waiting for permission to board could not read for themselves.

"The *Commodore* is not seaworthy, she is a floating coffin and the sooner the matter is brought to a test, the better. The author of these handbills is not afraid to meet the heartless man that would sacrifice human life for aggrandisement."

The ominous forecast was signed Frederic N. Smith of the Keystone Temperance House. Soon a murmur of gossip inched up the line. The steamer *Commodore* was known to the men of San Francisco. Captain Wright had bought ships in New York, including the *Brother Jonathan* which he painted, renamed the *Commodore*, and placed under the command of Captain George W. Staples on the north Pacific route between San Francisco and Fort Vancouver in Washington Territory, Portland, and Fort Victoria. The ship enjoyed a good trade. The fare from San Francisco to Victoria, sixty-five dollars first class cabin and thirty-five dollars in the steerage, was more than the sixty to twenty-five dollars charged by the slower sailing ships.

However, the ship had acquired a bad reputation, and these were the details that moved up and down the waiting line. Continuous service without overhaul and neglect of the ship's seaworthiness had made her an unsafe vessel. No insurance company would underwrite the risk guaranteeing her cargo. The ship was a lemon, a *clunker.* Before she departed, the humanitarian distributed these handbills informing us of the good reasons to hold out caution.

But Dr. Fifer was not swayed. He was committed to a course of action; speculation would not dissuade him. Nor were many of the waiting passengers affected by the new information. Only one man, dressed in coat and top hat, travelling with an infant and a wife who was obviously with child, left the line and reported to the wicket to request a refund. Obviously not a miner, he was in no rush. But the rest continued to wait for boarding to begin, shifting somewhat more on their feet, laughing somewhat too loudly with their neighbours.

If I was a Fool, I was not alone.

As Dr. Fifer's Chinaman and medical assistant, I knew before we left that the doctor struggled with fearful expectations and feelings of uneasiness. How he had detested being summoned to testify in court for his friends and against Dr. Cooper, a medical colleague, in a recent malpractice suit. How he suffered under the unending persecution by the Law and Order Party, slandering and threatening to kill him and all other members of the now-disbanded Vigilance Committee. When his marriage ended unexpectedly and unhappily, he had had enough of this new city where he had arrived as a New York Volunteer before the Mexicans capitulated and where he had established himself after the gold rush. He was fed up and refused to take it any longer. As soon as he heard the rumours of gold shipped from New Caledonia, confirmed by his friend Dr. Wierzbicki, now a federal officer in the San Francisco Mint, he began to put his affairs in order, in anticipation of his departure for the north.

In his travel·planning, Dr. Fifer was generous, leaving to me the choice whether I would accompany him into exile or remain in the city. He knew me well enough, though; he had already bought tickets for both of us. For thirty-five American dollars, I would travel as a steerage passenger. For his stateroom, Dr. Fifer paid nearly twice that much. Notwithstanding the Temperance House warnings, to us the *Commodore* was the best available transportation north. She was also our salvation, or so I thought.

.   The June 11th *Daily Marine Intelligence* of R. S. Martin and Son's from Telegraph Hill was terse: "At sundown, wind direction and speed: north-northwest, force 6, buffeting seas, rough. Precipitation and remarks: the weather haze all the day but very cold and clear night. Flood Tide. No inward bound vessels In sight from the outer station."

Undaunted by the uncertainty of the weather report or the warnings of the missionary, we embarked. "The *Commodore* has withstood the winds and the seas of the Atlantic and the Pacific Oceans for a good many years and will reach her destination without a problem one more time, Ah Chung." I could tell that he was convincing himself as he tried to impart confidence to me. Alas, this time, Dr. Fifer had miscalculated.

We stood at the railing together, watching the green hills recede in silence. As soon as the *Commodore* left the protection of San Francisco Bay, abandoned the Golden Gate to starboard behind us and headed into open waters, it became apparent that there would be difficulties. The vessel toiled labouriously against the heavy sea.

"Listen to that!" One of the passengers, the one in mechanic's overalls who had read the temperance handbill to us, cocked his head and pointed the sound out to us. "The ship's engines are making but six or seven revolutions per minute; she should have twelve." His knowledge was not reassuring to me, but a vintage sea traveller of Dr. Fifer's calibre was not to be inconvenienced by mechanical forebodings or minor storm warnings. He reminded me of his seafaring experiences. Had he not crossed the North Sea when he travelled from Bremen to Liverpool, and the Atlantic Ocean, from Liverpool to New York? Had he not sailed in the *Susan Drew*, a tub of a mere 750 tons burthen, dependent on wind power alone, from New York via Rio de Janeiro, rounded the Horn for Santiago de Chile, and up the Pacific Coast to Yerba Buena? I did not have the opportunity to mention my more recent voyage from Guangzhou to the Golden Gates of Heaven, as Dr. Fifer went off to the main lounge for a dinner of sirloin, new potatoes, garden-fresh peas, and a glass of wine. Since he was not concerned, I gave the matter no thought either. I had curled up on my pallet below deck by the time he retired to his berth.

Three days out on the open sea, we found ourselves in a sinking condition. As Dr. Fifer seemed to be the only medical man on board, passengers sought him out for conversation and advice. A Mr. Buckley, a practical mechanic and seasoned traveller who claimed to have been shipwrecked no less than three times, expressed his apprehension by giving full particulars of the condition of the ship.

"Before she left port," he noted, "she had a far too great amount of freight stowed and jammed full between decks. Some of the heaviest material, no less than 200 tons of it, normally stowed in the hold below, is placed there on the upper deck. All along the deck, forward and aft, those boxes and bales of merchandise piled up four or five feet high make it impossible to reach the wheelhouse except by climbing over heaps of freight—hogsheads of bacon and hams, boxes of salt, and no less than one hundred and fifty boxes of nails. All this makes the vessel top-heavy.

"Furthermore," Mr. Buckley claimed, "she is not fully provided with proper tools, pumps, or other various implements and the machinery indispensable to the safety of a vessel. Shortly after getting to sea, I examined the main pump forward of the engine and found it defective, looking more like an old farmyard pump than one of an ocean steamer." His observations proved to be prophetic. During the gale, Mr. Buckley and others managed to put the main pump in working order, repairing it with leather stripped from a Mexican saddle.

Each day out the *Commodore* pushed against steadily rougher seas. By four o'clock on Monday morning, conditions became so bad that Captain Staples ordered his men to throw the top deck load overboard. Bracing themselves against the buck of the deck, the men went to work as men only can when fighting for their lives. Mr. Abell of San Francisco was the first one to lighten the ship. He shot his four fine horses and proceeded to throw overboard the carcasses, harnesses, wagons, even his own clothing and other freight. He did it cheerfully, tossing crates without stopping to think whether they belonged to him or others. In an incredibly short space of time the deck was cleared.

Notwithstanding these frantic measures, the general expectation on board was that the vessel would flounder. As the sky darkened and the waves grew, tossing the heavy boat like a toy in a tub, washing the littered deck with surges of sea, some of the passengers sought refuge in cabins or on their pallets. Others came above to watch and pray. Some conducted themselves in a very creditable and stout-hearted manner while others acted like cravens and shirks, whether out of fear or paralysed by desperation, lying about on deck with their life preservers on. Some were so scared, they threw their purses and revolvers overboard.

Of the five lady passengers aboard, the chief engineer's wife distinguished herself by her coolness. The boatswain and the second mate behaved manfully and were exceedingly attentive to their duties, and the deckhands likewise, maintaining their posts, straining at their labours, creating confidence in those of us who watched.

As Mr. Buckley had pointed out, the donkey pump and the other pumps had not been in good order when we left San Francisco. The ship leaked badly, and had we been dependent altogether on the pumps to relieve her, she would have gone down. The crew knocked the heads out of liquor tierces and used them to bail out the water, hoisting them up by tackle. Besides the tierces, forty buckets were kept in constant operation, passed up and down by the passengers.

Altogether, nine horses and about two tons of assorted merchandise were thrown overboard. One passenger who had braved death a hundred times on *terra firma*, grew so desperate during the height of the gale as to hand the man standing next to him his pistol and beg of him to blow his brains out, preferring any death to that of being choked by salt water. The second man threw the pistol overboard and tried to cheer up the distressed man. But his terror was not yet over.

At five o'clock the men commenced passing freight out from between the decks, fore and aft. Gangs of three or four men were set to work at the pumps, and other lines were formed to pass water out of the engine room. By ten o'clock the water level was lowered, freeing the vessel from some two feet of water in the fire-room. Captain Staples gave the order to wear the ship around, to head back for San Francisco, but this was not accomplished until two o'clock in the afternoon when the gale abated in intensity. After the ship was wore about she rode easier, whether it was the beneficial effect of being lightened of her freight, the direction of the wind, or the angle of the waves breaking on her. The pumps were kept constantly going throughout her return. Now that I was aware of it, I could hear the engine running at the usual number of revolutions as she limped back to the dock.

During all the fear and commotion, Dr. Fifer had instructed me to make sure that none of his baggage was sacrificed. He spoke to the chief engineer who secured his valise containing medical instruments and medication, keeping it within reach on the upper deck. As it turned out, he was the only physician on board, and Captain Staples requested my master to tend to a number of injuries that occurred to the men whilst at work. One who had his collarbone broken received the time-honoured treatment of a figure-of-eight bandage; another sustained a crush injury to his hand and metacarpal fracture, a minor injury requiring splinting, and one sailor ran a nail under the cap of his knee, inflicting a painful wound. Dr. Fifer extracted the iron nail and bandaged the knee.

It was two o'clock when we arrived back in San Francisco and the vessel drew alongside Pacific Wharf. When the agent of the shipping line came aboard, he was surrounded by a large number of passengers who, in their excitement and anger over the loss of all their effects, threatened him with personal violence. "Refund! We demand our money back! Throw him overboard!" Chief of Police Curtis with almost the entire force at his command (he was short of good officers), boarded the vessel to quell the disturbance but his words seemed to excite the crowd to a still greater frenzy.

Shouts of "Hang him! Shoot him!" rang from the crowd of reckless characters from the city who had congregated at the pier as if for a lynching and were encouraging passengers to more violent conduct. One passenger, a Spaniard, drew his pistol. Finally, the police chief and a cordon of his officers escorted Captain Wright, the ship's owner, through the mob, into protective custody.

Before he departed, Wright advised passengers to call at the office of the company, at 111 Sacramento Street, opposite Knickerbocker's Engine House, at 12 o'clock, for a refund of their passage money. When the box office was thrown open at the designated hour, passengers rushed in with their tickets, and, on receiving their money, walked out through the side door. Dr. Fifer obtained a refund of our fare and was one of many passengers who expressed themselves perfectly satisfied with Captain Wright's promptness.

When the *Commodore* became overdue at Victoria, our point of destination, before word of our return to port had reached them, the Victoria *Gazette* wrote:

"The COMMODORE — It is now a matter of certainty that some disaster has befallen this vessel. She left San Francisco several days before the *Sierra Nevada* and *Pacific* for this port. The ship was to touch on the way at Crescent City and Columbia River. The *Republic* reports that she arrived at neither of these places and it is probable that she has not turned back to San Francisco and floundered in the severe gales that have recently prevailed on the coast. Passengers by the *Sierra Nevada* state they observed dead horses floating. The *Commodore* had, it is believed, 350 passengers who had boarded her with a well-founded dread of her unseaworthiness. She was, however, overloaded with freight, and being a weak vessel, has probably yielded to this strain upon her capacity. It is melancholy to reflect that the condemnation of the running of this worn-out steamer with which the San Francisco press has teemed for months, should have proved so unavailing; and surprising that in the face of such a reputation, anyone should have been sufficiently venturesome to trust their lives or property on board the ill-fated vessel."

Dr. Fifer read me this account sometime during the three weeks we waited in San Francisco for another steamer, the *Sierra Nevada,* to return to port and provide us a safer passage. He had not changed his mind about leaving as he was still on the hit list of McGowan's gang, the "Law and Murder" Party. However, the doctor also had many friends in the city who harboured him during our interrupted journey. For the time being, Dr. Fifer tempered his concern philosophically, concluding that, as in the practice of medicine, "the prognosis of the possibility to die is immensely preferable to the prediction of probability". He could tell from my face that I could not follow his logic. "The difference between possible and probable, Ah Chung. It is possible to be murdered by McGowan's mob. It is probable, indeed almost certain, to die by drowning should our ship flounder again." I found neither choice reassuring.

During the weeks we waited, our journey interrupted, we moved our bags from friend's house to friend's house before our place of lodging could become general knowledge. There was very little for us to do as the doctor had arranged for his friend Jules David of the Abel Guy Bank to manage the disposition of his business affairs. Mr. David was to sell the house on Washington Street and divest the portfolio of shares in their several joint business ventures, including the Pacific Farallones Fresh Egg Company, the Sitka Alaskan Ice Import Company, and the Bellingham Bay Coal Company. To pass time, Dr. Fifer and I walked around the harbour, still abustle with incoming ships waiting for their turn to dock. At each landmark, the doctor recalled his personal history of the place. "When we passed through here, back in '48, on our way to the gold fields, the cove was a forest of bare masts. Every able body had abandoned previous commitments and rushed to stake a claim. With no one to man the ships, the hulls settled at the bottom of the bay."

We strolled the Presidio where the doctor had laboured when the Volunteers first disembarked. "That was more than ten years ago, when the city was a fishing village called Yerba Buena, 'good grass'. How we hated this assignment, Ah Chung, breaking our backs at shifting the rubble of the ruins, between hours and hours of useless drill. Dr. Wierzbicki and I met here, though. 1847. He had shipped from New York on the *Loo Choo* while I was on the *Susan Drew*. The misery of the assignment to ready the ancient Spanish Presidio for American occupation brought us together and we have remained friends ever since." We wandered the hills in their green mantle of June, marveling from our viewpoints at the thousands of people where, ten years before, inhabitants numbered a mere few hundred.

One of the things we did not do was row across the bay to say good-bye to San Quentin where Dr. Fifer had found me and rescued me from my dank stone cell. It was my good fortune that his scientific arguments of applied phrenology had convinced the authorities that I had neither the face nor the skull of a criminal, when all my feeble protestations had fallen on deaf ears. I shudder to remember the cold and the damp, the knowledge that, had it not been for the doctor, my saviour, it is probable I would never have walked free again, that my bones would remain inside those walls still. Whenever I blubbered to express my gratitude, the doctor always brushed off his role. "Nonsense, Ah Chung. Science. Pure science, and justice. What is freedom without justice?" he asked, and I knew he expected no answer. Justice and mercy. Justice and mercy.

All those idle weeks, we walked the streets and trails like shiftless ghosts, severed from our former lives but not yet moved on to the new.

While Dr. Fifer was arranging reservations for another scheduled journey to the British Possessions, he picked up a copy of the *Daily Alta California* which had published a letter quoting Mrs. Douglas, the wife of the Governor of the Colony of Vancouver's Island. He read me the news:

"ADVICE FROM ONE WHO KNOWS: Mrs. Douglas, the lady of the Governor, is of Indian origin. She is an estimable person and willing to give advice to those who ask for it. Her gardener, an old Scotchman, who has lived with them for several years, has caught the gold fever and wants to be off to the mines. 'Do not start, Thomas', she said to him yesterday, 'until the end of the next month. Then the river will be falling several feet a day, as fast as it has risen, and then is the time to get the gold. There is plenty of it, and enough for a hundred thousand men. But if you go before that time, you will not be able to work for the high water. This advice is from one who was born and brought up in childhood on the banks of the Fraser River and who after her marriage, lived for years with the present governor at the various stations of the company. If this is not enough to inform people, then it is impossible to repress the premature rush hitherwards."

Dr. Fifer decided to heed the advice. There would be no mining activity in the gold fields while the snow was melting in the mountains; it would take another month for the water level to go down enough to expose the auriferous sand bars. Another letter confirmed that his decision was wise. The *Victoria Weekly Gazette* printed on June 13 a letter from a miner waiting at Fort Hope for the freshet to end, the high water to recede:

"I have been here for several days and have seen quite a number of persons from the bars above. From them I learn that there is but little doing in the way of mining; the river is too high, and but few persons are at work. There are about one thousand men here at present. What they will do if the river does not fall in the course of five or six weeks, is difficult to tell. By that time their provisions will all be gone, and there are but few who have money to buy anymore.

"I would advise all that think of coming here to remain where they are at present, for it will be at least six weeks before they can do anything here—perhaps longer. There is no possibility of getting above Fort Yale with a stock of provisions until the river gets lower. It is now at its height.

"I am well satisfied that there is gold here, and above; but whether it will ever be found in as great quantities as many imagine, remains to be seen. Quite a number are leaving here, cursing the mines. There are but few provisions for sale here.

"There is great need of an established system of local government here. A gambling house has already opened here; and if the means are not taken to suppress it, more will follow. Then, in this period of inaction, drinking and fighting will become the order of the day.

"There has been a considerable excitement here in relation to the killing of Cowry by Kerrison, and at one time there was talk of Lynch law being resorted to.

"An Indian was killed near here yesterday by a white man, who threw him into the water."

Dr. Fifer merely nodded at this news. "Creditable, Ah Chung. Creditable," he concluded. He knew the risks of a gold rush. "After I demobilized from the Volunteers, I rushed with hundreds of others to the gold fields of Sutter's Valley. The snow melt in the High Sierra does raise the river levels and did indeed at certain seasons cause the panners and sluice operators to shut down." I do not believe that he was beginning to hesitate; I felt at the time that he considered his experience in California would be something which gave him knowledge and expertise he could contribute to the new rush in another colony.

However, on one of the days when we were roving the streets of San Francisco's Chinatown, wandering between our old lives and our new, the doctor stopped outside a fortune-teller's stall. Captivated by Madame Swett's signboard, a painting depicting a man suspended upside-down by one leg, on impulse, he stepped inside.

Although I knew that Dr. Fifer was not a believer—"The Age of Superstition is behind us, Ah Chung. We live in a time of reason and enlightenment. Science, my man!"—he had also confessed that before coming to his decision to leave San Francisco, he had asked a former patient, Madame Jaune, whom he had treated successfully for venereal warts, to make some enquiries for him among her male friends.

"Your doctor friend should avoid getting killed by the 'Law and Murderers' and leave quickly," her advisors suggested.

"It looks as if the British will have their turn at a gold rush this time, a repetition of the California excitement of ten years ago."

"The Hudson's Bay Company's trading licence is expiring; they are selling off their assets."

"The Indians have absconded with all the Hudson Bay kitchen's spoons, ladles, pots and pans, to dig for gold."

"New Caledonia is probably a safe investment; the doctor will find law and order in the country."

As Madame Jaune was a banker's mistress, her sources proved

to be somewhat more realistic than those of the card-reading clairvoyant Madame Swett. When Dr. Fifer stepped slowly from her "office," he was pale and pearls of perspiration beaded his brow. I feared bad news, of course, although I knew that the doctor had merely succumbed to the siren call to amuse himself and to show me that he was not superstitious. When he finally shared his reading with me, several days later, he tried to brush it off. "Scoundrels all, Ah Chung. Just more *scheissers* relieving the gullible of our silver eagles."

And what had the soothsayer told him? I memorized his every word: "You will travel and be compensated by success through hard work."

"Of course, Dr. Fifer," I told him, "I could have told you that, and I would not have charged you thirty dollars."

But then he confessed that he had paid an extra ten and the diviner had warned him: "On Independence Day, beware of the bright sentinels of the sky."

"Hogwash," the doctor had asserted. I chose to remain silent. I could have said "By Independence Day, we will be long disembarked in British Territory."

I was such a Fool.

After waiting three weeks for the *Sierra Nevada* to return to port, we were happy to depart once again. She was an old steamer, built for 900 passengers. Still, her owners claimed her to be fast and safe, taking less than one hundred hours from San Francisco to Fort Victoria under favourable conditions. Again, Dr. Fifer reserved a berth for himself and steerage passage for me as his assistant. Again, as we walked aboard, we found the ship grossly overburdened with freight and passengers. However, during his earlier effort to re-book a safer passage, Dr. Fifer had learned that, in the surge of the boreal gold fever, all ships were overloaded and equally safe, or unsafe. Our choices were limited—we could go, or we could choose not to go.

Dr. Fifer expressed his concern at the mass of humans on board, altogether 1200, but the crewman he addressed only laughed. "We carried 1900 on our last trip, a record," he boasted. "Last year", he added, "we made the round trip merely once, San Francisco to Vancouver's Island. This year, at least fifty trips will be necessary, to meet the new demand." Dollars, supply and demand, he was implying, and the doctor resigned himself to what he could not control. If we were following in the wake of some 20,000 gold seekers, 20,000 had been delivered safely before us.

Hundreds of passengers, men, women and children, had been unable to secure berths or sleeping accommodations of any kind. They lay about on the decks and in the saloons and on the days of particularly rough seas, they moaned and cried in the abandon of despair and hopelessness. About the fifth day out, a woman passenger died, and on the evening of the same day, she was buried at sea. Captain Blethen read the funeral service as the corpse, sewed in canvas and weighted with iron, was shot over the side.

Conditions on the ship were abominable: the water was bad, the food was wretched, there was no attempt at sanitation, and the stench from the hold was unbearable. Only a few escaped an attack of seasickness; the doctor despaired how some would survive the journey. When I came down with *mal de mer*, Dr. Fifer treated me with small sips of cordial from a jug he had brought. He insisted that I move up from steerage to use his own berth where he could tend to me more effectively. He being experienced at sea was spared the affliction. I did begin to feel better, although the medicinal liquor was at ebb-tide mark by the time we sighted Cape Flattery on the tip of the Olympic Peninsula.

On the sixth night the head wind stiffened to a fierce gale. In spite of all that could be done to reassure the wretched people on board, many resigned themselves to their fate; few expected to see land again. That night two men, who had both come aboard healthy and strong, succumbed and were buried at sea the next morning.

The weather turned in the afternoon of the seventh day out; it was bright and warm. The wind died to a gentle zephyr, the sea calmed, and the steamer began to make fairly good time. The sick people gradually crawled from their hiding places, looking wan and wretched. They were loud in the expression of their thanks that they had come through the tempest with their lives.

The next morning was warm and pleasant; land was in sight. Gulls skimmed the surface of the waves. The captain assured us that we would reach Vancouver's Island the next day. Colour returned to many pallid cheeks and the lustre to many dull eyes. We were nine days on the way, and the discomfort had been great. It seemed a miracle as great as that of the Loaves and Fishes story that the *Sierra Nevada* had survived the heavy winds and waves that had beset her path to the north.

As the captain steered the steamer around the rocky point into the deep harbour and we reached our destination, I wondered at the different appearance of the place. Instead of the golden brown hills of the Golden Gate, green only in this one month of our hovering, here were rocks with trees twisting away from the wind, and tall evergreens. As the hired wagon took us into the settlement of Fort Victoria, the forest appeared transformed into giant stumps surrounded by tents. The straight wooden palisades around the fort stood out, and then, towering above the wharfs and tiers of buildings, the wooden steeple of Christ Church stood like a lighthouse, Dr. Fifer's beacon of civilization.

The crowds in the tent city seemed subdued. "Aye," the driver assured us as we approached a hotel, "they are still asleep, or still recovering from yesterday's festivities. Independence Day. Fireworks Night." Indeed, on the boat, noise-makers and lights had come out in the lounge the evening before, but the fear of fire at sea had kept the Roman candles, pinwheels, and firecrackers unlit. Instead, one of the passengers, a scientist from Austria, had gathered a crowd to stand at the upper railing and observe the sky. There were many stars, granted. The night watchers pointed out Hercules, the hero, almost directly over our heads, Polaris, the North Star, and the Bears, Ursa Major and Minor (those heavenly vessels of our childhood, the little dipper pouring into the big dipper). Orion, the ubiquitous hunter, was off in another direction, invisible at this time of year, the astronomer confirmed. But he insisted that a comet would arrive any night now. The passengers were so delighted to have calm sea and fresh air that they stood gladly until well after midnight and no one complained when the celestial visitor did not materialize.

When Dr. Fifer relayed this science to me, I rejoiced at the fiery star's failure to appear. I did not tell him that in my village, people know a comet as an omen of doom.

3

We had been spared the comet's evil omen on the arduous journey from San Francisco. We arrived safely, disembarked from the *Sierra Nevada*, and found a carriage to take us into Victoria. We alighted in front of the hotel, Dr. Fifer walking ahead, carrying his valise of medical necessities, while I kept an eye on the two heavy trunks.

What I would have done further will never be recorded—-"Boom! Boom!" A sound of heavy explosions greeted us from the direction of the fort. Dr. Fifer cowered, ducked, and gazed about in fearful confusion. I had seen this reaction in him before; sudden noises triggered alarm, evoked recollections of battle, of combat, of threats upon his life. Boom! Boom! At the brink of unthinkable anxiety, in the man once bitten by a snake, every rope arouses fear.

The explosions ceased and the doctor exhaled with relief. "Ceremonial, Ah Chung. Good. Could it be that someone in the fort is aware of the arrival of a well-known physician and his esteemed assistant?" I knew that he was making a little joke at our expense, to hide his embarrassment. He was, of course, well known in San Francisco, "the Athens of the Pacific". The newspapers had cited him, the doctor, numerous times for his accomplishments. However, his summons to testify as a medical witness last year, for his friends Mr. and Mrs. Hodges, in a malpractice suit against a colleague, Dr. Cooper, had left him with a taint of disrepute in his own mind, if not in the eyes of others.

In those early hours of our arrival in British Territory, the doctor continued to feign confidence, to pretend that the explosions had not triggered memories, either of murderous enemies or the prescient Market Street soothsayer—'Avoid Independence Day fireworks, the bright sentinels of the sky.' "It was probably some Yankee just waking up and finishing his celebration." I could tell that he had regained his composure and his sense of humour. As we walked into the hotel, a ripple of news washed through the lobby to us. The gun was a signal indicating that the Governor was preparing to speak to new arrivals.

In the jostle and bustle of transporting ourselves the few miles from the landing into the town, we had lost sight of one passenger with whom Dr. Fifer struck up an acquaintance on the passage. Among the 1200 aboard the *Sierra Nevada* headed for the gold fields of the Fraser River, he had met a twenty-four year old budding writer and newspaper reporter for the San Francisco *Daily Morning Call*, Mr. David Higgins. Mr. Higgins had planned to continue his journey with us but we lost each other in the melee of the masses streaming ashore. Higgins did catch up to us later, arriving in Fort Yale on Captain Wright's next voyage. He established himself in a rustic store on the bench above the beach where he resided for the better part of a year and during this time developed a casual friendship with the doctor. Perhaps the difference in age and experience was too great. However, this loss of Mr. Higgins proved to be prophetic; their relationship ended in disillusionment when the writer, after assuming the position of editor of a Victoria newspaper, published a rumour of a professional misadventure. When Dr. Fifer was attacked and falsely accused by a grieving mother, Higgins, to increase circulation, to sell more papers, had no qualms about publishing innuendo of the paltry incident.

The one-horse dray had taxied us up into Victoria but we found "no room at the inn," as Dr. Fifer phrased it. He arranged to store the trunks and we set out to find a safe place to lay our heads. We walked through the town, over rocks, through the trees, and into the fort to make inquiries which indeed proved fruitless. We learned that most of the company's unmarried employees boarded inside the fort; the houses of the married men and of the colonial officials were few in number and outside the palisades. Further back from the waterfront and the fort were the farms supplying eggs, milk, cream, butter, and meat to the small colony now hosting ten thousand transients representing every country on the face of the earth. Gold seekers, bearing their past lives and future destinies in one large pack on their backs, crowded every bit of cleared land. The rocks and fields were covered with miners' tents; the streets swarmed with impatient expectant humanity. "Like the monarch butterflies to Mariposa," Dr. Fifer remarked, recalling one of California's natural wonders. Then, as was his habit, he offered me another version. "Flies to the honey pot, Ah Chung. Like flies to honey." The miners, originally from around the world and now mostly Americans who had been ten years in California, had requested that Governor Douglas speak to them about the gold fields. To our great fortune, we had arrived in time, had heard the signal, and were present when the Governor addressed the crowd. In his person, Governor Douglas was an imposing figure, tall, swarthy, with a physique only augmented by the gold braid and ceremonial hat of his office. He stood on a platform moved towards the gates of the fort and lectured the multitudes arrayed among the outcrops below.

"My friends: You wish me to speak to you about Fraser's River, and get my advice about going there, and my opinion about the country. Now I will tell you all plainly, that I will not take the responsibility of giving any advice on the subject. You have all heard what has been said of Fraser's River, and I know nothing more about the gold than has already been told you by others.

"Had you sent to ask my opinion about Fraser's River before you left California, I would have told you, one and all, not to leave your quiet homes; not to give up the substance for a shadow, and to wait patiently until something more definite was known about the country. Now suppose I were to tell you so, suppose I were to advise you, one and all, to return immediately to your homes without going further, what would the answer be? Why, you would all refuse to do so. You would all say 'that course will never suit.' After the trouble and expense we have had in coming here, we must go the end, we must see the elephant. And perhaps you might think that I had some object to gain in keeping you from going to Fraser's River.

"Now I know, men, what you wish me to tell you. You wish me to say there is lots of gold in Fraser's River but that I will not say, because I am not certain of the fact myself. But this I will tell you as my own settled opinion, that I think the country is full of gold, and that east and north and south of Fraser's River, there is a gold field of incalculable value and extent.

"I have told our glorious Queen so, and I now tell you so, and if I mistake not, you are the very men who can prove by your courage and enterprise, whether this opinion be right or wrong. Remember I do not give you that statement as an established fact, but simply as an opinion, founded on what I have already seen myself, and heard from others who know the country.

"Now what more can I say to you, but go on and prospect, and in a few short weeks you will be able to tell me what Fraser's River is.

"Take mining tools and food in abundance: you will then be independent of others and may go to whatever part of the country you choose.

"I would not advise you to go beyond Fort Yale with your canoes, as the river is dangerous above that point. Neither would I advise you to take the Fort Hope road, as you cannot carry enough of provisions to last you over the journey. The route by Harrison's River is, I think the best, and they are now preparing to get a road open to that way, in fact, I expect to see teams and wagons on the twenty-mile portage that divides that river from Anderson's Lake, before many months are over. That is a safe and accessible route at all seasons to upper

Fraser River.

"Let me say one word about the Indians. They are all friendly but still have an eye to your things; do not leave them exposed, get on with them as quietly as you can, and government will protect you. Be careful of your revolvers, and be not too ready to use them in your own cause. The law of the land will do its work without fear and without favour. Therefore, appeal to it in all cases, let it do justice between man and man, let it defend your rights and avenge your wrongs. Now my friends, go on and prosper, there is hard work before you, and I hope you will be repaid with rich strikes and big nuggets."

"Amen," I heard Dr. Fifer murmur under his breath. We looked around at the ragged crowd standing silent and attentive. Still Governor Douglas spoke on:

"One word more about the views of government. The miner who acts in submission to the laws and pays the Queen's dues like an honest man shall be protected in person and property, and as soon as good and trusty men are found, measures will be taken for the conveyance and escort of gold from the mines to this place. Every miner will give in his own sack, and his own weight, and have it addressed and sealed in his own presence, and get a receipt for a sack said to contain so much gold dust. It will be deposited in the public treasury at Victoria, and delivered to the owner on producing the deposit receipt. There will be a charge made for the expense of conveyance, but that will be a small matter compared to the security of your property.

"I now wish you all well and shall not detain you by any further remarks."

Dr. Fifer graded the governor's address as honest, realistic, and instructive. He liked what was said about respect for authority being rewarded by the protection of British law, "without fear and without favour". I had heard him discuss in better days with his San Francisco friends over cigars and brandy the mistakes they had made in

California, how great men are controlled by their own right conduct but, to control lesser men, laws are necessary. The news that the colony was preparing to hire the necessary "good and trusty men" as administrators was reassuring to Dr. Fifer.

We left that assembly and, having explored all there was to explore of the small settlement, proceeded back towards the harbour to stake a plot to lay our heads that first night. We picked a rocky bench beneath a sheltered outcrop with a view of the water and the security of the fort to our backs. We felt safer where crowds would deter foul play. Then, still tired from the journey, we organized our possessions and wrapped ourselves in our blankets.

After listening most of the night to noise and rowdiness all around us, still tired from the journey, we were finally able to sleep. We lay that first night on beds of knotty fir boughs.

Awaking late, making our toilet where we could (as for bathing, there was always the harbour), we set out around the noon hour to eat at the Bayley Hotel Restaurant of which we had read in San Francisco. Luncheon cost each of us a dollar, and for a glass of water to wash down the food, we paid fifteen cents. Water was scarce and just as dear as Hudson's Bay rum. For the evening meal, I prepared our dinner of bacon, beans, and flapjacks over an open fire.

More miners arrived, by the thousands, it seemed, off every sail and steamboat that glided in. Most stayed close to the small inner harbour, awaiting passage on the next available vessel departing for the mainland. The Hudson's Bay Company freight boats going as far as Fort Langley carried as many miners as they could cram on board. Men talked of finding their own way across the remaining ninety miles of ocean waters. Some busied themselves farther inland and up stream beds, attempting to construct makeshift crafts, but the crossing was known to be dangerous.

We learned that during the weeks we had waited for passage in San Francisco, the American Pacific Mail Steamship Company had contracted to furnish transportation across the open waters to the mainland as well as up river on the Fraser as far as it was navigable, a total distance of close to two hundred miles. We remained in Victoria only long enough to arrange passage on this new service to the interior. To get to the gold fields required travelling on two different vessels for a total fare of twenty dollars. The seaworthy side-wheeler *Wilson G. Hunt* took us across the strait to Fort Langley.

Crossing the Strait of Georgia was a breeze compared to the storm of our difficult seven days into Victoria. These waters were different from the open seas; in places fast currents and eddies came together from different channels. In other places, there were islands and groups of rocky outcrops around which the captain steered. There were places where muddy river currents entwined with green-blue ocean waves and tides. In colour, in composition, where the salt chuck melded with the river's load of sand and silt, it swirled and marbled like the powders and tinctures I pulverized and mixed in the mortar to prepare Dr. Fifer's medicines.

Everywhere on this crossing, land was visible. The passengers pointed out the snow-capped peaks, the cone spewing smoke and steam had an English name—Mount Baker—after an officer on Captain Vancouver's crew. The waters and islands bore Spanish names, of men who had arrived before: Juan de Fuca, Quadra, Galiano, Saturna. The channel we sought into Fraser's River had not been charted by the Royal Navy, Captain Vancouver having sailed by in the fog and missed the passage completely. The day we travelled was clear and bright, making the darkness of the treed shoreline more impressive than oppressive.

We arrived at Fort Langley after one night on board, and transferred our luggage to Captain Wright's *Enterprise,* a smaller flat-bottom sternwheeler, better adapted for river travel, able to out-manoeuvre the cumbersome sidewheelers, to better negotiate the fluctuating water levels, narrows, and treacherous currents to Fort Hope.

On this little vessel, I was able to observe the types of people who would be our future neighbours, perhaps our patients. Although we were all modern-day Argonauts, the miners were hirsute, with unkempt hair and beards that would put the prophets in Dr. Fifer's Bible to shame. They sported high boots, a wide-rimmed slouch hat, and coarse red, green, or blue shirts tucked into their pants. Each of this motley crowd of bonanza hunters carried a pack, supplemented by a pick and shovel. They wore a leather belt from which were suspended a Bowie knife and a revolver.

In contrast, Dr. Fifer and I lacked tools and weapons and were most unsuitably dressed; I had anticipated cold, wearing my city frock coat, wool trousers, and boots; however, only my head felt the cool breeze as I never like to wear a hat atop my braided queue. Most surely, the doctor's attire attracted the captain's attention, for he wore his dark *Cassimere* jacket over gabardine trousers, a black silk velvet vest and an embroidered Mexican linen shirt. On his feet he had a pair of scuffed but clean brogans instead of high boots. His gold-rimmed spectacles and a "Prince Albert" golden watch fob gave him away as a well-heeled, learned, and cultured person, while his eyes revealed a glint of humour and a shine of serenity. His bearing of respectable dignity made him appear taller than his actual inches.

Once we were on our way, the Captain left the wheel to his assistant and came down from the pilothouse on the upper forecastle to converse with passengers. Captain Wright is a big burly fellow who towered above us; both Dr. Fifer and I had to look up to speak with him. After pointing out how the huge steering wheel in the pilothouse was connected to the rudder by means of chains running in grooves along the steerage deck, the captain guided us towards the stern to explain other specifications of his pride and joy.

"The heart of the ship is the steam engine," he began; then, pointing to the boiler sitting well forward on the deck, "the engines are a high-pressure type, which can put a severe strain on these boilers. A faulty boiler or even excessive boiler pressure can mean a serious explosion. On the other hand, we often need to utilize every possible pound of steam to master difficult rapids. We store a cask of bacon with the firewood, for an emergency," Captain Wright laughed, "in case we need additional steam." I know from my own kitchen duties how fat can fuel a fire.

"The furnaces are on this level, the main deck," the captain continued our guided tour, "to make it easier to feed the fire, cords of firewood are stacked here. The long steam pipes leading to the engines at the stern give off ripples of heat all down the main deck. That is why this deck level is used only for non-perishable freight." I noticed, as we inspected the main deck level, that "non-perishable freight" included Indians, Chinamen, and Negro passengers.

"The length and beam are proportionally very great. She is 115 feet long, with a beam of twenty-one feet; the hull is flat-bottomed and draws sixteen inches of water when light, and twelve or fifteen inches additional when loaded. She can carry eighty tons of freight on waters as shallow as twenty-six inches. The paddlewheel is twenty-one feet in diameter and spans the entire width of the boat. The individual paddles immerse to a depth of sixteen inches." From the deck we strained to see the details as he explained them. "The hull is quite straight down, to the wheel here at the stern, although the bow is 'shovel-nosed'. Fort Langley is the exception; at most of our landings, there are no wharves, but I can run her bow up on the bank and lay a plank ashore almost anywhere. Then, I just throw her into reverse and the paddlewheel takes her back to midstream, and we're on our way."

Dr. Fifer mentioned that he had seen steamboats 'hung-up' on the sandbars of California rivers. "It is no exaggeration," Captain Wright agreed, "that I've actually had to 'walk' the steamer over a sandbar on its paddlewheel. I can take her between snags and close to bluffs, where side wheels would be knocked away."

After our guided tour, Dr. Fifer excused himself to go above to the saloon deck, which was fitted up with a few staterooms and a dining room for upper level passengers. I stood at the railing on the main deck, watching the river and the shore as the crew went about their work. "Stand by with the trip-pole!" I heard when the swift current threatened to turn the boat about. On the shout "Trip!" the heavy pole, attached to the ship's side by a swivel, was plunged into the shallow water. The first time, the ship was brought up by it and swerved into the bank. Farther upstream when the call came again, the bottom must have been hard and rocky, or the water deeper than was thought, for the trip pole did not hold. Away she flew again, backwards, down the river, until brought up against the bank or across a snag. Then the captain's skill with steering and with feeding the right amount of steam to the engine took us back into the current.

Captain Wright knew what he was doing and he did find his reward for his investment. I heard later that he was once paid $25,000 for a single run from Victoria to "Murderer's Bar" near Hope. Another tale told how his other ship, the *Surprise*, was frozen in the river. The passengers had to proceed on foot through deep snow to Hope. That was before the captain took his business to Washington Territory. Tom Wright's *Surprise* or Bully Wright's *Enterprise* were the best known steamers on the Fraser River and carried a substantial portion of the early traffic.

Left to myself, I explored our main deck. At the stern, sitting on a wooden crate, an elderly Indian man, wearing heavy wool trousers, rolled up at the ankle, and a heavy grey wool pullover shirt, was working a block of red cedar in front of him on the deck. Using a knife like hunters carry to process a carcass and a rock for a mallet, he would split off a slice of cedar, a miniature shake, trim it to hand size, and rub the planes and edges to ensure smoothness and the absence of slivers. He noticed my attention and motioned me to take one, nodding and smiling. The twinkle in his eyes made me homesick for my grandfather whose face I had not seen for more than ten years.

Since the old man could tell that I was confused, he made a

digging motion, and then a scooping gesture, patting something into the imaginary hole he had dug. But the utensil seemed too delicate for mining. I was still confused. To explain further, he took the shake delicately on one side and pretended to wipe his ass, at the same time repeating the word "swites" which I understood from no language that I knew.

"Swites?" I mimicked, and he was so pleased with my repetition that he insisted I take his offering, which I pocketed with a bow of thanks. It was weeks later, when Lucy Allard stopped into my kitchen one afternoon and saw the swite lying on a pantry shelf. After she quelled her bubbling laughter, holding her hand to her mouth, the young woman clarified the object's true function. And that is how I, red in the face, learned what this tool is used for.

Although I had observed Indians, Chinamen, and Negroes taking advantage of the lower steerage deck fare on the *Enterprise*, there were also two White women who stayed together. They were checked upon at regular intervals by a gentleman who left his table in the saloon and shared his flask with both ladies. One of them was not well, seeming weak and nauseous, but she did not refuse the swigs he offered. They were dressed fashionably in voluminous skirts with a matching jacket, high neckline, puffed sleeves, and high laced boots. Were it not for my experience around the docks and for receiving women patients in Dr. Fifer's San Francisco practice, I would not have recognized the occupation of these two as working ladies, accompanied by their protector who had purchased the cheapest fare available. All three were heading, along with the rest of us, to find their own pot of gold in the fields of New Caledonia.

At the other side of the deck from where the women watched, I observed a loquacious Negro man who had pulled out another crate and with a stained white towel over his forearm was calling out "Last chance! Last chance!" He did a little jig, snapping scissors in his right hand, singing something about Dixie. Although the gentle rocking of the vessel on swift water precluded shaving, the barber was offering the hopeful prospectors what could be their last chance of a haircut for several months or years. The unkempt appearance of the miners we could see on the bars was the best advertising he could have had. Men lined up for his service.

On that first trip in early July, we stopped to drop freight at the mouth of the Harrison River on the north shore and the Chilliwhack on the south bank before the river started to narrow and gravel bars appeared more frequently midstream or along bends. Dr. Fifer came down to watch with me as shoreline and mountains moved in, crowding closer towards the deep channel. Together we watched men working the sandbars, standing where the water lapped the shingle, dipping gold pans into gritty water, swirling them to speed the separation of gravel from gold. Campfires and tents staked their territory. Some of them waved as we chugged by; others refused to be distracted, even by the calls and greetings of the eager passengers on board. "Any hot spots? A pay streak? Bonanza? Is that your glory hole?"

Dr. Fifer provided running commentary as we passed. "See the trees, Ah Chung? Cottonwood. Dr. Wierzbicki's paper on locating gold makes the point that oak trees indicate the presence of gold. These men will want to move farther up river soon."

The river began to curve north around the base of a snow-capped mountain. Before we reached Fort Hope, we passed Cornish Bar, Murderer's Bar, Last Chance. "Such names, Ah Chung. What evil are we moving into? Is this the River Styx drifting us ever deeper into Hell?" I did not think at the time that the evil is not in the landscape but rather in the men flocking to it. But Dr. Fifer was oblivious. The passing beauty made him loquacious; he answered his own question. "I think not. We are not drifting into Hell. It's getting better, really. You can see for yourself—the flat lands, the breadth of forest between water and hills is narrowing; sandy soil is yielding to a rise of cliffs; we are penetrating granite and hard rock, climbing into the mountains. See the waterfalls? Upstream will be canyons. That's where the gold originates, as those ancient rocks cooled. The secret mother lode from which fortunes spring. I think my friend knew that the wink of quartz, the glitter of feldspar, are better indicators than a stand of oak. Quartz and gold are cousins. Or, as the alchemists used to say, forged in the same crucible."

I fingered the lucky worry stone I always carry in my pocket. Black as coal, but smooth, solid, hard, and shot with white lines of quartz in streaks as graceful as if crafted by a master calligrapher. "So then, are these panners here slaving in vain?" I asked.

"No," the doctor responded. "They'll find flour. Gold dust. What they call 'colour.' Nuggets even, anything big enough to pick out of the pan with their tweezers. Anything that may have been weathered out of the bedrock, and transported downstream by the water. Every time the water level changes, there's a chance that more alluvial gold has been deposited. *Placers*, the 49ers called them, from the old Spanish, *plaza*. Meaning 'this is the place.' The smart ones will look on benches that were under water in the freshet, and in crevasses where the heavy metal settles, and just downstream from a big boulder or any other impediment to the water's flow.

"Anything that slows it down makes the water drop some of its load." The doctor liked to hold forth. "A confluence, where waters meet, or a branch, where an arm veers off are both good prospects. Look in the roots of reeds and grasses and snags; look in the moss on the higher rocks. The moss is like a green Golden Fleece. In the olden days, when the gods lived with men, they used a sheep fleece to trap the gold, to sieve it from the water. That's the Fleece the Argonauts were after." I knew of the Argonauts from Dr. Fifer's reading of the labours of Hercules to me. The doctor went on. "The lure of gold brought the heroes together, and spurred their voyages of war and discovery. It is true what they say, that 'gold is where you find it'. However, you are more likely to find it if you know where to look."

As the waterway narrowed further and braided into separate channels and appeared to disappear into the mountains, the captain's whistle, three short and one long blast, told us that we were approaching Fort Hope, the terminus for our steamer journey. Captain Wright steered his vessel around a wooded island which loomed black in the waning light and nosed the prow into a sheltered bend below the Hudson's Bay Company buildings.

With regret we said good-bye to our captain, and walked up the narrow gangplank, M. W. Fifer, M.D., and I, Ah Chung, enduring the critical stares of the crowd on the riverbank above us. We inquired at the Hudson's Bay post about the best way to get to Yale. Alas, we found confirmation of what the Governor had told us miners: there was no "best way." River transportation, although a risky undertaking also, was preferred to taking the pack trail on either side of the Fraser River, fighting the dense underbrush up and down steep inclines. In contrast, the journey by water required no physical exertion but demanded that we as passengers sit immobilized for hours, without shifting weight, in unstable dugout canoes, at the pricey fare of two dollars.

. Annoyed at what seemed like an outrageous fee and at how the authorities allowed this scalping of travellers, Dr. Fifer directed me to place our effects in the large dugout manned by Indians offering their service. Our canoe already contained considerable freight, including a blacksmith's forge, destined for Fort Yale. Our Indians, Uslick Sha-en-Khmethen and Indian Joe supervising, assured us that they had hauled all kinds of goods and passengers upriver. On the previous trip, they had transported a heavy cast iron door portal for the Gold Commissioner's vault. The size of the freight had made it necessary to tie the contraption crosswise on the canoe to allow room for the paddlers.

A few days ago, they reported, their freight canoe had carried four passengers, one of them by the name of Friesach, an inquisitive mathematics professor from Salzburg who never ran out of questions. I wondered if this was the scientist aboard the *Sierra Nevada* who had guided the night watchers on their lookout for the comet, the night before we docked on Vancouver's Island.

We were seated in the canoe, about to cast off, when, at the last minute, the clerk of the Hope Magistrate, a Constable Chisholm, came running with a package. Scanning our faces, he handed the parcel to Dr. Fifer, saying: "Would you see that Captain Sanders, the magistrate at Fort Yale, gets this?"

Dr. Fifer accepted the sealed missive, feeling self-important to be entrusted with an official communication. He took it as a favourable omen, as providential, until the Indian crew explained that the slipshod secretary had missed the regular mail boat to Fort Yale and that our canoe about to leave was the last one for a day or two. The paddlers already knew that the Hudson's Bay posts in Forts Langley and Hope had received similar dispatches, and that they contained copies of the proposed Colonial Council's Indian Act forbidding the dispensing or sale of spirituous liquors to Natives.

On the river, the paddlers' progress against the strong current was slow. They avoided the fast flow of the middle of the river and kept to the side eddies. All along the Fraser, wherever a bench or sandbar appeared, miners were encamped, waiting for the water to fall. "Union Bar," the men called out the new place names, as we approached or passed. "Trafalgar Bar. 54-40. American Creek. Texas Bar. Emory's Bar." The miners occupying the sand, waiting, were expecting to be able to make a fortune, to scoop up the gold by the handful and live at ease forevermore. "The larks one hopes to catch when the sky falls, as Higgins would say," was Dr. Fifer's first remark. Then he looked at me as if to translate: "When pigs grow wings, Ah Chung, pigs will fly."

The lulling dip of the paddles into and out of the water was the only sound. The paddlers battled the rapids at Trafalgar Bar and the currents at Two Sisters Rocks and Strawberry Island. Shortly before reaching Fort Yale, we passed a place of particularly intense mining activity, a bar to our right, which would be the left bank of the river. "You stand in the river, the current pressing your back, facing downstream. On your right-hand side, it is the right bank; on your left-hand side, the left bank," the doctor instructed. From the canoe, Dr. Fifer counted seventy-three solid wooden houses and one tent on the benches. He estimated several hundred miners and their helpers would be at work on the beach at first light. We had reached the notorious Hill's Bar, the infamous settlement peopled by the rowdy boatmen from San Francisco.

The paddlers had become less talkative as they laboured farther up river into the darkness of the night, the darkness of our yet-to-be-revealed future. A red blush rose in the night sky; when our canoe rounded the point, we saw that the fiery glow emanated from the burner of a mill where trees are sawed into timber. From this point we could see the black outline of our destination, the gold rush centre of Fort Yale rising in rough tiers from the river, above rocky cliffs and the beach along the water. In the sooty light I could make out the prominent dark profile of the Hudson's Bay Company warehouse on the upper bench. Here too, as had been the case in Fort Victoria, makeshift tents seemed to have sprung up like mushrooms on the rocks.

"No room!" the paddlers assured us. They insisted that they and many others offering the same service had brought so many gold seekers to the old fort site that no accommodations were available. Our red-shirted companions were undaunted. I was less enthused about another night rolled in our blankets and canvas on a bed of knotty boughs.

When the canoe's prow moaned onto the pebbly beach, our ordeal of nearly eight hours came to an end. The crew made fast to one of the large shore boulders; the passengers, after sitting rigid for hours, afraid to move lest we capsize and drown in the frigid waters, came alive. The crew helped us ashore, assisting by carrying those who hesitated to get their leather boots wet. We stretched, stiff, tired, wet, and blue with cold.

The Indians, notwithstanding the hours-long labour of inching the deeply-loaded dugout against the strong current, requiring the use of both hands to hold the paddle, unable to fend the tormenting midges off their nostrils and eyes, displayed a surprising change in deportment. As soon as the vessel scraped the ground, their silent hostility had changed to a jolly euphoria. Uslick Sha-en-Khmethen had difficulty containing his partner, Indian Joe, who was raucously laughing, uttering words in their language with a snicker that he tried to but could not suppress. *Shites. Swites. Whites. Shit. Shh. Shh,* sounds I could not decipher. Hardly having set foot on the ground themselves, they shoved off into the darkness. Echoes of their hilarity rippled across the water.

"*Schadenfreude,*" I heard the doctor mutter, I have since learned the meaning of the term: "Malicious delight in anticipating the misfortune of others." Dr. Fifer had a gift of being able to read men's hearts but by then he had lost his taste for instruction.

Perhaps his loss of patience that night meant simply that his attention was elsewhere, taken up by a cause more discreet, more personal and timely. Without distinction of social station or upbringing, without regard for education, wealth, profession, or privacy, the physician and surgeon from California's "Athens of the Pacific" and his Chinaman assistant followed the example of thousands of arrivals before us. With our pants down, aggravated by myriads of buzzing flies and mosquitoes, we squatted and unburdened ourselves.

Once relieved, breeches up again, no one showed compunction. Attending to first things first had wiped away social distinctions, forging us into comrades-in-arms on a singular quest. However, as we busied ourselves, the vanishing light turned the canyon into darkness. Movement was futile; there was no choice; where we had come ashore, there we had to settle for the night. The annoyance of bluebottles and mosquitoes was a small price to pay; we had reached hallowed ground, our stepping-stone to a fortunate future.

I could sense how tired my master was despite his ambitious plans for the morning, when he would attend to the safe delivery of the sealed letter and call at the Hudson's Bay post to inquire about a place for a medical office. Preparing his bedroll, Dr. Fifer had sniffed a suspicious unsavoury scent. Although his medical training had taught him to associate bad air with disease, he forced himself to ignore the olfactory alarm, allowing darkness to muffle the stench the same way it made invisible its origin. Content to have reached his destination, we rolled into our blankets, head and face covered against the bugs, and drifted off to sleep.

The growling of my empty stomach, the pestering of pesky insects, and the mattress of hard, shifting pebbles poking into my sides, awoke me before sunrise. In the grey light of dawn, I got up to build a campfire and to prepare breakfast. Try as I might, the fragrance of fried bacon, freshly baked bannock, and boiling coffee did nothing to mask the pervasive smell. Morning's milky light soon revealed the source of the stench. We had lain with the squalor of ubiquitous human metabolites, our own freshly deposited *ejecta* and those left behind by the thousands of our predecessors. "Shit!" I heard the men mutter as each in turn made his discovery. "Shit!"

Dr. Fifer was fastidious by nature, a medical man to whom cleanliness was next to godliness. To his colleagues' amusement in San Francisco, he had established in his waiting room rules for keeping people with repulsive conditions separate from regular patients. Boots with dog poop on them had to be left outside. He had also pioneered a wrought-iron washstand in his office, enhancing his commitment to hygiene. Dr. Fifer had learned from experience; ten years earlier he had survived *morbus typhi*, acquired, he was convinced, from eating contaminated grapes. Confined to hospital for several months, he had resolved never again to take food he thought unwashed.

Initially, the doctor was full of fortitude; however, when he awoke to the villainous *fetor of ordure*, or, "As we Americans call it, Ah Chung, the smell of shit," his disposition changed. With the substance caking his brogans, his gabardine pantaloons, the backside of his fine *Cassimere* coat, Dr. Fifer experienced no small degree of mortification.

Seeing that he was so disconcerted, I offered to clean his clothes and boots, which I did with the aid of the still mysterious *swite* tablet I had received from the old Indian. I scraped and washed the befouled coat and pants as best I could before we set out, less heroically, for the Hudson's Bay Company post.

As we stomped up the steep bank, still in a foul mood, the doctor was accosted first by a heavily-set fellow, Thomas Yorke, who blocked his way while insisting that our party be guests at his recently completed "hotel". Pushing through, a second scalper introduced himself as Captain Seidenstriker, who importuned the doctor to stay at *his* hotel and restaurant, "newly established." Evidently the canoe paddlers' assertions that there was "no room" had been part of their little humiliation.

The crude approach of the two Fort Yale residents had struck Dr. Fifer at a precarious moment of sartorial embarrassment. He abruptly declined both enticements, knowing the reputation of such hotels, *rancherias,* along the gold trails—that they were often infested with lice and rats, and usually offered sleeping space for men wrapped in blankets on dirt floors. His first encounter with the two peddlers huckstering cheap lodging to anyone seeking shelter, regardless of colour, race, or scent, was interpreted as a snub. The doctor had made his first enemies in British territory.

We climbed upward, oblivious. Reaching the Hudson's Bay emporium, Dr. Fifer introduced himself to the storekeeper, Ovid Allard, and made the necessary inquiries. Mr. Allard, as is his wont, was only too happy to assist. He proved to be a valuable ally and future friend.

4

Knock. Knock. Knock. KNOCK.

Go away, woodpecker! You are too early. Pick another tree, another door. You have not taken possession yet.

Oh, no. Am I talking to imaginary birds now? Careful, Ah Chung.

I have had another rough night, with many ghosts chasing away sleep every time it approached. Last night, stars falling while a condemned man in chains awaits his fate, the reverend, distraught like a chicken without its head, the hangman, hovering like a vulture, my evening peace was destroyed. Everything was overshadowed by Jehil Hoadley Hale's gallows. That bizarre scaffolding crowning the grave of my beloved Doctor Fifer drew too many strangers; phantoms followed me home to my bedchamber.

Tap. Tap. Tap.

Again! The door. I am coming. I am coming.

I open it; I peer both ways, yet no one is waiting. Another paper, tacked to the panel. EVICTION NOTICE! Not again! I know what it says. "Vacate these premises!" The magistrate's clerk, Mr..Tennent, is becoming more persistent. I must hurry, pack what is mine, leave, disappear, or they will be forced to evict me themselves. The building is for sale. The estate. House and contents belonging to the late Doctor Max Fifer of Yale, British Columbia. Posters have been tacked up; the notice is published in a Victoria paper; Reverend Crickmer has read it.

I have not finished packing. What is mine fits easily into one valise. The rest, the simple furnishings—beds constructed here, shelves installed after we bought the house, stove, table, chairs, washstand, examining table, the office desk—along with the medical instruments, cooking pots, basins, pitchers, chamber pots, cuspidors, must all remain as part of the assets. Yet I am tempted to pack those things that the doctor left to me to manage. His medicine bottles, his powders and tablets, even the mortar and pestle which only I used, and the collection of dried roots, bark, and leaves I gathered myself or traded with the healer, the medicine woman from the Indian village.

What would a stranger know of these implements? Of Dr. Fifer's tools, his instruments? Or of his medical texts? Who else could even name a stethoscope, the new duckbill *speculum vaginae*, the silver catheter, the hard rubber syringes with their brittle gutta-percha tubes, blood-letting equipment, scarifiers, lancets, forceps, tooth pliers, the arrow extractor that I now use in the kitchen. Who would be able to identify the saws to amputate fingers, toes, arms, or legs, if they were to appear in a jumble box at a public auction? Or to be found as a curio left in a barn?

What will happen to this venerable old mortar and pestle which only I used, to grind the doctor's many concoctions until the apothecary suppliers began selling the powders ready-made? Like the arrow extractor which has been transformed into a kitchen tool, this mortar's function has changed. As a vessel, it is not the right shape for cooking or drinking from, and too small for a wine-bottle cooler. The top is too narrow for a cuspidor or a chamber pot, although we did use it in the surgery to collect fresh specimens. Is it doomed? The midden is no place for a crucible of such mystic provenance, tossed out with other discards—leaky tea kettles, burned-out pans and pots, leftovers and scraps. Like the arrow extractor which has been transformed into firewood tongs, will this reliquary be degraded into an inferior utensil? To save the vessel, I place the mortar with my valise.

I have managed to clear the top of Doctor Fifer's desk. I have sorted the papers, now filed into the many pigeonholes. Bills and expenses. Outstanding Invoices. Personal correspondence. This is the slot where he put his letters from Mr. David, his accountant, and the sad news of Dr. Wierzbicki's death of Christmas last. And the address of Dr. Rattray, the writer from Edinburgh who had visited Yale with Lady Franklin's entourage. This envelope contains newspaper clippings, some yellow and brittle, dating as far back as our San Francisco days. Expendable. The patient files, I am told, must remain, as part of the estate. But this largest file contains his duplicates and draft copies and one or two personal responses to Yale Town Council business. These I will wrap in the leather portfolio and take to Mr. Allard as soon as there is enough light on this special day.

I keep the folder under my coat against the morning's rain. Before my feet leave the boardwalk outside the Hudson's Bay store, Mr. Ovid Allard sees me coming, he looks up from the ledger as he sits at his high stool behind the counter.

"Ah Chung! How are you? You are up early too. I could not sleep as we await all this morning's terrible excitement to come to an end. What else is there to do but work?

How are you managing?" I know he means "managing the packing". I do not wish him to see how difficult it is for me, managing alone in this place.

"I am still packing, Mr. Allard, thank you. The clerk nailed another notice to the door. It woke me up this morning." I place the leather folder on his worn counter. "I think I should leave these with you, for the Council business."

Mr. Allard nods a thank you and removes the file to his desk behind the counter. "Ignore the eviction notices," he counsels me. "No one will expect you to leave before the hanging is over! If they do find a buyer quickly, you are always welcome to bunk out here, in the back, until you can arrange your transport."

I bow my head to thank him, a habit the doctor was always trying to get me to change. "Speak up, man," he used to say. "There is no need for you to appear subservient!" But habits return when we are tired or distressed.

"Ah Chung, you look like a man who has not slept in days. Almost as bad as the first time we met, but I must admit, you smell better today."

Mr. Allard is trying to dispel the brute nature of the day, to cheer me, reminding me of happier days, the first day we met when the doctor sought him out to inquire about establishing a practice, whether a hospital was needed, and where to deliver the brown package thrust on him by the Hope clerk.

"At first, you know, Ah Chung, I feared that your Doctor Fifer was another of those pompous city-slickers who arrived with the whisper of gold, one of those who thinks his own shit doesn't stink." He laughs at his own joke. "I told him that we already had a doctor, Dr. Crane, who demanded payment in gin and cash, and refused to be called out for dead bodies, but then Doctor Fifer defended the man, and defended the premise that payment is required. I think to myself, 'These people. When will they learn? We do things our own way here.' But after I got to know him, the doctor reminded me that in a free country, a capitalist country, people have to pay for the services they receive."

"You never had to pay?" I ask, to encourage him to go on.

"No, I never pay. The Governor and Company of Adventurers of England trading into Hudson's Bay, known as the Hudson's Bay Company, looks after me, and my family. When I told your Dr. Fifer, he pointed out: 'You are lucky.'

He explained that unlike the miners, I had benefits as an employee of the great HBC——since Here Before Christ." Mr. Allard laughs again, as he does every time he repeats this expression. "But, the doctor said to me, miners have no company to provide a doctor and medicine for them; and doctors and other professionals have no salary from a benevolent company. Their skilled services must be paid for by the patient directly. You know, Ah Chung, I had not thought about that before Doctor Fifer told me. But we had no professionals here, before the gold rush."

Although everyone is aware of what will take place today, Mr. Allard laughs again, yet, I'm not sure why, until I understand his reason: "It's easy to promise free service when none is available, not counting Doctor Crane." He alone knows how different things are now, how different they were before the little golden butterfly from the north arrived in the San Francisco mint. Have I not heard him complain more than once about the plague of locusts, the predatory flies who came and defiled his paradise?

"You know, Ah Chung, that first morning, arguing about what is right and what is wrong, I could tell that the doctor was pretending that the state of his clothing did not matter to him. I could tell he was tired and upset, but it did make him the same as everyone else. All the travelers who arrived at night slept on the beach, with the same result. It did not bother me. But I was wary when he said he was a doctor, and that he wanted to set up practice. I began to wonder why such a man, who could hang his shingle anywhere, why would he choose to come here, along with all the riffraff?"

Mr. Allard has begun to reminisce and I am content just to share his company, to listen.

"We already have a doctor in business here;" I told him. "Dr. Crane is working out of the California Hotel on Front Street. To tell you the truth, we've had not had much luck with doctors. This one reeks of liquor and will do house calls only if served a large gin first. According to the *Victoria Gazette*, the police there arrested Crane several times for being drunk and disorderly, and the magistrate fined him five shillings for stealing two bottles of gin, *Aged Thomas* brand, from Mr. Muir's store on Langley Street. Threatening the owner with a knife brought a quick end to Dr. Crane's medical career in Victoria. And Dr. Fifer, trying to defend him, he says to me: 'Surely we cannot believe every thing they print in the newspapers, Mr. Allard!'

"On your first day here, Ah Chung, I tell Doctor Fifer, your master, I says: 'Last week, there was a bad storm up the Canyon; trees fell and floated down the river. A miner arrived on the trail from Sailor Bar, looking desperately for a doctor. There had been an accident: a stranger on his way downriver was using his loaded gun as a walking staff when he fell over a tree that had come down across his path. The trigger caught on a twig, the gun went off and he shot himself in the thigh.' And Fifer says: 'Did Doctor Crane go?' and I says: 'We cajoled him on his way with a drink of *Highou*, a diluted whisky spiked with ground red pepper and flavoured with camphor, from company stock. By the time the party reached the scene, the stranger had died, having bled to death. All Crane did was pronounce him dead. He wanted to know about the man's effects, and his friends produced some letters and a poke of gold dust. A pair of gold scales was procured and from the dead man's purse the doctor weighed out $150 worth. He took that as the fee for his service, returned the black bag to the miners, and went on his way home. Us folks here considered the doctor's action greedy and heartless, and the word soon spread."

Mr. Allard continues to talk, as if my waiting ears were all that were needed to open the sluice. "This Doctor Crane's *a cheval donné*, the best gift horse we could get, a good-for-nothing who couldn't hit the wall with a handful of beans. Medical services in Yale were *en échec*, lamentable; we would make do with whoever visits briefly. Some were vagabonds, claiming to be healers, who cared more about getting paid than about the patient's welfare; they tried to get something for nothing. The worst was that at times of real need for medical help, none could be found. For serious conditions we preferred the long canoe journey to see Doctor Bradshaw in Hope."

I remember how Doctor Fifer tried to soften Mr. Allard's indignation that day. "You folks may be judging this Doctor Crane too harshly," he chided. "We don't know what unfortunate circumstances drive

73

a man to drink; Doctor Crane exhibited a sense of duty and did not refuse to go when the call came for help. At the scene, like a doctor would, he likely tried his best to stop the bleeding and revive the victim; alas, he could not save the stranger's life. You can't pin the blame for the miner's death on Doctor Crane! I suspect some travelling mountebank has fooled you, promising cures that cannot be had for love or money. No doctor, not even *Anno Domini* 1858, can guarantee a favorable outcome; he can only do his best.

"As for helping himself to the fee," Doctor Fifer continued lecturing, "the doctor did what you and any storekeeper do every day. Is it not common practice to reach into the customer's poke, using thumb and finger for the pinch of gold dust? Crane did better: he used scales to be accurate. Based on the fee of sixteen dollars or the equivalent in one ounce of gold dust for a regular office visit, Doctor Crane charged the going rate, fair and commensurate with the services rendered. I would have billed the same, regardless of the outcome."'

"I did not believe him at the time," Mr. Allard went on. "I lumped them all together—travelling healers, dentists, lawyers, schoolteachers, ministers of Christ with no credentials, peddlers selling bogus parchments, and doctors. But when I said as much, my words seemed to touch a sore spot with him. The good doctor took one step forward and leveled at me: "*Monsieur!* I'm a charter member of the Medico-Chirurgical Association of San Francisco where I was in private practice for more than ten years, a physician and surgeon with experience in surgery and medicine as a full time hospital stewart and later as assistant surgeon in charge of a military hospital.' ·

"'Were you a doctor before you came to America?' I asked him, because I could hear something of the old world in his speech." This seemed to set your Doctor Fifer off again. He began to try to explain to me how he became qualified. He said: 'I started my career in California. After the Mexicans drove out the Spanish *gachupines*, the troops departed, ending the country's occupation, and the doctors also left. The country was free but without physicians. It was a thorny problem for the Mexican administration; they made up for the deficiency by allowing any doctor to practice as long as he had worked as an apprentice under a senior physician. After the United States conquered California in 1847, they left well enough alone; the Mexican system seemed to function. It sounds as if, strangely enough, here in the north, you face a doctor shortage similar to the one in the south. Your government, I reckon, should do what the Mexicans did twenty years ago.' He said that, Ah Chung, on his first day here!"

It is true; Dr. Fifer held strong personal sentiments about the controversy between informally trained apprentices and regular, university-educated doctors. Ten short years earlier, as a founding member of the Medical Association, he had taken a stand defending the rights of those doctors who could not present a recognized diploma, he argued successfully in favour of a united medical profession. Both classes of physicians had amalgamated in the San Francisco Medico Chirurgical Association. They held joint scientific meetings and all their physicians contributed competent valuable service.

But that first day, Ovid Allard had remained skeptical. Why would a physician, with impressive credentials and a good reputation in a world-class city, stoop to arrive in company with the boatmen of San Francisco, the scumbags and bobtails of society? What concealed motive lay behind the selfless offer to help in the solution of the local doctor shortage? After his experience with Dr. Crane, Mr. Allard was not going to be made a fool of twice.

How could the ordinary Hudson's Bay store keeper have known the reason behind Dr. Fifer's relocation, how his membership with the San Francisco Vigilance Committee and its subsequent disintegration had forced him to forfeit practice, family, friends, and fortune?

"Yes, you must understand, Ah Chung. I was prejudiced, I was suspicious. In my position as clerk in the Hudson's Bay store, I am not getting scalped easily. Once burned, twice shy. But along comes Doctor Fifer with his side of the story, and my confidence in the medical profession is restored. He had arrived in California before the gold rush, you know. He knew what was about to happen here, what was already happening with ten thousand tents pitched on our little flat and up on the bench land. 'There will be others after the miners,' the doctor predicted. 'Families. Businessmen. Government officials. Men of God, and their wives and children.' 'Tis true. He showed me the larger picture; he looked to the future, like Governor Simpson or Chief Factor Douglas. Yet with his experience, and his business acumen, he also brought the compassion of a care-giver, well suited for the community, and heaven-sent for our family. Thank God I convinced him to stay. Little did I suspect how soon we would need his services."

With this, Mr. Allard's face goes dark and I know he is remembering his little daughter Sara. But he continues to recall his first encounter with Doctor Fifer.

"Your master was looking for a place to hang his shingle. I knew his dislike of Yorke or Seidenstriker class hotels and was certain he had cash on him. I asked him straight out. 'If you are prepared, Doctor, to put up with this charlatan Crane as your local colleague, I can arrange a private accommodation in a good location, ideal as a medical office and dwelling, with a wooden floor, better than any hotel. It's a brand new house on Front Street; the builder, Jehil Hoadley Hale, would let you have it for cash,' I said."

I remember how, at the name Jehil Hoadley Hale, Dr. Fifer's face brightened, his hesitancy disappeared; he extended his hand and said "Done," although this time he did not share with Mr. Allard that Hale was a previous patient in San Francisco. The two men walked immediately to inspect the house, whereupon the doctor promptly paid in cash, as the astute Mr. Allard had surmised he would. While counting out the gold eagles, he quick-wittedly alluded to the fiasco of that morning: "Does the price for the house include access to the privy, or do I have to use the beach?"

"'Do I have to use the beach?' That's what he asked me." Mr. Allard laughs again at the memory of his friend's first joke, of how they had both held their noses in the same exaggerated gesture.

Doctor Fifer and I moved in on that same day; in no time had I set up the office to commence practice. But I do believe that it was not until the crisis of the unfortunate Sara that the two men bonded as friends. "You became friends, I know."

At my simple statement, Mr. Allard nods agreement. "*Oui, monsieur.* We became fast friends." His eyes fill with tears again and he turns to gaze over my shoulder, towards the rough crooked stair that leads up to the family's living quarters. And then he begins to ramble, almost as if I am no longer present.

"You know, Ah Chung, I blame Gallagher, for what happened to Little Sara. Silly, I know. It is just more satisfying to blame a scoundrel like him than to blame God. Or to blame the doctor, as my wife did. I blamed Gallagher, and Lucy blamed herself. But my wife Justine blamed the doctor; sometimes, in her heart, I fear she blames him still.

"Mr. Allard," I say, "I knew this Gallagher, in San Francisco, "Not really 'knew' him, but I watched him escorted, in manacles and chains, with other convicts, five gang members, for deportation to the Sandwich island of Maui. Nobody expected that he would make his way back, to British Territory, in such a short time. 'Bad news' Doctor Fifer called Gallagher. 'That man travels fast like bad news,' he said more than once."

"Bad news. Yes, Ah Chung. He said the same thing that night. Gallagher slipped back in to British North America on the whaler *Glencoe*, and quickly became the head honcho of New York Bar, after the two previous owners were found dead. Our Lucy said they saw him, she and Sara did, the same day Sara got sick."

"Yes, sir, I remember letting her in and alerting the doctor. Our first real emergency call—a sick little girl."

Mr. Allard continues his recall of the fateful night. "Sara had been ill when they returned from berry-picking, but we just assumed that it would pass. Children often get upset stomachs, and especially if they are excited and when they over-eat a new food. She was my sixth, Ah Chung. By the time you've 'gat that many babies, you don't worry as much. But she was still too sick to eat supper, and when we put her to bed, instead of a soothing sleep, her distress increased and her stomach was sore and hard, like nothing I have ever seen before. That made Lucy run for Dr. Fifer."

Mr. Allard nods and his eyes tear as he talks. "Doctor Fifer entered the sickroom. He had come so quickly he had not stopped for coat or top hat. 'Do we know what happened?' he asked, speaking to anyone who might answer. And Lucy, who was sweet on him even then, blurted out in great detail the story of their journey. 'Yes, Doctor Fifer. I took my little sister to visit Erastus Champlain, a Quebecois like Papa who has a nice garden business there across the river, with pease, new potatoes, young carrots, and other fresh vegetables. *Tite* Sara wanted to look for wild strawberries, and I let her go, thinking nothing of it. She would be going uphill, away from the river. Late in the afternoon, the ferryman brought us back. Sara was already feeling ill. 'Did you eat too many strawberries?' I asked her and she shook her head, '*Non.*' But then she said '*Pomme de terre. Pomme de terre.*' You know. Potato. And I said, 'What? Pere Champlain's potatoes?' But she shook her head again. I fear she found a potato some miner had used to bake his gold. Oh, Doctor Fifer, is it possible that a potato could make her so sick? Can you cure her?'

"'Was she sick at all, before today?'" Mr. Allard recalls Dr. Fifer asking. "Maman looked at me and I looked at Lucy. Lucy said, 'She was the sweetest baby, Doctor. She never cried. But in the last little while, she has not been herself. Instead of *Ma Petite* Sara, Papa started calling her *Ma Petite Diable*, she tested us so. No! No! She'd refuse to eat what we were eating. She'd fly into a temper. She would scream in the night, and walk about in her sleep. Do you think something has been happening before today?'

"'It's possible, Lucy,' Dr. Fifer told her. 'If she were ingesting something that was not good, over a period of time, and then an overdose today, perhaps that would explain her symptoms. But we can only speculate, as long as she cannot communicate. And yes, a potato could cause this, if it were a potato laced with mercury, after it has been baked to separate the gold. The mercury infuses into the potato with the heat. I have seen the symptoms before, but only in animals who consume the miners' garbage without suspecting.'

"'It was a sad dinner our family had this evening,' I said to the doctor that night. 'I tried the medicine we carry in the store, prepared by Doctor Helmcken, the Company's head doctor, in Victoria. But it was useless; she chucked it up and became worse. Before she went to sleep, she told her mother that the potato she had eaten had been cooked by a fellow whose description would fit that of Martin Gallagher. She had watched him at his fire. She was hungry, so she ate the discarded potato when he wasn't looking. She had no idea it was laced with mercury. Mercury is poison, is it not, doctor? We never used to carry it; I only order it now since all the miners ask for it.'"

"'Mercury should never be ingested, Mr. Allard,' Dr. Fifer agreed. Then he asked: 'Has Sara had any previous medical intervention? Has she seen a doctor before?' When I answered in the negative, he proceeded to examine her. We had laid her in our own bed where she seemed to fade from sight, white as the pillowslip. She was asleep yet a sound like a moan escaped with each outward breath. Dr. Fifer put his hand to her forehead, then lifted an eyelid to peer into her eyes. He held the bedside lamp closer to her to check the colour. He put his face to her face to sniff her breath. He looked at her tongue and her teeth. He held his fingers to her wrist to count the pulse.

"'Tachycardia. Fast pulse,' he said, and 'Irregular,' and 'Shallow' after listening to her breathing. He tugged at the ruffle on the bottom of her nightdress and raised it to her armpits. I could see a flush, like a child with the measles, and remembered that she had complained of itching. The doctor asked if she had passed her water and asked to examine the chamber pot. He checked the colour, swirled the liquid in the pot, smelled it, and then touched it with the tip of one finger and tasted it. 'Scant; brownish; no foam; no smell of rotten apples; no sweetness,' he said, seeing that his actions were meeting with disapproval from *Maman*.

"Then Doctor Fifer pulled out his stetho.., his listening tool, he put the earpieces in his ears and the ivory mouthpiece between his teeth to hold the instrument in place and free the hands. He moved the chestpiece over Sara, listening to her chest and abdomen. I could tell, he heard nothing. He checked the instrument for obstruction by ear wax or an ear wig, blowing into the chest piece to test it. Accepting that the instrument was functioning, he concluded that the sounds were absent, that the silence he was hearing signaled inactivity within the young body. He mumbled 'Total absence of *peristalsis*,' and then, 'Paralysis of the intestines. The silence of the grave. Sinister.' He turned to me and said quietly: 'Sir, perhaps you may wish to attend to Mme. Allard?' You see, Ah Chung, my wife was becoming more agitated every minute; she could tell what the doctor was thinking.

"I went to my wife, to try to quiet her, as the doctor continued his examination. I could see Sara's stomach sticking out; the doctor tapped it with his fingers; it sounded like a baby drum. He leaned over her, placing his right ear directly where his fingers had just been, holding up his hand to demand silence, listening, listening for the faintest sound of life inside her. I could tell from his expression that he was not hearing what he wanted to hear. And at that moment of highest intensity, of life or death, that's when the pounding started, on the door below, and I had to leave. When I got back, my baby was already gone. *Défun*"

"I too remember that sad night. Doctor Fifer had instructed me upon leaving our house, 'I can manage this call by myself, Ah

Chung, stay in bed, get a good night's rest.' When I got up the next morning, my master's blankets were undisturbed. "He had spent the entire night at the bedside of your little girl." I did not say to Mr. Allard how upset the doctor was when he did come home. During the difficulty of making a diagnosis on an unconscious child, the inability to prescribe any antidote, the feeling of impotence, of useless hands, unable to prevent the young life from slipping through his fingers, then, the nocturnal intrusion of Captain Snyder disrupting his treatment, had frustrated him so. "You have my sympathy, Mr. Allard; be not ashamed of your tears."

"After his initial examination of Sara, your master sat with us all night. Mme. Allard told me later that he had not given up; he continued to examine Sara after I left the room. He had informed Maman that he must make one more test. He showed her his finger, and she objected. "*Non!*" But he continued, apologizing 'I am sorry,' while he moved Sara on to her side, into a fetal position he called it, and lubricating his forefinger with lard from the jar Lucy brought for him. Placing his other hand on Sara's abdomen, he explored inside her. Upon removing the finger, he held it up to look. No pus; no blood. 'The good news is, we can spare her the surgeon's scalpel, but I'm afraid Sara's bowels are paralyzed, probably caused by poisoning, with an unknown substance.'

"During my absence, dealing with the "Black Guard" at the ground floor, Lucy comforted her mother. She watched the doctor administer drops to relieve Sara's pain. He asked to close the window, to keep out bad air which he called *miasma*, from the room. They watched her breathing becoming so shallow as to be barely perceptible.

"What made my little princess' death even more upsetting was that I could not be with her in the final hour and that she could not die in peace. We had been hearing for weeks talk of war up river, between the Indians and the American miners. Bodies, decapitated heads, arms, legs, you name it, had been floating downriver.

"Chief Spintlum is a smart man; he knows just how to play tricks with our heads. You know, he took me hostage, ten years before that, when I was building the fort? He said then that it was because we did not ask them their permission first. That's the kind of man he is. Proud. He expects people to behave properly. I could not imagine him starting a war. I've never known one Indian to harm a white man, not around here, anyway. They are our friends and partners now, up river and down; there would be no fur trade without them. They are a gentle people, but there proved to be some truth to the rumors. The rumors that the chief had united tribes north of the Boston Bar and they were defending themselves, and especially their women, from the disrespect of the Boston men."

Justine Allard is Cowichan herself, which makes Mr. Allard family to many of the communities downriver. Mr. Allard understands the chief's desire to protect and defend the women.

"Bang! Bang! Bang!" He says it in such a deep voice, impulsively striking the table with his fist, that I know it is the sound of a heavy hand hitting a solid door. "It was about midnight when Captain Snyder hammered on the door of the store. I was still dressed, sitting up with Sara and the doctor; in that state I had to leave my dying child and went down to answer. ."

'Guns, Allard. We want all the guns you've got.' 'What are you talking about?' I asked, and this Captain Snyder explained about the death of miners up river, the body parts floating by, the terrorizing of the men on the bars, their impatience with the interference from the Indians, just as the water level had gone down and the claims were at their busiest. 'Vigilance,' Snyder said. 'We can't wait for your precious Chief Factor to bring in law and order. We're prepared to do it ourselves. We need guns and ammunition.'

"Although little Sara upstairs was on my mind, I wasn't buying their tactics. I suspected they had brought it on themselves. I knew the Chief Factor Douglas was big on doing things the British way, and not letting Americans take over. Yet my mind surely was not set on suing for peace and quiet with a gang of rowdies. I loaded them up with a pile of old muskets from ten years before, most likely to be a flash in the pan, and sent them on their way. We were holding a vigil upstairs; I wanted those men out of my house. Out of my store. Out of my town.

"I hurried back up to the vigil room to tell Dr. Fifer, but when I got there, I could see immediately that my little Sara was no longer breathing. Justine, crying and rocking the child's body, cringed when I touched my hand to her shoulder. Lucy signaled me to wait, to let her look after her mother in this crisis."

'The next morning, I filled in Doctor Fifer and apologized for the nocturnal disturbance, thanking him for his prompt and thorough attention and his sympathy. It seems, that night of terror and grief brought us closer, and we became friends."

"I was confused, however, when he replied: "Thank you, Ovid Allard, for not telling them I was here.' I didn't understand. He tried to explain to me how, as an American, a known member of the Vigilance Committee, of the 'Stranglers Party,' a veteran of the Mexican War in California, and a veteran of the Indian Wars against YoSemite, they might have tried to recruit him. 'You fought in the war?' I asked him. He began to tell me his stories."

"He was no swashbuckling war horse of a doctor, ready for a gunfight anytime. That night he confessed that he never was much of a hero or a soldier. After the New York Volunteers arrived in California, set to take the country away from Mexico by force, Volunteer Fifer never saw any combat. He was anxious and happy to avoid all hostilities. He said he spent a good amount of war time in the hospital, first as a patient with typhoid fever, and then he worked his way up to the rank of Hospital Stewart.

He had apprenticed as an apothecary before leaving Germany, 'and his work blended well with what he already knew,' was the way he explained it to me.

"After peace with Mexico, he went gold seeking with most of the other veterans. He suffered from typhoid fever and dysentery. He said he had to be carried to the gold field on a litter, too sick was he to walk. It was then that I understood his passion to clean the beach, to dig latrines, to get the residents of our ten-thousand-tent city to take better care, or disease would inhabit the town. Remember, how he put up such a stink? Tried to prevent Governor Douglas from stepping right into it? Sent me, of all people, downriver in a canoe alone, to intercept his Honour and warn him of the potential humiliation? I caught Douglas and his party at Emory's Bar and explained the situation. Old Square Toes did not want his boots browned. He outsmarted us all, setting up camp across the river. You remember, Ah Chung?"

I nodded, and Mr. Allard continued, hardly stopping for a breath.

"That night of our vigil Doctor Fifer also talked about his own days as an Indian fighter. In California too there was trouble with the Indians, YoSemite and his tribe in Mariposa country. The governor of California Territory organized a battalion of miners; Doctor Fifer ended up in charge of the Mariposa military hospital. The Indians there had their own way of instilling fear. 'They had a diabolical new secret weapon to fight the whites. They made arrowheads from glass shards of old junk whisky bottles from the deserted camps of libative miners; the resin glue would dissolve, separating the arrow shafts. The embedded glass arrowheads were translucent, invisible, impossible to locate in the body except by feel; if you touched them during surgery, you cut your fingers; if you removed them, their sharp edges cut the soldiers' nerves and arteries, causing paralysis and internal bleeding; if left, they were designed to cause rankling in the wound. But he said he was glad they had defeated YoSemite and that there was peace.

"He told me how he opened a practice in San Francisco and would be a successful doctor to this day, had he not made the mistake of his life. He joined the Vigilance Committee who soon became notorious for their overzealous enforcement of the rule of law. Their motives were commendable; they wanted to suppress crime, but soon they used methods that were excessive, perhaps even criminal. The Vigilance Committee soon became notorious for their overzealous enforcement of the rule of law. Our good Doctor Fifer confessed that he cringed every time a suspect was sentenced to be hanged, although it was the only punishment available for murder, except for banishment, transportation to the Fee Jees or the Sandwich Isles.

"When the opposition Law and Order Party under Ned McGowan gained sway, the situation became dicey for Fifer. McGowan and his men were worse than the Vigilance Committee and, the doctor said, he lived in constant fear they might come and shoot him. Well, you know the rest of the story, Ah Chung. San Francisco's loss was Yale's gain."

I nod my head in agreement as Mr. Allard continues.

"I know he was disappointed that not being a British subject, he was ineligible for the new government appointments in British North America. We should not have held his American citizenship against him. He was a gentleman with much to contribute, and a valuable addition to our new country. We two were akin; both strangers from elsewhere, with different cultures and mother tongues. We both had to learn the language of the country; we were both determined to make this our home. After that dark night, we were brothers. Above all, *le docteur, il est mon ami. .*" He sighed: "*Etait. Etait.*"

Listening to this solid testimonial from an upright man from Quebec puts joy into my heart. In the eyes of Ovid Allard, we, the doctor and I, a Celestial servant, had come from the south, from a place where lynch law and the Colt revolver reigned supreme. However, he recognized us for what we really were—exiles, professionally qualified, looking for a suitable location to apply our skill for the good of the new country.

I remember how dejected Dr. Fifer was, the morning he returned from Allard's. "The only thing worse, for a doctor than losing a patient,

Ah Chung, is losing a child patient," the doctor confessed. "Little Sara Allard never had a chance. Whatever she ingested, it shut down her whole system. While Allard downstairs quibbled with Captain Snyder's vigilantes, doling out muskets for the great Indian fighters, upstairs, Sara's respirations ceased. After the raucous warriors had departed the store and clambered down to their boats or up to the portage, there was heavenly silence; the only sound remaining was the distant screeching and the hum of the sawmill across the creek, cutting the boards for little Sara's coffin."

Dr. Fifer had seemed to need to tell the details of that night. "Despite his grief about the child," he told me, "Mr. Allard had the presence of mind to take precautions, in case the outdated muskets would let them down and the fighters would be overpowered, in case their opponents triumphed and pushed south into town. After Justine quieted and dried her tears, she and Lucy washed the tiny body one final time and dressed her in a soft white gown. Ovid wrapped her remains in a striped point blanket and carried her into the cellar. 'Help me hide her, doctor. I don't want anyone to desecrate her body.' And I helped him dig a shallow hole in the dirt floor of the cellar. Bundled in to it, and covered over with rough planks, she will be safe there until these troubles are over. I believe that, in his fatherly grief, being able to do something, anything, was better for him than having to sit there with her lifeless corpse.

"I have seen a good number of people die, Ah Chung," the doctor said to me, "from illness or injuries, inflicted on purpose or by accident. All, perhaps even suicides, have their place and intrinsic justification in society. When I look at the dead faces of former patients, they have become strangers, different, unapproachable, belonging to another realm. They reject us, the living, by no longer according us eye contact or bodily response. Yet they demand our respect, having attained the existential privilege through a brute biological fact.

"Death forces us to concede that we have reached the edge

of knowledge and must admit defeat. I cannot offer treatment to a patient whose problem cannot be diagnosed. I do not know the cause of this little girl's death. The limitations of my knowledge, of what I am able to do, these make me realize that, in our presence here, we are walking on thin ice."

I do not think Doctor Fifer meant that he was afraid of falling through thin ice and drowning. I think he meant that the golden curtain across the gates of heaven, the veil between this world and the mysterious beyond, is very very thin.

5

Done. Delivered. Dr. Fifer's town council file is now safely with Mr. Allard. We talked about the past, our arrival here in Yale, in the summer of 1858, the beginning of his friendship with Dr. Fifer, of how it grew after Little Sara's death, adding more grey to this fateful morning. Indeed, we are both stricken by the ebb of life, and we are both mourning our losses. Contrary to what Reverend Crickmer counsels, that excessive grief verges on selfishness, I can see that bereavement at the loss of his young daughter Sara still haunts this father after three years, that his sorrow is no more diminished than is mine five short weeks after the death of my master.

Mr. Allard's reminiscences have melted the snow pack, creating a flood of memories of our work here. Although I did not see Little Sara, either while she was ill or after she died, I observed the impact of her death also upon Dr. Fifer, who was the caring doctor. Yet I know that not all his patients met such sad ends. Some of the accounts before me attest to happier outcomes.

Although treatment files are private and confidential, as part of the doctor's business they are considered, I am told, part of the estate. These documents, in Dr. Fifer's meticulous calligraphy, must remain here. I shall do a quick review, tidy them, and sort them, perhaps, into categories of Female Patients, Indians, Royal Engineers, Miners, Citizens.

Patient: Mrs. Thomas Yorke
Diagnosis: primipara, uterine inertia
Treatment: amnio-centesis
Outcome: Live birth, Mother and Child well.

Yes, I remember that night. October 21st, 1858, a good eight weeks after Sara Allard's death. I was fast asleep on my cot by the pantry when urgent knocking woke me up. The caller was a woman, about thirty years old, a domestic, scantily dressed, barefoot in slippers, clutching a shawl over her nightdress. Out of breath, she stammered: "Please, Chinaman," entreating me. "Please send doctor...come to Mrs. Yorke's 'ouse; she's 'avin' a bad time; it's the baby; it's her first one, it won't deliver!"

I roused Dr. Fifer immediately, helped him dress, handed him his case. He knew the woman, a midwife from town, and greeted her. "Hello, Miss Maguire. Who is it?' She answered, and Dr. Fifer followed her up the street.

Finding the patient in the family room above Thomas Yorke's primitive hotel, the doctor recognized a primagravida, in the final stage of labour, and progressing poorly. Dr. Fifer ruptured the woman's amniotic membranes; the fruit water gushed forth, drenching his trousers, but enhancing her labour contractions; soon the head of the child engaged in the inferior strait, and she delivered a healthy male infant. Johanna sacrificed her red silk hair band to tie the cord. The womb contracted readily upon the placenta, which expelled intact. (These are the entries I took from the doctor's records).

"It is good that you came for me, Miss Maguire," he praised the woman he knew as midwife, although with obvious problems of her own. They sat the rest of the night providing intensive care to mother and newborn. When Dr. Fifer finally made his way home, trudging along the riverbank, half-asleep, a fresh morning fog cleared his dreaminess. Nature had given notice: overnight, a startling transformation warned of the coming change of season. A successful birth, a happy occasion, the invigorating nip foretelling winter—it all boded well.

Yet, he paused; the possible dangers, the high risk at the time of confinement, the many things that could and often did go wrong—occiput-posterior presentation, cephalo-pelvic disproportion, a shoulder arrest, a twin pregnancy, a tear of the symphysis pubis—all these complications could require professional assistance which was unlikely to be available to him here. Dr. Crane was often incapacitated by drink. Miss Maguire's condition made her availability even less predictable. For the first time, the doctor questioned his decision to move to this bucolic frontier. Was this step detrimental for his medical career? Could he not better achieve his ambition—always to render the best of medical care—in a community with a hospital? But his doubt was short-lived. Who refuses to eat because he fears choking?

That night, when the outside air had changed, the vegetation had turned golden yellow, red, and russet, and thin ice covered the puddles. The crackling under his feet as he sleep-walked home and the cold air vapourizing his breath as he exhaled, reminded the doctor that he was in a colder climate. He inhaled deeply. Wide awake then, he recalled where he had been one year before, the milder clime, and, alas, the adversity under which he had struggled at that time. One year before, leagues far to the south, he had attended a caesarean operation, a foolhardy procedure with unfortunate results: A stillborn baby, the mother's permanent disability, and his own forced implication in a malpractice suit against the surgeon, a professional colleague. To top it off, the patients filing the lawsuit were his personal friends.

In stark contrast, last night's straightforward delivery of the Yorke baby, the first child born to immigrants on the shores of this Fraser River, was a joyful event. Amidst the ongoing revolution in the profession and the rapid advances in the science of medicine, he had retained the timeless quality of the healing art—real compassion, the gift of understanding patients' sufferings and celebrating with them the joys of convalescence and recovery. Coming home that chilly dawn, after the night of the Yorke birth, while I served him a bite to eat, Dr. Fifer shared these profound thoughts with me. So tired was he that I helped him out of his boots before he fell onto his cot and was fast asleep.

It took me some time to learn from the doctor details of the failed caesarean birth that had led to the malpractice suit in San Francisco. The patient, Mary Hodges, a family friend, had insisted upon Dr. Fifer's presence during the surgery even though she had changed to the more illustrious Dr. Cooper as the attending surgeon. Dr. Fifer, there to render moral support to his friends, agreed to administer the chloroform, a treatment for painless childbirth popularized by the English Queen. But Mary Hodge's was not a simple birth; she would require a deep anaesthetic for a major operation. The risks faced during the anaesthetic were those of cardiac arrest and of aspiration of vomit, but trusting the flexible stethoscope to monitor the heart, and keeping her fasting, ("nothing to eat or drink after midnight, no, Mary, not even a sip of water!") he proceeded in confidence, applying castor oil to her eyes against injury by chloroform. He made certain of a wooden spoon nearby, to pry open the jaw if necessary. He applied the chloroform from a brown glass bottle, marked *Trichloromethane*, to a wire-and-cloth mask over the patient's face, at a trial-and error rate of twenty drops per minute. Abruptly, when deeply obtunded, her breathing ceased, she was choking on her tongue that had slipped back into her throat and was too slippery to grasp. She clenched her teeth, powerful enough to crack a nut, over his fingers, down to the bone. Her face turned a dark purple colour; it was now life or death.

Dr. Fifer used the wooden spoon to force open Mrs. Hodges' jaw. Without breaking a tooth, he managed to free his fingers. He retrieved from his pocket a Hunt's safety pin and, despite her short neck, reached and pushed it quickly through the fleshy tongue and closed it. He attached a string and pulled the slithery tongue forward, relieving the respiratory obstruction. She was breathing freely now; her colour returned to a live, pink appearance. But now hiccoughs interfered with the delicate balance of regular respirations. Dr. Fifer described to me the moments of sheer terror on the operating table, how the patient's spasmodic inhalations would not furnish enough anaesthetic. She woke up and struggled, feeling the pain, drawing up her knees, calling for her mother, thwarting the surgeon's attempt to make the abdominal incision.

When, finally, Dr. Cooper managed to open the abdomen, it became obvious that his diagnosis of twins was incorrect; there was only one infant. Attempting to justify the unnecessary surgery, the doctor immediately revised his diagnosis to "contracted pelvis." However, the high dose of chloroform to anaesthetize the mother had knocked out the baby *in utero*; the infant, once delivered, failed to breathe and died. Dr. Fifer felt guilty, having applied the chloroform, but he was angry that Dr. Cooper's sloppy pre-operative workup resulted in a misdiagnosis which had led to the unnecessary risk of surgery, and a stillbirth. And Dr. Fifer was angry at himself for not having disregarded Doctor Cooper's objection and double-checked the diagnosis before agreeing to the procedure. The sound of two separate heart beats would have confirmed the presence of twins. "Even you, Ah Chung, would have known better." I remember Dr. Fifer's frustration about Dr. Cooper's over-confident and self-aggrandizing nature from earlier dealings in the medical association. The malpractice suit filed by the Hodges against Dr. Cooper, in which Dr. Fifer was summoned to testify, brought disrepute to their fractured medical community.

Patient: Higgins' Assistant
Diagnosis: undiagnosed full-term pregnancy
Treatment: uncomplicated delivery
Outcome: Mother well; Child taking the breast.

Johanna Maguire attended another patient with Dr. Fifer. This time it was Mr. Higgins, store owner and agent of Ballou's Express, who called to ask the doctor to hurry. A young man Higgins had taken a shine to, Harry Collins, who had come to Yale to search for his brother and had been bunking in the back room of Higgins' store, had suddenly taken a bad turn. Johanna herself had shown a peculiar interest in the young man, taunting him for his supposed softness, his inability to keep a job, or to hold his own with the other men. With Johanna present, and Dr. Fifer called, the reason for the youth's softness became apparent.

Not until Mr. Higgins moved to Victoria did he draft accounts of his adventures in Yale and forwarded them to Dr. Fifer for his comments, explaining that he planned in the future to publish them in book form. I do not know whether Dr. Fifer responded, but I see that he has filed some of Higgin's stories in the patient files.

One afternoon, nearly four months later, young Harry feeling very sick, as if he would die, sought my help, and I put him to bed in my own bedroom. As the Maguire woman was in the store, calling for mail, I delegated her to see how he was getting on. She was inside for about five minutes and then, coming out, she asked me to go at once for Dr. Fifer, the leading surgeon at that time.

"The bye's very sick. He's all of a shiver. I think he's got the cholery morbus." Whereupon I hurriedly summoned the doctor and was about to enter the sickroom, when Johanna barred my entrance "for the good Lord's sake, shtay out. The bye must be kept quiet."

The doctor came to her assistance and added his entreaty to hers. As I was fuming and fretting over the impudence of keeping a man from entering his own room, the doctor came out with a puzzled look on his face.

"Really," he commenced, "this is a most remarkable case. It beats everything. In all my experience I never saw anything like it. How long have you known Collins?"

I told him about four months.

"Humph! Really, this is extraordinary—most extraordinary."

What he would have said further will never be recorded, for at that moment the shrill voice of Johanna Maguire was heard: "Docther, come quick!

Come quick!"

The doctor rushed inside and in five or six minutes came out again. He put his hand on my shoulder and looking me full in the face said solemnly: "It's my duty to tell you that Harry Collins is no more!"

"Mercy!" I cried, shrinking back. "Not dead? Not dead?"

"Well, no not dead; but you'll never see him again."

"If he is not dead," I said, greatly agitated, "tell me what has happened or why I shall never see him again. You should not keep me in suspense."

"Well," said the doctor, laughing heartily, "he is not dead. He's very much alive. That is to say, he is doubly alive. Harry Collins is gone, but in his place there is a comely young woman Harriet Collins, who calls herself the wife of one George Collins who is now above the canyon hunting for gold. She has just been delivered of a handsome baby girl that weighs at least seven pounds."

The story soon spread. Recently married to a man who left for the gold fields to make his fortune, left alone with abusive in-laws, the young woman had followed her husband, choosing her disguise for safety, but her journey ended at Yale. The story turned even more joyous when the missing "brother" showed up in town and was re-united with his bride and their new offspring.

Patient: Alice Durant
Diagnosis: pneumonia
Treatment: the tincture of time, bed rest, nursing care, good
                 nutrition
Outcome: recovered

Another evening that first fall, Dr. Fifer was called out to a shack just back of the town. Alice Durant, a girl of about fourteen, was gravely ill, stricken with pneumonia. As Dr. Fifer approached the cabin, the girl's father, very much under the influence of liquor, met him at the door.

"Doctor," he began, "Allie is dyin', shore. There ain't no hope for her," and he sobbed tearfully.

"Nonsense," said the doctor, "she'll be all right in a few days. All you've got to do is to leave her alone and not bother or frighten her."

The man put his face in his hands and turned away. The one-room cabin was divided in the middle, the kitchen / living room partitioned off by a piece of unbleached muslin that stretched from side to side of the shack. Behind this curtain the stricken girl lay. As the good doctor was about to draw back the curtain, the sound of a person praying halted him. In a soft sweet woman's voice the doctor detected the rhythms of the Lord's Prayer being recited, and a stammering, feeble voice responding. Then the woman's voice gently said: "Dearie, say this after me: 'I know that my Redeemer liveth, and that he shall stand in the latter day upon earth.' "

At the sound of a woman weeping, Dr. Fifer parted the muslin and entered.

"Ah, docther, sure I'm glad ye've came. The poor chil' is very sick, indade. Sure, I think she'll not be long wid us." It was Johanna Maguire's voice.

"Where's the other woman who was here, the woman who prayed? Tell me, Johanna, where is she?"

Johanna replied: "She hopped out o' the windey as ye come in."

"Nonsense! Where is she?"

"Go find her yerself," and with a savage and offensive oath, her face twitching, she grabbed the doctor by the shoulders; repeating the vile words, she flung past the doctor and ran from the room and the house.

The girl, Alice Durant, was very low indeed, but some of the ladies of the town took an interest and nursed her back to health. In a course of two or three weeks, she was able to travel down the river in a canoe, and the doctor saw her no more.

Patient: Johanna Maguire
Diagnosis: intermittent insanity
Treatment: kindness, tolerance, observation
Outcome: unknown

Johanna Maguire herself remained in Yale. Gossip had it that she arrived here the same year we did, although perhaps just before the time of Thomas Yorke's birth. She had come from San Francisco, in the company of Captain Harrigen, a known "procurer of women", but when the Captain continued north, Johanna remained in Yale.

The woman gained notice by her regularly calling at Mr. Ballou's Express office. That first year, Ballou's was the only reliable means to send letters; he also shipped all the gold treasure. She would enter the place and enquire if there were any letter for Johanna Maguire. The clerk examined the "M" pigeonhole and handed her a letter, and she, after reading it, asked if someone would change a £5 Bank of England note. She was referred to Mr. Hicks in the Gold Commissioner's office on Front Street. After that, nearly every week, the woman applied at the freight office for a letter addressed as before. Sometimes she was rewarded with a missive, but often there was nothing for her. Whenever she received a letter, it always contained a £5 note, which she hurriedly exchanged at the Gold Commissioner's and hastened back to her home at the upper end of the village.

Johanna Maguire always spoke with a broad Irish accent, and there was nothing in her language and appearance to indicate that she belonged to any other than the peasant or uneducated class. Indeed, often she would be in a quarrelsome, irritated, mood, which showed on her face and in her body movements. Her eyes would blink continuously, she would utter snorting and grunting sounds, her forehead would frown, she would thrust her head sideways and shrug her shoulders at the same time. She would come close to others and seemed to have the urge to touch them as though she felt she would become lost. If she became worse, there was "swearing like a trooper", as Dr. Fifer called it, and if she had whisky to drink, she was out of control with the utterance of the most profane and obscene words, repeated loudly as though she had no shame at all. On at least two occasions she was seen using pieces of furniture on the heads and bodies of some miners who had done something that irritated her while in the house.

There was also word that she had been charged and sentenced in Victoria the year before, for using obscene language in public. The fact of her broad Irish accent, and the fact that she waited regularly for mail from the old country, made the doctor begin to suspect that there was more to her story than the obvious and all too common reason that women fall into prostitution and sought the protection of scurrilous pimps.

About three weeks after the departure of Alice Durant, who had recovered from pneumonia, Dr. Fifer was taking his usual evening walk with Higgins, the newspaper writer he had met on the *Sierra Nevada*. The day had been warm. There was a slight rise in the river, and numerous floating trees had begun to make their appearance. The sun was just sinking behind Mount Lincoln in the back of Yale, and the chill evening breeze had come up when they heard a scream, a woman's scream in mortal agony or fear. They turned and saw Johanna Maguire running along the trail towards them. At every step she uttered a wild shriek and beat the air and her breasts alternately with her hands. As she drew nearer she pointed with one hand toward the river and screamed rather than spoke: "Please, gentlemen, there is a man afloat on a tree. Please save him! Get a boat! Get a boat!"

And, indeed, in the boiling, surging stream of the river, a man was seated on the trunk of a huge tree, waving his arms and apparently shouting for help. His voice could not be heard above the raging of the wild torrent, but he was waving in a frantic appeal for assistance. They at once ran down to the beach, shouting the alarm as they went. Some men manned a boat and put off to intercept the tree. But the night closes quickly in this narrow canyon, and darkness intervened before any meaningful effort could be made to save the man, and he must have passed to eternity at the first riffle below Yale, for tree and man had swept out of sight before the boat got well under way.

Johanna, who was still greatly excited, continued her lamentations, but what struck all as peculiar was that in her excitement she spoke the most perfect English. There was not a trace of the brogue, and her language gave every evidence of good breeding. As her excitement wore off she seemed to recollect herself, and presently lapsed into the broad drawl and with an obscene curse in condemnation of the fruitless effort to save, she walked up the face of the bench and disappeared.

"Max," said Dr. Fifer's friend, "that woman wears a mask. She is not what she wants us to believe she is." The doctor remembered the incident at the sick girl's bedside and the mysterious woman's gentle voice that cited the prayer. He agreed that there was a mystery about Johanna that needed an explanation.

Early the next summer, it would have been 1860, after Higgins had relocated to Victoria, he reported on a police court trial held there, Judge A.F. Pemberton presiding. To his surprise, whom should he see seated on the bench usually assigned to witnesses but Johanna Maguire. She was in a deplorable and fearful state. Her face was battered and bruised, her eyes were blackened and she was doubled up with her bodily stiffness. A bloody rag was tied about the lower part of her face; it would be hard to imagine a more deplorable spectacle.

In the prisoner's dock stood a former Hill's Bar miner, "Ned" Whitney, previously a college graduate, member of a church choir, and usually known to be as regular and reliable as a good watch. During the rush to Fraser River he fell in with the Hill's Bar crowd and they spoiled him as they spoiled everything and everyone with whom they came in contact. Whitney, it came out in court, had accompanied Johanna to Victoria where they lived together in a small cabin on Humboldt Street. They both got drunk, and after a verbal altercation he beat and blackened his consort until she became the spectacle described.

As is often the case, the woman did not want to charge Whitney. She gave evidence in the prisoner's behalf, saying that she alone was to blame, and he was left off with a light fine, which the woman paid.

That same evening, Johanna was found at a small house on Humboldt Street, alone and in a high fever, with breathing difficulty. Among many injuries, bruises from contusions, three ribs had been fractured. A search was made for Whitney, but he had left the country and was never captured.

Johanna Maguire, thinking she was about to die, confided details of her past history—that her parents were each other's cousin, that in early life she was a welcome and frequent visitor at Dublin Castle, and that she was connected with one of the highest families in Dublin, a family with an historical record and a lineage that dated back several centuries. She confided that her family had sent her away to San Francisco from where she came to Yale with the general influx of adventurers. The relatives would support her with a weekly remittance as long as she would stay away because the family were embarrassed by her bouts of uncontrollable offensive language and her bad behaviour to which she was subject with increasing frequency since the age of nine years.

Thus did we learn that Johanna was really a cultivated woman who had superior advantages in her youth. She disclosed to her confidant a mass of correspondence and some jewelry of antique design and considerable value, and directed that in case of her death, they should be sent to a given address in Dublin.

When she had sufficiently recovered, she sailed for San Francisco and we never heard what became of her.

It had taken Dr. Fifer some time to make the connections, between the pious prayer he had overheard, and the foul-mouthed woman he encountered so frequently on the streets of Yale. It was Higgins who had pointed out the obvious to him—"Surely, she's a remittance woman, paid by her family to not darken their door?" "Of course," the doctor realized. "And the reason for her exile, surely, is her condition. I am convinced, Higgins, that her affliction is not a moral weakness but rather something organic, like a complex tic. Her behaviour is surely a symptom of illness, probably some neurological condition. Unfortunately, I would require a more complete medical history and consultations with someone who has witnessed the progression of her deterioration, before I could suggest a diagnosis."

. Indeed it is the case that part of the appeal of our healers' calling is the opportunity to solve mysteries, to apply what limited knowledge we have to sort out the chaos, to help train the butterflies to fly in formation.

Patients: Gambling and Dance Hall Ladies
Diagnoses: infections, blocked uteri, haemorrhoids, syphilis, gonorrhea, venereal warts.
Treatments: tincture podophyllini, nitro glycerine ointment, mercury sulphide powder, salt of mercury, mercury ointment, calomel, douches, sponges, rue, tansy syrup, savin, ergot, Chichester's Pennyroyal Pills, laudanum, quinine, bandages, dressings, splints

Gambling is common in mining towns including Yale. The very nature of the mining occupation is a gamble. Gambling is considered a problem of moral rectitude, not a secular concern. Only the clerical authorities like Reverend Crickmer castigate the vice and corruption: "The existence of certain grave social evils is not to be denied. Such is the degrading concubinage with women, a vice that is happily on the decrease. Gambling, that curse of the mining communities, has been hitherto largely practised at the mines." Reverend Lundin Brown from Cayoosh was one of the early champions of action.

In Cayoosh, gambling may have been practised at the mines on the Lillooet, but such was not the case here. When the Reverend Crickmer arrived in Yale in May of 1860, he found himself missionary and pastor in a town where, out of sixty buildings, fourteen were bars, drinking and gambling places, open for all kinds of vices, even on Sundays.

Not unlike the San Francisco of the early 1850s, Yale had become a haunt for sensual pleasure, which, for the medically trained, means a natural place for certain diseases to thrive. Consequently, Dr. Fifer's medical activity expanded from caring for acute injuries and diseases of deprivation more to treatment of disorders of the organs of passion, the results of that "degrading concubinage", in both men and women.

Is it for reasons of privacy and decency, or because these ladies are transient, with names and faces changing regularly, that Dr. Fifer has left this file as a summary?

Patients: Yale Indians
Diagnosis: victims of debauchery
Treatment: social measures, resettlement, separation
Outcome: stalemate

The first summer we arrived, the *Gazette* printed an account of Martin Gallagher, an American gold digger·resident on Hill's Bar, molesting a Native woman after bribing her husband with a bottle of whisky.

Even Mr. Allard had complained to his friend about the unwanted attentions his daughter Lucy was receiving from miners such as Mr. McGowan. But Lucy, although a half-breed girl, did not live in the Indian settlement and enjoyed the protection of her father's home and position.

When Reverend Crickmer preached of the social ills of his little town, he used Lundin Brown's allegory of two rivers, comparing the larger but muddy and turbulent Fraser with the crystal clear Thompson River to the two races, Whites and Natives. The larger, more fierce, rolling and filthy stream of the sinful Whites was gradually polluting, absorbing and destroying the unsophisticated children of nature. He decried the horrible influence of the Whites' blackness and lust upon the unwary Natives, tempting them to copy their desire for possession of wealth, gambling and drinking, and destroying their own race by active debauchery.

With the increase in the transient population, the state of morals in Yale continued to decline. Available ladies moved out of the 'dance halls'; prostitutes, by-passing the Indian Liquor Act, served as go-betweens in the sale of whisky to the Natives, and the demoralization resulting from the drinking of whisky increased reliance upon the prostitution of Native women.

On August 25, 1860, the Yale Town Council held a special meeting to discuss the abuse of liquor and its catastrophic after-effects. Two council members, Reverend Crickmer and Dr. Fifer, who both faced almost daily the destructive result of alcohol inebriation, expressed their concern for the health and the social life of the Natives. Governor Douglas' Liquor Bill had been introduced in the legislature and passed unanimously, and the proclamation "forbidding the sale or gift of intoxicants to Natives" was posted conspicuously at the Gold Commissioner's office. Making laws was one thing; enforcing them was another problem entirely.

The new liquor law made our first New Year a "draughty year". But the imposed temperance did not last; the next New Year's Day the colonists celebrated as usual again, in what Dr. Fifer referred to as a "Bacchanalian manner".

In their meeting, the Council resolved to advise Governor Douglas about the conflicts between the local immigrants and the neighbouring Yale Indians. Their letter submission recommended the Natives' removal to a suitable point below Yale, for winter quarters, and the Town Council's introduction of a curfew restricting the Indians from visiting the town after certain hours of the day.

The governor rejected the proposal. He was aware that the local Yale government, including their mayor, was composed almost entirely of Americans. He added a lecture on respect for human rights and speculation on further social adjustments in the community which had annoyed Dr. Fifer to no end. Ideals versus reality, he had fumed, but thought better of putting his feelings to paper again.

Copies are in the Correspondence file.

Patients: Royal Engineers Sturtridge and Colston.
Diagnosis: rheumatic fever, heart problems, broken limbs, rashes, waxy legs
Treatment: herbs, oil of evergreen, willow bark tea, digitalis, extract of witch hazel.
Outcome: relief; referral

Yes, this unexpected group of loyal British patients arrived at Christmas of our first year. Before the official proclamation of the new mainland colony of British Columbia in November, 1858, in response to the apprehended war between the miners and the Indians that August, and because of the aggressive stance of many American miners, Governor Douglas had requested the services of a contingent of Sappers, military men with specialized engineering training. First and foremost, the Royal Engineers represented what Dr.

Fifer called the "vanguard of civilization". Ready and able to enforce British law, at the same time they were trained to scribe the markings of human progress upon this uncharted territory by surveying town sites, building churches, training residents and supervising their building of trails and roads, or constructing breakwaters, canals, and pilings to prevent obstruction to navigation.

Richard W. Sturtridge: Sturtridge was a member of the Royal Engineer crew working in the frigid current of the Harrison River, installing yellow cedar pilings and brush to prevent the tributary Chehalis River from clogging the steamboat passage with spring debris. He was in the icy water over and over again, submerged to the chest. Often his body was so numbed, clammy, and stiff with cold that co-workers had to pull him out because he could hardly move. The prolonged exposure to cold caused him to develop very painful and swollen joints, making him no longer suitable for this work.

He consulted the force's medical officer who diagnosed his condition as acute rheumatism (rheumatic fever). The doctor had him taken off the demanding project and recommended a dryer climate for his recovery. Thus, Sturtridge received transfer papers to the Yale construction crew of the Royal Engineers who were engaged in widening the Douglas Portage, the old footpath between Yale and Spuzzum.

Even in the more arid climate, Sturtridge still suffered from swollen joints. Stiff and in pain, he reported sick and was examined by the military medical officer at Hope, Staff Assistant Surgeon Dr. John Seddall. The quinine he prescribed helped initially. The swelling and pain in the joints subsided and Sturtridge could swing his road builder's pick again. After a few weeks, however, the drug lost its effect even when the doctor doubled, then tripled the dose. Quinine was costly; even worse, the higher dose caused an itchy rash to cover his entire body. Dr. Seddall had nothing further to offer from his military medicine chest and candidly told Sturtridge that he could not help.

Meanwhile, the rheumatic condition did not abate. Every morning when Sturtridge arose, his joints were so stiff, swollen and sore that he had difficulty getting off his cot. He felt weak and short of breath. Toward the evening his legs swelled and the skin assumed a whitish, shiny appearance. When placing a finger onto the flesh it left a depression as though the flesh were candle tallow. The Sapper suffered from oedema of heart failure.

In his misery Sturtridge decided to look for help elsewhere. At the Hudson's Bay post he spoke to Mr. Allard, who recommended Dr. Fifer. Sturtridge decided to consult him as a private patient, hoping that his ministrations would be superior to those of the military physicians. He told the doctor about his stiff joints, the unpleasant side effects of the quinine and how little good it had done him.

Fifer noted how the patient hobbled into the office from pain in his knees and ankles, and he felt the hot, seized-up joints. He could see the patient's difficulty in putting on his trousers, the painfully swollen fingers trying to close the buttons.

From his California apprentice days, Dr. Fifer remembered the name of a Dr. Gaulthier. A hundred years before, this "Canadian Physitian" had discovered an evergreen rhododendron plant, later named after him *gaultheria procumbens*. It contained an oil which might help Sturtridge's pain. The plant grew in the mountains near Hope.

The extract, called oil of evergreen, was rubbed on the soldier's painful joints, and it gave miraculous relief. Sturtridge also had to drink a bitter-tasting tea that the doctor directed me to brew from the bark of the willow tree, *Salix alba*, and the poplar tree, *Populus alba*. Willow and poplar trees grow abundantly on the swampy shore of Kawkawa, a mountain lake near Hope. Dr. Fifer obtained the medicine by having natives dry the willow bark before they brought it to him. When the tea became unpalatable and made the patient nauseous, the doctor resorted to the administration of pills. He showed me how to pound and grind the brittle bark into a powder in his apothecary's mortar, then sprinkle the medication with a half-dram of powdered cinnamon and liquorice for flavouring. Compounding it with gum myrrh as a binding agent, I rolled the substance into pills, to be taken three times daily, with food.

To treat the wax-like swelling of the soldier's legs, Dr. Fifer dispatched me to have the Natives collect the woolly leaves of *digitalis lanata*. The pretty flowering foxglove graces the banks of the river. The doctor had experience in treating patients with leg oedema. The medical proverb "Foxglove for waxy legs" attests to the diuretic effect of digitalis.

To relieve the hot skin rash, Dr. Fifer used a watery extract of the fragrant witch hazel, *Hamamelis virginiana*, which he had imported from San Francisco. He had stocked this medication in anticipation of the arrival of the "itch", a tormenting condition that predictably returned each winter's end. It affected whole families, all members at the same time, whenever people huddled closely during the cold season.

A French doctor claimed to have discovered an almost invisible skin mite, *sarcoptes scabiei*, as the cause of the "itch". Dr. Fifer found his witch hazel compresses to be effective; other physicians, however, unconcerned about harmful side effects, continued treating the disease with bleeding and, since the irritated skin of scabies resembles the skin rash of syphilis, applied a generous layer of mercury ointment. The oedema of Sapper Sturtridge responded well to the digitalis medication. The swelling of his joints and the rheumatic pain went down under treatment with the salicin pills. Under the good doctor's care, the private returned to the rest of the crew engaged in widening the trail to Spuzzum. To his comrades, he spoke well of Dr. Fifer and his skill in prescribing the miraculous medicine. Thus, it was no surprise that the knowledge of Dr. Fifer's talents spread. Two more members of the Royal Engineers consulted him and received satisfactory treatment of their illnesses.

Following his treatment of Sturtridge's rheumatism, the doctor submitted his account to the authorities. Since he knew the stinginess of the British military, he calculated that initial modesty in his fees would appeal to their parsimony. In his first bill he omitted all charges for professional services and requested only reimbursement for the cost of the medication. Speculating that his low fees would meet their approval, he then could build a good relationship with the common soldiers. When his services were more in demand, he would ask for more appropriate fees.

Despite its modesty, Dr. Fifer's bill arrived at an unbefitting time. News of Dr. Fifer's success had reached the ears of Dr. Seddall and his colleagues. The British doctors were not amused by their soldiers' drifting to the American medicine man in Yale, rather than reporting for medical attention through proper channels. How dare this civilian Yankee challenge their medical skills, undermine their reputation, and corrupt their men with his esoteric nostrums!

The main cause for their rancour was patriotic. Dr. Fifer was an American and posed a threat as a potential enemy and invader. Furthermore, from their medical point of view, Dr. Fifer did not display a diploma to prove formal medical training. Rumour had it that this quack got his doctor's degree not through a medical school but as an apprentice and mere hospital stewart.

The British medical officers with their university education knew nothing of the conditions during the early days of colonization in California. Apprenticeship training was often the only method of medical learning, and the knowledge gained by practical experience was considered invaluable. A medical apprentice in California, after serving two years, received full recognition as a doctor. Dr. Seddall and his colleagues did not realize how enthusiastically the people of Yale had welcomed this supposed charlatan from the south.

Dr. Fifer himself was oblivious of any animus against him. By submitting his account in good faith he merely sought recognition from the military, equal to what the people of Yale had accorded him so openly. Negotiating with the military was obviously more difficult. What became of the account he sent to Dr. Seddall, the military medical officer, Dr. Fifer never learned. Its receipt was never acknowledged.

It did surprise me though, with my master's past experience in the military, his knowledge of 'military competence,' and the proscribed way that an army does business, that he even tried to collect. The men themselves had no cash with which to pay; the force provided its own doctors and had no budget for any unplanned or unauthorized duplication of services. Even if the commanding officer had agreed, how many months would the doctor have waited for London to say yea or nay?

Sapper Colston: With the number of indigent local patients depending on his care and his potions, Dr. Fifer had his hands full of freeloaders. The medicines on his shelves were a dwindling supply. He could not afford to dole out drugs and services to a British military unwilling to pay extra for the health care of their men. His tiff with the British authorities came to a head on September 8, 1860, when a rock slide, set off by a blast, tumbled down on the trail above Yale, nearly burying Sapper Colston. The soldier, in a state of shock, supporting his crushed limb with his good hand, staggered down to Yale, seeking the nearest medical assistance. Dr. Fifer provided emergency treatment only, referring him back to the medical officer for amputation of the crushed finger. On the following day, September 9, the doctor informed Colonel Moody by letter that he declined further treatment of the soldier because of the lack of common courtesy of a response to the previous bill. Colston's commanding officer reprimanded his man for abandoning his tools and directed a dockage from his pay for his two and one half pound steel pickaxe, marked number 791.

Initially, when the construction party of Royal Engineers arrived at Yale, there had been rejoicing among the businessmen. Dr. Fifer, with the Yale Town Council, had welcomed the sappers warmly and intended to establish good relations with the military. The Victoria

Colonist took note and praised his enthusiasm when he proposed that on completion of the Douglas Portage the Yale merchants treat the Royal Engineers to a dinner of appreciation. That was six months before.

At the conclusion of the trail improvement project, nothing more was said or done about a banquet for the military guests. Dr. Fifer was miffed. If Colonel Moody would not afford him a reply to his medical bills, then he, Fifer, chairman of the Yale Town Council, was not willing to wine and dine his troops.

Patients: Fraser River Miners

Diagnoses: death by drowning; death by falling; death as a consequence of a blow or blows to the head; broken fingers, toes, arms, legs; scurvy; pneumonia and other disease of the lungs; rheumatism and other inflammations of the joints; various fevers; dysentery and other diseases of the digestive system; heart ailments as a consequence of all of the above; arrow wounds; lacerations, contusions, concussion and other assault injuries; gunshot wounds.

Treatment: splints, bandages, amputations, better nutrition, spruce tea, folia digitalis, laudanum (tincture of opium), quinine, mercury ointment, nitro glycerine ointment, etc.

Quinine is our miracle drug, the panacea for all the ills, especially for alleviating fever and pain. However, it is very expensive. In San Francisco, one lot of quinine sold at auction for precisely fourteen times its weight in gold.

Floaters: The first patients Dr. Fifer was called out to attend were floaters, unfortunate miners who had slipped off the rocks or sand bars, tipped out of a canoe, or perhaps met some sort of foul play and ended in the cold embrace of Mr. Fraser. Dr. Fifer soon trained the townspeople that, for someone who was already dead, his services would be redundant. If the circumstances seemed suspicious, they were to call a policeman or the coroner. It is too late for a doctor. Later, he made arrangements for a standard fee for his services as a coroner, on the understanding that he would attend to the body in a suitable location (usually the bar or table of one of the gambling establishments) during suitable business hours.

The miners who escaped the water's embrace were still subject to many afflictions. As he had experienced in California, working in the mines was hard labour. Often a prospector sifted through a ton of sand and gravel to find an ounce of gold. Each type of operation, the dry diggings of the ravines and hillsides, and the wet diggings of the rivers and creeks, offered its own distinctive hardships and hazards to health. In the wet diggings, those we had observed from the sternwheeler as we made our way up river, the coldest, most elementary method was panning the placer. Washboards were replaced by the gold pan. The miner filled the shallow pan with sand and gravel and sloshed it gently back and forth in the stream, pushing the waste material away and leaving, hopefully, a few grains of the heavier gold. To "wash" one pan, the miner had to submerge his hands for ten or twelve minutes in water that was usually ice cold. Alternatively, the prospector might work from the bank, bending down to wash from an awkward back-straining angle, or else he might squat in the streams submerged up to his thighs in the chilly waters.

Another river mining method involved team operation of a rocking cradle or a sluice box, an open-ended box mounted on rockers. Sand was shoveled in by way of a hopper and water poured through while the cradle was rocked vigorously from side to side. This movement was to wash the lighter sand away while the heavier gold particles lodged against the cleats or riffles along the bottom of the box. Similar in principle was a device called the Long Tom. It consisted of two coffin-shaped sluice boxes mounted one on top of the other. A perforated piece of iron served as a sieve between the two boxes. The system was more efficient than panning but also more arduous. Continuous shoveling of sand and pouring water were what got good results.

The finer gold, appearing as gold dust or flour, required coarse blankets so that the particles were caught in the cloth. Dr. Fifer related on our journey up river how the legend of the Golden Fleece probably originated in ancient times when sheepskins were used as sieves. Most miners were successful at the beginning, when the gold fields were not crowded. While some made two to three hundred dollars a day, it was more common to make strikes of forty to fifty dollars, with rudimentary equipment.

Those miners with the better-paying claims tended to re-locate during the winter rains and snow, back to Victoria or to San Francisco. Those who remained along the river were less wealthy and often suffered from an illness that had not been seen since the Royal Navy discovered the prophylactic effects of lemon. Dr. Fifer recognized their bleeding gums, joint swelling and pain, widespread bruising under the skin and into the tissue, associated with anaemia, and general weakness as heralding scurvy. "In this day and age, Ah Chung. In this day and age." Men died from this form of malnutrition, if not from the primary symptoms, then from the inevitable cognitive impairment and lack of judgment that accompanies it. Or from the equally dangerous risk of misdiagnosis. The symptoms of scurvy were frequently diagnosed as gangrene and treated with unnecessary surgical amputation.

The British Navy have rid themselves of scurvy since an Act of Parliament in 1844 made the daily issuing of lemon juice mandatory. Here in Yale, lemons are in short supply. The Indians seem to survive quite well on a diet staple of salmon. For miners, Dr. Fifer always asked me to boil up some tea made with tips from evergreen trees and the patients who followed his directions usually recovered.

Scurvy was often the underlying cause of many of the existing diseases—rheumatism, dysentery, malaria, erysipelas, brain fever, and intermittent, remittent, and continued fevers, the latter assuming a typhoid character. However, most of the treatment required by miners was surgical, and often of a terrible nature. There were many disastrous accidents resulting from inadequate working conditions, lack of safety regulation, lack of enforcement, lack of government. In the dry diggings, great rocks frequently rolled down the steep mountains. Unsuspecting miners working in the river bottoms were crushed to death. Unwary new arrivals fell into the numerous pits of the prospectors that honeycombed the canyons and bars. Accidents also included stab and gunshot wounds, shattered limbs and compound fractures, even of thighbones.

Such injuries taxed the ingenuity of the surgeon, forcing Dr. Fifer to act quickly and without counsel or consultation. Although ether and chloroform had been available in San Francisco, emergency surgery and reduction of fractures on the mining bars still required the old standbys of whisky and opium, with the patient being tied down or held down by the strong arms of friends. Neglected conditions could turn into complications—pain, infections, gangrene. In California it was estimated that one in five miners died young; very few succumbed to old age.

Most of the gold seekers continued working while ill; many left the gold fields with a constitution broken down for the rest of their life. Others suffered from the imprudent excesses of their limited social interactions, involving excessive drinking, fraternization with unhealthy partners, gambling or other business dealings with violent unsavory characters.

Although Dr. Fifer defended Dr. Crane's right to charge for his services, I never knew him to refuse to treat a miner, or anyone else, because of their inability to pay. He always asserted that "he was here to help those who had money as well as those who did not.

Patient: Edward Stout
Diagnosis: lacerations
Treatment: Excising Seven Arrows
Outcome: successful extraction, poultices

August, 1858, a few nights after Little Sara died, when Captain Snyder and his men returned from their expedition to Boston Bar, Edward Stout sought Dr. Fifer's assistance to treat lacerations on the skin of his shoulder, arms, thighs, and back. This was the one time that Dr. Fifer used the arrow extraction tongs in Yale. The doctor noted that the arrowheads were crafted from obsidian and chert and not the deadly whisky-bottle glass which Yo-Semite had employed against intruders in his territory ten years earlier. Edward Stout was one of five survivors of the McLennan party decimated by the Indians above China Bar. Although Mr. Stout claimed that Chief Spintlum had spread word that the projectile tips were dipped in a mixture of rattlesnake venom and deer's blood, and that wounded comrades had died of convulsions after turning black, this patient made a complete recovery.

Patient: Magistrate Sanders
Diagnosis: Nose laceration due fo bear mauling
Treatment: Rhinoplasty, plaster brace and bandage
Outcome: healed successfully, with only a slight bump

Magistrate Sanders was mauled by his pet bear which bit off his nose on the very morning he was to wed. The laceration healed well, albeit with a slight bulbous deformity at the tip. The wedding proceeded as scheduled.

Patient: Jules David
Diagnosis: assaulted with a wooden club, scalp lacerations, fractured nose, contusions, possible concussion
Treatment: cleansing, bandage, laudanum
Outcome: disorientation, memory loss, nasal deformity, breathing trouble

After McGowan's attack on Mr. David: the injured patient received our emergency treatment and was dispatched from Yale immediately. Dr. Fifer was unable to follow up upon initial treatment of September 11, 1858.

Patients: Dance Hall Ladies' Clients
Diagnoses: infections, uterine blockages, swellings
Treatments: mercury, acontin applied p.r.n. (*pro re nata*).

Patient: Ikey Dixon
Diagnosis: contusions following an assault
Treatment: bandages
Outcome: recovery

Mr. Dixon was assaulted the week of our first Christmas in Yale. He recovered from his beating physically, although he remained fearful of further harassment and retaliation.

Patient: Edward (Ned) McGowan
Diagnosis: urinary obstruction
Treatment: insertion of a catheter, dilatation
Outcome: relief

Mr. McGowan left Yale (Hill's Bar) shortly after his treatment by Dr. Fifer, in February, 1859. During the eight months he lived in the district, he was the aggressor in two serious assaults with fists and clubs and was responsible for more than one gunshot wound.

Patient: Robert Wall
Diagnosis: priapism, infection of the testicles, excessive libido.
Treatment: application of aconite ointment.
Outcome: relief of symptoms as long as supply of salve lasted.

I remember Robert Wall's face, the first time he came to see Dr. Fifer in March, 1860. The young gold miner showed pain and embarrassment as he entered the office. His claim that he had "strained himself" while moving his heavy sluice-box made little sense. "Probably an acute case of haemorrhoids", was Dr. Fifer's first impression. After persuading the reluctant patient to disrobe, the doctor could see that he had intuited incorrectly.

Dr. Fifer gathered some details for the personal history. Robert, "Bob", Wall, son of a Belfast Coastguard man, had come to San Francisco in 1852, too late for the California gold rush. He worked as a cattle drover until joining a group of boatmen who moved north with news of gold in the British Territories and took up mining at Hill's Bar. More recently, he had been mining near Twenty-One Mile House, between Lytton and Boston Bar.

Bob Wall's problem proved to be bizarre. He confessed to an inordinate obsessive sexual urge, without relief from self-pollution. All the gold mined from his claim he had spent on prostitutes. Now there was burning when he urinated; even worse, he suffered from "flowing of his seed in large quantities without emotion". At such times he would be quite mad and grow aggravated. At other times, he said he would be sluggish for days, stupid, like a bear in hibernation. His waddling gait was due to painful testicles which had swelled to an enormous size. The continuous pain caused an irritation of his manhood, and in his shame Robert was unable to suppress its unchaste turgidity, what the doctor called *priapism*, after some Greek god of creative potency.

Robert Wall begged the doctor for help out of his misery and admitted that he had no money or gold to pay. His mining partner James Griffin had borrowed $180 off him and bought a half lot close to the doctor's office to start a tin-man shop. The business made money but not enough to pay back the loan. Robert promised to pay his bill as soon as Griffin would return the money lent to him, or else, from the first pay dirt of his claim once he was well enough to work again.

Fifer agreed to help. When he examined the patient he noted his painful groin swellings, buboes, which were fluctuant, aching to be drained. The doctor incised the boils. The patient experienced great relief when the yellow pus of infection gushed forth.

While it was one thing to treat the painful groin swellings, to relieve the young man's compelling indecent desire required quite different therapeutic measures. Dr. Fifer referred to a paper by Ringer and Broca, which he had reviewed when he was editor for the San Francisco medical journal. Describing the therapeutic applications of the drug aconite, the authors recognized the substance as a deadly poison if taken internally, however, they claimed good results in "deadening the sensibilities" when applied externally. Dr. Fifer pondered whether aconite might not relieve Robert Wall's harassing engrossment. He directed me to grind up two grains of root of wolfbane, *aconitum napellus*, in his apothecary's mortar, and to work into the bowl six drachms of cerate, purified bees' wax. Dr. Fifer directed Wall to apply the ointment to his scrotum and priapic phallus three times a day. "Don't let the smell of horseradish trick you, Robert; the drug is a powerful poison for your inside, it's good only for the outside. Use the medicinal finger, the ring finger; it leads directly to the heart. Work the salve well into the skin, the acorn, too. You'll feel prickling like nettles and a burning like a fine, easy glow. Finally, there will be numbness of the skin, that's the drug working. You must be careful, wash your hands after you have used it."

Wall thanked the doctor and left, again promising to pay soon.

The ointment was effective. Within days, the drug deadened the sensory nerves, and, *mirabile dictu*, the resulting flaccidness made self-abuse unrewarding. The lymph nodes in his groin dried and healed.

After some weeks, Robert, who had followed the doctor's advice, ran out of salve. The tormenting lust returned. Penniless, he had not worked his claim, had not paid Dr. Fifer, and could not bring up the courage to face him to ask for more salve. He decided to consult Dr. Crane at the California Hotel. Making a scapegoat out of his benefactor, he complained: "That Fifer has made me sick, doctor. Ever since he treated me I cannot satisfy women or myself. I am now the butt of all the ladies. Wherever I shew my face, they jeer after me: 'Cultus Man, Cultus Man! No good. No good!'

"If only you had come earlier, Robert, I could have helped," feigned Dr. Crane. People in Yale knew that Dr. Crane was envious of his rival's success and would discredit him whenever he could. Crane saw a great opportunity to condemn Fifer. "It's too late now; he has ruined your brain. The operation has made you impotent, having cut the cords of your testicles and your penis. Fifer has poisoned you medically, and his knife has made you impotent for life!"

Robert Wall, frail at the best of time, inflamed by Crane's criticism and provocative statements, bought into the fantasy. "I know why he did it. Three years ago, Billy Burgess, Tom Toole and Frank O'Dyle asked me to go and rob a ranch in California. I refused. They came to British Columbia. These three have taken revenge and bribed Fifer to maim me for life. I hear the voice of God; the Almighty is telling me to kill the doctor for it."

Wall's paranoia suggested that he was suffering from a "paroxysm of madness". His belief in Dr. Crane's insinuation that his illness was from another doctor's treatment was irrational. Hearing that there was no hope for cure must have been like a death knell. In his already confused mind, he withdrew into a state of melancholy. Unable to work for at least a year, he roamed the colony like a lost soul.

A catastrophic event, such as a sudden bereavement or other kind of loss is often followed by depression. If unresolved, the despair can change to anger, which in turn is often directed against, transferred to, the most suitable person close at hand. We had heard the rumours of Wall's accusations and threats. Yet, knowing their source, what could we have done? What is the treatment for madness?

This patient, Robert Wall, as a result of anger and untreated depression, assaulted Dr. Fifer with the help of a newspaper and a pistol on July 5, 1861.

If only I had taken heed, before we left San Francisco, or after we arrived in Victoria. That summer Donati's Comet made its appearance.

Patient: Ovid Allard
Diagnosis: Ejaculatio praecox
Treatment: acontin
Outcome: satisfactory

After the grief of Little Sara's death, and some conflict in the marital bed, Dr. Fifer's friend Mr. Allard had approached him about a problem he had never before encountered during conjugal relationships with his wives. He was having difficulty with the timing of disengagement, and premature seminal spill deprived him of the kick of fulfilment.

Dr. Fifer listened to his friend's lamentations, of how the many months of quasi-self-denial had availed him to naught and how the youngest of the family was the result of untimely withdrawal. The doctor recognised indications of declining virility. He wanted to help and speculated that the drug that helped Wall's over-excitability would perhaps cure his neighbour's reverse problems if applied in extremely diluted state, according to the homoeopathic principle.

Patient: Mr. Langley, S.S. Yale passenger
Diagnosis: facial and scalp lacerations
Treatment: cleansing, salves, bed rest
Outcome: recovery

The steamship *Yale* was built in Victoria in the spring of this year. Although it is common knowledge that the boilers of these steamboats have a propensity for sudden blow-ups, "sending a score or two of parboiled passengers to an inconvenient altitude," as one writer puts it, a consortium of businessmen pooled their resources to back this venture. They saw it as a way to ensure Yale's upper hand over Fort Hope as the transhipment point of goods going north to the gold fields of the Canyon and the Forks. If their project were to fail, surely this community would be doomed as business and its profits would pass it by.

On Easter Sunday, April 14, 1861, the *Yale* was pushing upstream towards Yale against the strong current of the Fraser River. It was her first voyage to the head of navigation and was meant to be symbolic. In all its new gilt and splendour, the vessel passed Fort Hope, announcing its presence with a blast from the whistle. As the Yale was negotiating the riffle at Union Bar, the sound of a loud boom and the rattle of doors and windows brought the people of Hope out on the streets. On the steamer, eye-witnesses, passengers in the saloon, reported later, "the cabin floor raised and then fell in, at the same time, the hurricane roof fell upon us, cutting our heads more or less, and blocking up all means of escape towards the forward of the dinner table." Details of the tragedy spread up and down the river, how they all "quickly made for the windows and doors in the after part of the cabin, and got to the roof of the hurricane house, and there beheld a scene that baffles all descriptions, and such as I trust I may never witness again."

Under the stress of the load against the current, the overheated boiler had exploded, burst, and shattered those parts of the ship it flew through. "Five or six human beings, their faces streaming with blood, and presenting an awful appearance, were struggling for life."

Killed were five white men, including her captain, Smith Jamieson, Joseph Growler, Joel Osburn, fireman, Samuel Powers, and a coloured person, name unascertained. The body of the cook, although seen in the cookhouse, was not recovered. There was a report that seven Chinamen were aboard and six lost. Others say there were only three aboard and one of them was saved.

"Of the passengers, Messrs. Langley, Stevens, and several others were cut in the head and face and bled freely. Some of the injured crew were James Ellison, boatman of Hope, who was carried up into the air to a great height and then plummeted into the water. Engineer McGreary, who was in the engine room, injured his arm. Mr. Smith, the mate, was standing on the guards by the side of the boiler and was blown overboard. Thomas King, a deck hand, was blown into the water and lost his leg below the knee. He afterwards had the stump of bone sawed off by Dr. Bradshaw of Hope, assisted by Dr. Oliver, a fellow passenger. It is feared, however, that King will die."

The current swept the shattered vessel below Hope where survivors were rescued. James Ellison had been with Captain Jamieson in the pilothouse almost directly over the boiler where it received the full force of the blast. Ellison was blown high in the air but landed in the water with only bruises. Another passenger, Samuel Powers, a blacksmith of Hope, wasn't so fortunate. He was also blown high in the air, but landed on shore against a rock, gashing his brains out. When found, his body was perfectly naked.

No trace was ever found of twenty-six-year-old Captain Jamieson. Other survivors included purser F.J. Barnard and Captain Irving, who was a passenger. Shortly before the explosion, he was in the pilothouse with Captain Jamieson and offered to steer while Jamieson ate. Jamieson laughingly remarked that he would not trust his boat to an opposition pilot. Irving went below and just sat down to dinner when the vessel was demolished. Captain Jamieson was a

Scot, one of six brothers, five of whom came to the Pacific Northwest. All became steamboat men, with tragic results. Smith was the third brother to die in steamboat mishaps on the Columbia and Fraser Rivers.

In the days that followed, word arrived that the steering wheel and the top of the pilothouse of the Yale were picked up by the Indians below Harrison River. A piece of the boiler, weighing ninety pounds, was found four hundred yards from the point of the explosion.

When the intelligence of the steamship disaster reached Yale, inhabitants rushed down in canoes to render assistance and to help inter the dead. Dr. Fifer hired a canoe and reached the place of calamity within the hour. There was work to be done in helping Dr. Bradshaw who had his hands full looking after the injured.

From his days as hospital stewart, Dr. Fifer had considerable experience in the management of major explosion injuries. In Los Angeles, in 1847, he had treated similar injuries in soldiers caught in an explosion. In a false alarm, the guard had lit a fire of burning tar to search out intruders. The flames accidentally spread to the guardroom where small arms, ammunition, and powder kegs were stored. They caught fire, resulting in a huge explosion which killed four and injured seven soldiers. Dr. Fifer treated the injured brought in by horseback and on donkey carts, covered with blood, suffering from fractures, with white bone jutting from a gashed arm or leg, from blast injuries, from crush injuries caused by fallen walls, and from shock. Some of the men were groaning; others were quiet.

No proper anaesthesia was available then. Surgeons amputated by cutting the soft tissues and then sawing the bones with quick deft movements. Pain was managed by doping the patient up with laudanum and whisky to the point of coma. Held down, the patient could hear and see the cutting, sawing, and other excruciatingly distressing things. Mercifully, many fainted. The maximum safe time for such procedures was fifteen minutes. The surgeon had to know exactly what he was looking for and what to do when he found it. He needed the qualities of an eagle's eye, a lady's gentle hand, a lion's heart, and a greyhound's speed, to work fast, with bold strokes of the knife or saw, so that there would be only one short moment of agony. Dr. Fifer was treating a young private with a compound fractured thighbone which required removal of the crushed leg. Either the dose of laudanum or the shock of the amputation proved fatal; the soldier died on the wagon, his makeshift operating table.

The steamship explosion at Hope resulted in injuries of similar nature and magnitude. In addition, steam and hot water burns required dressing and treatment for their pain. Dr. Fifer felt his experience in treating major trauma would be welcome. However, to his great surprise, he was received coolly. He returned early to Yale, bringing with him in his care Mr. Langley, a passenger who had received facial lacerations,

The medical aid which he had offered at the scene had been trumped by political bitterness. The people of Hope had observed the resplendent steamer, named after the rival community, passing their town on her maiden voyage; they heard the ship's provocative whistle. They were resentful of the good fortune of the Yaleites, a good fortune which could have been theirs had they not sided with Doc Chisholm and opposed the road tax suggested by Governor Douglas a year before. Now the tide had turned; they could revel in the ill fortune of their neighbours.

Dr. Fifer's rushing to the scene of the disaster was not altogether altruistic. Like the other enterprising businessmen of Yale, Oppenheimer, McRoberts, Kurtz, Power, and Barnard, the doctor was a shareholder in the failed project. Indeed, a good part of the freight on board was his property. He was anxious to see for himself what of his investment could be salvaged. He had put his entire fortune into the venture. Neither ship nor cargo was insured.

Of course, nothing remained. The supplies he had ordered to begin to furnish a small hospital were nowhere to be found. The loss of the freight in fire and flood was the swan song of his dream of a modern medical facility for Yale.

Of course, Dr. Fifer never witnessed the accident, so perhaps it never crossed his mind that this disastrous explosion may have been "the bright sentinels of the sky which the clairvoyant had predicted. As for me, Fool that I am, I prefer to believe the fortuneteller referred to the Fourth of July fireworks we all watched, the night before Robert Wall walked into the doctor's office with a Derringer under a newspaper. That was the day after the eclipse. Our life in Yale starts and ends with celestial portents. For did it not begin with the bright arrival in the sky of Donati's Comet, with its prominent dust tail, curved like a long scimitar? It was Mr. Jules David who pointed out to us this coincidence of timing, in one of the newspapers he brought with him, on that happy visit in early September, before he too required Dr. Fifer's professional services.

6

The only person from San Francisco who came to visit us here in Yale was Mr. Jules David, both friend and business partner to Dr. Fifer. Although the call took place almost three years ago, to me it still seems like yesterday. The doctor and I were both anxiously listening for the whistle announcing the steamboat's arrival that day, as I made up an extra bed for Mr. David in the doctor's examining room, the realm of "Poor Yorick," the doctor's phrenology skull. This very skull, set upon a shelf, would stare down at our guest, whether he was awake or sleeping. What was it Dr. Fifer had said to it whenever he joked about this phrenology cranium? "Alas, Poor Yorick. I knew him well. A fellow of infinite jest." I do not think of "infinite jest" when I look at this scribed memento of death. Jest is a joke, something to make us laugh, but this skull signals no tease, no rude reproach, no funny story or mockery. The once-inhabitant of this cranium, this anonymous man, saved my life—I feel only gratitude towards it. The reason for my cognizance is an oft-told tale, one which Mr. David had surely heard before from his friend while in San Francisco, yet the version I remember best is the one Dr. Fifer narrated at his guest's special request, on his first and only visit.

That day, almost three years ago, began innocent enough in an ordinary way, with a friendly knock and greeting.

"Ah Chung!" Pete Charlie called out at the back door before he stepped into the kitchen. He plopped a large fish onto my work table.

"Chinook," he said, by word of explanation.

"Chinook?" I repeated. That was our first summer in Yale, and I had not yet learned the names for all the different kinds of salmon, and the different times they make their way home, back from the sea to the river, back to the people. I had walked to the Indian village that morning, to inquire about fresh salmon to prepare for Dr. Fifer's first visitor to our new home. Pete arrived in no time at our house with a freshly caught Chinook. Thanks to the doctor's quinine, Pete had just recovered from the shakes of "river fever". He promised to bring some dried and smoked salmon the next day.

I had just slit the belly of the fish when Dr. Fifer arrived home with his guest and friend, Mr. Jules David from San Francisco. The gentleman was, as expected, a passenger on the morning steamboat and Dr. Fifer had gone down to greet him on the beach and to escort him up the hill to our first home and office on Front Street. They set Mr. David's travel bags inside and went for a walk to tour the town, Dr. Fifer pointing out the high points: the Hudson's Bay Company store and warehouse; Ballou's Express freight office; the gold commissioner's vault with the drop hole in the top of its solid dome where the miners deposited their pokes with their names attached; the land commissioner's tent; the sawmill; the miners' staked claims; the tents for ten thousand gold seekers; the Indian village. By the time they returned, Mr. David had regained his land legs and "worked up a vicious thirst," for which Dr. Fifer was well prepared, having already arranged for a prodigious supply of Mr. Allard's brandy.

As I busied myself with preparing both a light lunch and an evening feast, Dr. Fifer and Mr. David attended to the doctor's accounts at the outset in order to be able to enjoy a relaxing visit. The first order of business was the monies realized from the liquidation of the San Francisco real estate and the company shares. Mr. David began to explain: "I would have shipped the money sooner by Wells Fargo express; however, I learned that the San Francisco City Coroner..."

Dr. Fifer, with the wink of an eye, interrupted him: "I heard of the Coroner, his removing jewelry from the bodies of victims."

Jules David confirmed: "Kent was fired; he went north and opened an express business out of Victoria under the name of Kent & Smith for Wells Fargo. That's one good reason for me to bring the cash to you personally. Selling your shares of the Sitka Alaska Russian Ice Company was not a problem; the quality of the San Francisco drinking water is deteriorating; the table ice from the Sierra Nevada mountains is rust stained, melting to yellow water. Our Alaska ice is like crystal. The share value has nearly doubled."

Mr. David continued with the business details. "The Market Street stand of our Fallarone Island Egg Supply Company is doing well. The eggs are fresher than those from a chicken farmer. Our men cross over to the island the night before and smash every egg in sight, thus guaranteeing freshness of the morning eggs for breakfast.

"The mining stock of the Bellingham coal mine on Puget Sound in Washington Territory has risen in value because of the increase in crime in San Francisco. The citizens have demanded better public safety; the new gas streetlights call for more coal to produce the gas.

"The sale of your house on Washington Street brought in extra cash. Here it is; I have kept a 5% commission." Mr. David handed Dr. Fifer an envelope stuffed with money which he placed immediately into this hidden compartment in his desk drawer, nodding his thanks as he did so.

The friends moved on to a general discussion of the stock market. They congratulated themselves on not having invested in the Atlantic Cable Company which had created such a stir in all of North America in August, when it completed a link between Europe and America, making communication over the wires almost instantaneous. After one month, trouble downed the line and finally, just the week before the visit, scuttled the whole project. "You'd be surprised," Mr. David hinted, "at how many people you know who lost many thousands of dollars." Mr. David had brought a souvenir with him, a section of cable mounted in gold, sold by a New York jeweler. "Trust me, Max. This will be worth more than the shares by the end of the year!"

Dr. Fifer picked up the curio and examined it. "Who would have thought," he mused, "when I was labouring in New York harbour to lay cable across Buttermilk Channel to Governor's Island, a mere twelve years ago, that I could have made my fortune chopping it up and selling it to the gullible?"

"The power of advertising, Max. Do we not ourselves, sell ice in winter?" Mr. David winked, and both men laughed at their own good fortune and quick wits.

More somberly, Mr. David explained how the political climate in San Francisco had never recovered; as a former member of the Vigilance Committee, indeed its chief financial officer, Mr. David remained a target of invective and threats, and the best way out was a new start, to relocate, as he had done when he had left Paris to seek a new life in America, a new world where he hoped the prejudices against his race would not follow him. Although he had been born in Lyon into a well-off Jewish family, and studied medicine in Paris at the Sorbonne University and the hospital for destitute women ("built at the site of the old powder factory, hence its name Salpêtrière," he added in explanation of the institution's name), in America he had made his career as an executive agent for the Paris-based Abel Guy Bank.

Hearing our guest speak of "relocation," Dr. Fifer and I realized that Mr. David did not intend to return to San Francisco. "Mr. Guy, the president of the bank, is in accord with my plan to move; he sees me as a bridgehead for a branch office in the British Territories. In contrast to your furtive exit, Max Fifer, a festive and excited crowd attended the embarkation of Jules David. There is safety in numbers; Mr. Guy, in the company of his lady friend and her fräuleins of entertainment, saw me off."

This was how Dr. Fifer and I learned that Mr. Jules David planned to set himself up in business in Fort Victoria. The fact that he was unmarried made the change easier. He had already begun by renting office space and placing notices in the local papers. Placing his trust in the British system of law and order for protection, he seemed not to care that his eye-catching advertisements would reveal his whereabouts to everyone, including his mortal enemies.

"I traveled on the steamer *Pacific,* well booked with passengers and her holds crammed with freight. The voyage was uneventful until we reached Astoria. There, our captain spotted a disabled sternwheeler stuck fast on a sand bar at the mouth of the Columbia River. We helped free her, and towed her to Victoria, where we were two days late."

"Two days late, you say, Jules?"

"Indeed, Max, I stepped onto British soil with a sigh of relief, free like an English lark, free at last from the threats of McGowan and his Law and Order gang. The town of Victoria is small, about five hundred inhabitants, mostly British, around one hundred very neat houses. As you have seen, of course. Yet, on the streets, I recognized a number of San Francisco city sharps, looking around for deals, contracts, and privileges they can pounce upon. But the Governor, your man Douglas, now, he's too smart for them. Did you hear that he even called Ned McGowan on the carpet, chiding him for his too boisterous arrival, telling him to his face that he expected him to respect the Queen and obey her laws? Ha! McGowan, respect the Queen?!"

"Yes, Jules. Rumours of Ned's presence or his imminent arrival are still 'ubiquitous'."

"In Governor Douglas' Victoria, there is No Gambling and No Prostitution allowed. For entertainment, people go to dance halls, and they hold outdoor picnics. Everything is quiet and orderly."

I looked at Dr. Fifer and he looked at me as I served the tea and some ginger biscuits and then the doctor said "Victoria must have quieted considerably since we were there two months ago."

"Perhaps the rowdies have all moved on then. Today, there are no taxes to pay; those wanting to sell liquor have to buy a license, which is $100. I went to the passenger agency of Freeman's Express to inquire about you, Max, and your Chinaman, and learned that you had wasted no time—tickets for the gold fields at Yale. And now, here I am. I've caught up with you."

As Mr. David chatted on, Dr. Fifer smiled and poured more brandy from the decanter. "Opportunity, Max. Victoria is a place of opportunity. Growing by the hour; new arrivals require land transportation, baggage handling from the deep harbour into the town, lodging and meals. Business is going to mushroom: there are opportunities for brokerage services for shipping consignments, a seamen's employment office, an agency for passenger tickets. Inertness," he said, almost to himself, "inertness is a great characteristic of the English. With the spirit of the progressive Yankee, soon Victoria will equal, if not surpass, San Francisco."

Mr. David detailed his idea of deluging the public with a multitude of services, all directed through his office. He had located a reliable artesian spring in the vicinity of the harbour and purchased it on the spot. Eye-catching ads would overwhelm the shipping companies with the offer of fresh drinking water for their vessels at low rates. He had paid a visit to the *Victoria Gazette* on Government Street to arrange front-page advertising for a proposed credit institution. He would offer help to those who had spent their last dollar on the purchase of passage; he would strip them of their belongings for a few dollars, without compunction. Another ad offered his services as a broker on commission; his seamen's employment office would conduct business with "fidelity and dispatch".

Mr. David had another more far-fetched scheme. Mattresses were expensive because of the high import duty imposed on Kapok fiber. He had found a promising substitute that he expected would become a best seller. Pulu, the furry growth from the base of fern stalks, *genus cibotium*, was not a floss or fibre and, therefore, free of the high import levy. The pallets were softer, kept their shape better, and were much, much cheaper. Pulu mattresses were manufactured at a factory atop an extinguished volcano on the Isle of Hawaii. As he had done in San Francisco, Mr. David planned to import the mattresses once the ads created the demand. "With Pulu, everybody can afford to sleep in comfort." We heard some months later that the pallets did not last, that the stuffing crumbled to poppy-seed-sized chaff, resembling termite droppings that, indeed, turned out to be just that; the mattresses were riddled with the varmint.

Mr. David also planned to construct a depot for the American Russian Ice Company. "Will the citizens of Victoria not appreciate the luxury of crystal-clear Alaska-cool refreshments, just as the well-off people of San Francisco do?" He expected the newspaper advertisements to do their work while he was visiting with Dr. Fifer in Yale. Before boarding the steamer for the mainland, he had called on the printer once again, to ensure that there would be no confusion about the Victoria address. "Jules David, on Wharf Street, opposite Freeman's Express." Customers would be waiting to place their orders when he returned to Victoria; nothing was left to chance.

From his baggage, Mr. David retrieved a tight roll of newspapers, peeled off an outer layer, and displayed a proof copy of the Victoria advertisements of which he was so proud. Beneath this outer stratum was a bundle of San Francisco dailies covering the two months we had been away, recent copies of the *San Francisco Evening Bulletin*, the *Alta California*, and the *Herald*. "The news may be outdated, Max, but it's a treasure of mementos and a consolation for a homesick exile."

As they settled in to their reading, I placed biscuits, butter, cheese, sliced cold meats, and a pot of mustard sauce on a tray and set it where they could serve themselves.

Page by page they leafed through the papers, stopping to read aloud to each other as they came upon articles piquing their interest or requiring updates. They read the report of the coroner's inquest on Captain Ames Reynolds who had committed suicide in his room at the Central House on Clay Street. Mrs. Jane Savage, proprietress, gave testimony: "He told me that he lost his position in the San Francisco Branch of the United States Mint because he openly expressed his views against the Vigilance Committee. He insisted that he heard their bell ringing, indicating that they were after him. He appeared out of his natural mind; from his conversation, I knew he was insane."

Julius Knapp, being sworn, stated: "I am a hair dresser in the Metropolitan Saloon. That afternoon, about 3 p.m., I went to Dr. Fifer's office and saw Captain Reynolds sitting there, barefoot; he had thrown away his brogans. I saluted him; he seemed very much troubled and asked me if I had heard anything about the Vigilance Committee being after him. I said no. Dr. Fifer persuaded him to go home; the doctor and I went with him to the Central House. The doctor gave him some medicine and he laid down for about two minutes. Then he jumped up and cried out: 'There they come!' The doctor persuaded him to lie down. We left after about five minutes and heard that about three quarters of an hour later the Captain had taken his life."

Dr. Fifer added details he remembered: "During an interval of sanity, the Captain came and implored me to speak on his behalf to Judge Loff, the head of the Mint. He begged me to use my position and ask the judge to reinstate him. I felt sorry for his wife and the eight children in Philadelphia and went to see the judge who agreed to take him back as an adjustor of coin. But when Reynolds came to work he was as tight as a tick. He was too far gone. When not drinking, he was very much afraid of the Vigilance Committee and in his delusion said they had charged him with a crime although there was no charge against him. In the end, Reynolds hallucinated that the Vigilance Committee were after him, and in the panic, while labouring under a state of mental derangement, cut his throat with a pen knife."

Dr. Fifer went on, adding more detail: "Dr. Williamson and I performed the post- mortem; our report describes an incision on the right side of the neck, midway between the angle of the jaw and the collar-bone, which penetrated the jugular vein and carotid artery and had severed the pneumogastric nerve. His death resulted from haemorrhage. In our opinion he suffered from delirium tremens as he had several times before. He was given to the habit of dissipation. Like all cases of alcoholism, Reynolds required a lot of my efforts, but often there is nothing a doctor can do."

A sharp knock on the back door interrupted my kitchen preparations. I wiped my hands and opened the door to Mr. Tennent, the town clerk, who stepped in and asked for the doctor, adding: "The men at the beach have pulled up a floater, quite far gone. Magistrate Sanders has ordered a post-mortem to rule out foul play."

I called Dr. Fifer who advised them to leave the body where it was and to cover it to ward off flies and animals. The examination could wait; he would perform it in good time. No medical man hankers for the task of examining human bodies in a state of decomposition, particularly when he is sitting down to dine with a friend. Nor was post-mortem work Dr. Fifer's intended *raison d'être* in Yale. As a newcomer, however, he did his best to comply with the authorities' requests, expecting they would call him also for less fulsome and more rewarding medical services.

He returned to his guest in the office; I heard him apologize for the interruption.

"Do you get a lot of that here, Max? Floaters. Dead patients?"

Dr. Fifer welcomed the opportunity to speak of his work. "It has been hectic. I have so far treated a lady's migraine headache which caused her to leave her stomach contents, all of it, in front of the office—the town dogs took care of the puke and other *dejecta*—while two drams of laudanum, on an empty stomach, fixed her headache.

132

At 3 a.m., a cattle drover with a bad toothache and swollen jaw knocked at the door. The culprit molar was drawn; a liberal dose of laudanum did the rest. Rufus, a miner's pet dog who had erred onto the site of a powder charge that went off prematurely, was another patient. My care was *pro bono publico*, of course. It was the silence before the storm. On Friday, I tried for hours to save the life of Isaac Miller who was mortally wounded by another miner, Henry Post, in a terrible, savage, bloody fight over claims at Madison Bar. Yesterday, on Sunday morning, I was called after another attempt at murder had been made. I did all that could be done to relieve the victim's suffering, before he too passed on. This floater is the third fatality in the same number of days. The post-mortem can wait until tomorrow as long as the body is kept cool, out of the sun."

"No doubt, I'll read about it in the San Francisco papers next week in Victoria," Mr. David predicted. "With such an influx of people from California here, news from the British Territories is a hot item in San Francisco; it may concern one of the boys from home who has gone for the distant gold, an acquaintance, a friend, or a relative who met his fate or fortune." With this premise, Mr. David moved back to the log of rolled newspapers.

As I brought in the additional servings of tea and brandy that Dr. Fifer requested, he, turning pages, began to read aloud: "Here is the article about the tragedy of the Ogsbury family and their three nice boys. One of them, ten years of age, was bitten by a pet dog, which had been raised in the family and of which the children were very fond. Nothing was thought of it at that time, not until a hog, which had also been bitten, was seized with hydrophobia and died. This alarmed the family who at once procured a tea made from white ash bark. The youngest boy drank this freely, but the other, who has since died, could not be induced to drink it. On Thursday, the oldest boy complained of slight indisposition and I was called in and pronounced the case hydrophobia. The poor boy had every indication of the fearful malady and suffered greatly from spasms and convulsions, requiring two men to hold him, although but ten years of age. He continued to suffer thus, until the evening of Saturday, when he lay quietly and died. The brother of the deceased, also bitten, is now at home in the hands of a Mr. Clow, who is said to have been successful in treating this terrible disease. By the time I left, no symptoms of the malady had manifested themselves in the survivor; but, as it is positively known that he was bitten, the family live in fearful apprehension."

I began to clear their lunch dishes. It pleased me to see their delight in each other's company. The liberal servings of brandy, the pleasure they were taking in sharing the newspapers, made the afternoon a picture of comfort and contentment. Mr. David laughed as he read out a letter printed in the *California Evening Bulletin*, written by Police Captain Donnellan who had also moved to Yale from San Francisco. Donnellan stated that "Doctor Pfeiffer is doing well at the new location in British Columbia." Dr. Fifer chuckled, pleased to see his name, oblivious to how such well-meant publicity might pose a threat or danger to himself or others.

When he came across an advertisement for the People's Opposition Omnibus Line, Mr. David saw it as an opener to a delicate discussion. "Louis Maillet, the omnibus driver of the Red Line from Kearny Street to the Mission Dolores, was going up the road to the Lone Mountain Cemetery with his team of four horses. He was going too fast, trying to pass the omnibus of John Logue's People's Opposition Line. The vehicles collided, and his vehicle broke the spokes of their wheels."

Mr. David continued to read: "The People's Opposition Line driver, John Wintringer, had fourteen passengers on his bus. They were on their way to the Mission. Fortunately, nobody was injured. Louis Maillet was arrested, brought before the Judge and fined $10 for reckless speeding while under the influence of alcohol.

"The speeding fine, however, was only the tip of the iceberg of his perpetrations. Preceding the accident, Maillet had consumed a large amount of whisky and then visited and forced himself on a certain Louise Rotand at her house. The neighbours heard her exclamations of 'Mon Dieu! Mon Dieu!' and a sort of stifled groan but thought nothing of it as such sounds were frequent in that neighborhood." The article further stated that after sexual relations, Maillet stabbed Miss Rotand with a double-edged knife, lacerated the left lobe of the liver and severed the descending aorta. The doctors found semen in her. Mr. David continued to read: "The inebriated Maillet, unconcerned, went to the stables, took the horses out, and resumed his daily bus circuit as though nothing serious had taken place. Had it not been for the traffic accident, the person who murdered Louise Rotand would not have been discovered." .

Dr. Fifer remembered the circumstances well: "It is true. The Rotand woman did not survive. Together with doctors McCauley and Heiver, I performed the post mortem that revealed a lacerated liver and the right emulgent artery severed at the level where it enters the kidney. She probably bled to death quickly." Dr. Fifer made no further comment; he stated only findings commonly known through the newspapers. However, Mr. David had also known the victim, and my servings of brandy-laced tea had loosened his tongue.

"Miss Rotand was a professional. I favoured her on occasion myself. After one visitation, I noticed burning on urination and discharge. She was an attractive girl, that Louise, but I hear she was diseased."

"Do you fear that you may have acquired maladie anglaise, French gout, gonorrhea, my friend?" Dr. Fifer had picked up on his friend's dilemma. "I am sure you know, Jules, that all I can talk about is what the papers publish, not what my patients tell me in confidence. She called herself Victoire, was a native of your country, from Paris, a rather prepossessing personality, and about twenty-seven years of age."

The doctor mentioned nothing further although I remember Louise calling at our office in San Francisco. Dr. Fifer treated her for an intimate injury, a nasty tear, incurred during her notorious sessions of *ménage à trois*. That was not long before she was killed. In the end, Dr. Fifer concluded: "She can claim to have died by the sweat of her loins."

Mr. David found John Edwards' obituary. "He was a good man, that Edwards," Mr. David remembered, "a member of the No. 4 fire engine, employed for some time at the Bank Exchange. Always helpful, Edwards was trying to remove some offensive pictures from the wall in the barbershop adjoining the theatre when he fell from the ladder, striking the floor violently. He was removed to the house of Mr. Parker, his brother-in-law."

"Indeed," Dr. Fifer confirmed, "he was injured because someone tried to save him by holding his feet up, so the body came down first and fractured his ilium, the upper portion of the pelvis, on his right side. The bone fragments cut into the bladder and the escaped urine caused mortification of the tissue. He was passing pure blood. I referred him to his physician, Dr. Sawyer. He had a poor prognosis and died a few days later."

One particular note Jules David found in the paper affected him more than any other. Scratching his ear and seeming to glow at the memory, encouraged by a swig of Hudson's Bay brandy, he mused: "Ah, the mysterious Josepha Dela. A Spanish lady. I have tried in vain to learn more about her but the press has been unusually discreet. Miss Dela kept an elegant establishment across from the International Hotel on Jackson Street, between Kearny and Montgomery. According to the police report, a Mexican gentleman, Jose Gardonio, entered her saloon and struck her, without provocation, with a long dirk-knife, below the right nipple. Officers Baker and Gayton took her to the station house and called in a doctor."

"Indeed, Jules, that doctor, c'est moi. Josepha was a regular patient; she paid her medical bills promptly." But the doctor held back intimate details; disclosing them, even a thousand miles away, would be an egregious breach of professional confidence. He had probed the wound; Josepha was lucky; the knife passed down and to the side through the right breast without entering the thoracic cavity. He had applied a *Scaltetus* bandage to her chest. She survived the attack. The doctor added details publicly known. "Her attacker Gardonio got a break in court; he was not charged with murder because Josepha recovered from her injury. However, Judge Hoffman warned him about drinking and sentenced him to six months in the county jail."

I was happy to hear that this lady recovered from her injury. She was always pleasant and paid promptly whenever I took Dr. Fifer's bills to her, and there was always an extra dollar for me, "because she appreciated the services of my master".

Jules David was also glad to hear the report; he expressed relief that the lady would be all right. To dispel a suggestion of personal interest, he pretended to be amused: "I hope the scar will not affect her professionally."

Dr. Fifer knew that Gardonio's vicious attack left Miss Dela with infection, purulent discharge, and persistent oedema of her right breast and arm. She had a difficult time during her recovery, requiring continuous poultices and periwinkle compresses. However, all he was willing to share was: "There was nothing erotic about the breast laceration." He understood his visitor's intimate proclivities and his secret anxiety. "Friendship or not, Jules, the Hippocratic vow forbids disclosure about one patient to another, even after death."

Embarrassed, Mr. David was quick to change the topic: "Is it not astonishing how small causes can lead to serious consequences? One of our bank clients," Mr. David stressed, as if to say no such oath applied to him, "Mr. Joseph Lewis, was a successful operator of the Railroad Restaurant on Commercial and Clay Streets. His dining business flourished until he was assaulted, and that assault took place on the day after he raised the price of porterhouse steaks from 39¢ to 50¢. Did the police call you?"

"They got me up early, about five o'clock. It was an emergency; the officer let me use his horse and his police rattle; carts, drays, and hackneys heard me and pulled up, allowing me to pass." Dr. Fifer had taken the bait. "At the scene, I found Lewis in a state of insensibility. We took him to the station house. The wound, obviously caused by a bullet, was in the right chest. There was no bleeding, the pulse was thready and he was breathing very poorly. I probed the opening and found no resistance but could hear air whistling in and out through the hole in his chest, like a ruptured bellows. I plastered the opening and advised Officer Riley to take him to the County Hospital immediately. On Saturday, Dr. Holmes, the resident physician, informed me that Lewis had died from *pneumothorax*, air trapped in the chest. To this day, the murderer has not been found. Raising the price of a meal may be avaricious, but is no reason to shoot the cook. What will the murder do to the price of sirloin or pork chops?"

Mr. David read about the effects of chloroform. "Didn't Miss Ida Morgan die from taking chloroform?" he asked.

"You have a good memory, Jules; the lady suffered from *tic douloureux*, trigeminal neuralgia; she had come across the Bay for a visit, from Berkeley, and was in good health before taking the medication. The action of the chloroform seemed to change her blood to water. She had inhaled it during a previous attack and had felt good effects from it. The chloroform in the fatal instance was pure, and the usual quantity was given on a sponge. One application did not produce insensibility, and, at the patient's request, the sponge was again placed to her nose. After a third application, she attempted to get up but failed, and her head rolled to the side of the chair. She was then placed upon a lounge, breathing heavily, but soon her breathing became easier. She never spoke after being removed from the chair. The jury's verdict was that she came to her death by chloroform. Although it was a pure drug and properly administered, the jury cautioned the public against injudicious use."

"So how do you cope with that, Dr. Fifer, with untrained citizens telling the physicians and doctors what to do?"

"You may have misread, Jules. If patients are using the drug by themselves, the effect is self-limited because overdosing would make them unconscious and terminate the administration. Death by chloroform has frightened a number of people who now say that instead of an anaesthetic and die, it is better to suffer the pain of an operation and survive. One of your countrymen, the writer Alexandre Dumas, has started a campaign against the use of anaesthesia for surgery and warns against chloroform in high concentration and also against addiction to the substance." After a pause, Dr. Fifer continued: "I think I know what went wrong with Miss Morgan. Mr. Leipnitz, the druggist dispensing the drug, admitted to me that he had run out of amber-coloured bottles and dispensed the medication in a clear glass bottle. Miss Morgan left it standing in the hot sunlight, and the chloroform turned into a poisonous substance, phosgene, that killed her. Adding an ounce of brandy to the chloroform would have prevented the decay and saved her life."

Dr. Fifer continued: "A new anaesthetic, called Amylene, is said to be much safer. Little and Company in the Apothecaries' Hall on Montgomery Street keep it in stock. They sell it to physicians only, because of the potential abuse."

"Do you mean Miss Morgan was abusing the drug?"

"No, Jules, that is not what I mean. I believe it was an unfortunate accident, which could have been prevented. I do not believe Miss Morgan was using the drug to excess. She had a legitimate complaint. However, criminals have begun to use chloroform as a weapon. Did you read the story?" Dr. Fifer began to read aloud. "Last year, during a night in June, two bold and daring robberies took place by the aid of chloroform. This should teach all persons a lesson—to see that their houses are properly secured at night. After the robbery, Mr. Folly and his wife felt very stupid and singular when they awoke in the morning. The other couple, Mr. Hopper and his wife, upon awakening in the morning, experienced singular feelings as though they had been partially suffocated. A French woman named Bertha Hornitas was robbed of $7,000 one morning before daylight. The robber administered chloroform to her, and she was so much hurt and injured, that she was scarcely able to speak during the forenoon."

Dr. Fifer ceased reading and added his own details to the story. "Dr. Tewkesbury told me of a Mexican female in the upper part of town who was robbed one night, by having chloroform administered to her. She remained insensible for a long time; it was feared that she could not be resuscitated. Medical aid, however, was called in, which saved her. Her name was Loitendres Peres; she was a hard-working washerwoman. The robbers got sixteen dollars for their trouble."

"A washerwoman, you say?" The mention of the woman's occupation reminded Mr. David of another. "Did you read about Anatola Touissant, in Upper Canada? She has been convicted of the murder of her husband and was sentenced to be hanged in April. When she was diagnosed with a pregnancy, a jury of matrons—empanelled for the purpose—decided that her execution would destroy an innocent life. The hanging was deferred until July, after the baby was born."

Dr. Fifer commented: "What may pass as mercy strikes me as refined cruelty."

"Isn't that the nature of the beast, my friend? Which of our many foolishnesses would not be recognized as cruel and unusual, if we were to think clearly on them?" Mr. David was beginning to sound somewhat sentimental.

"Yes, Jules," Dr. Fifer paused, rubbing his chin, "and here is proof of your statement. I know all three doctors involved. Listen to this: 'Doctors Hitchcock, Angle, and White were attending a duel of Messrs. Ferguson and Johnson, during which Ferguson's thigh was struck and the bone fractured, whereas Johnson was slightly wounded on the left wrist. The doctors were able to extract the bullet from the thigh; they had to remove a portion of the bone, about an inch and a quarter long. Since the injury was a compound and comminuted fracture of the femur, the doctors decided on an amputation at the thigh level, the only method known to save his life. It was obvious that Johnson would be charged with murder if Ferguson should die. Ferguson refused the mutilating surgery. Finally, weeks later, the patient acquiesced and it came to an amputation. By then he was so weak that he died on the table. Johnson, the dueling partner, was fortunate. Although charged with murder, Judge Coon dismissed the case because Ferguson had waited too long before allowing the amputation.'"

Dr. Fifer turned his attention to another paper. "And here is another tragic incident. I had to perform the autopsy on the body of a fellow doctor and subsequently attended the inquest."

"Was that Dr. Sponeyk?"

"The very same, Jules. A mysterious state of melancholy. Dr. Sponeyk, a native of Strasburg, Germany, aged thirty-five years, and a physician by profession, arrived with his wife on the ship Gray Feather and took a room at the Globe Hotel on Dupont Street. His wife proceeded to stay with a relative in Marysville where she still is, to the best of my knowledge. After her departure, the doctor grew low-spirited and drank more than he ought to have. One Saturday evening he took his medicine chest to his room and seems to have taken a quantity of morphine."

"He died of an overdose?"

"It would seem so," Dr. Fifer responded. "Coroner Kent, still in office then, obtained a brief history of the last three months of Dr. Sponeyk's life, throwing some light on the causes that led to this melancholy event. In October last, Sponeyk and his wife had embarked in New York on the Gray Feather with 134 other passengers. He was a skillful physician and was solicited by the owners of the ship to come out as the ship's physician. The owners charged him and his wife the regular price of passage, but gave him a 'permit' to attend to passengers on the ship, for which he could charge."

Mr. David nodded; that sounded like good business practice.

However, Dr. Fifer went on: "Before embarking, the passengers of the ship were informed by the owners that a ship's physician was employed by the ship. The doctor had many patients during the voyage, but when he presented his bills to the passengers, they were indignant because the ship-owners in New York had represented the doctor as being hired by the ship, and therefore they considered he was not entitled to charge for services, and he was not paid. When the passengers sued the ship for breach of contract, Dr. Sponeyk put in a claim also against the Gray Feather for fraud. Although Sponeyk had lost many hundreds of dollars by misrepresentation of the owners, Judge Hoffman threw out his claim, and the doctor was left penniless. He fell into a gloomy mood from which he did not recover and which caused his suicide." Dr. Fifer concluded: "It shows the frequent mistakes we doctors make, focusing solely on patient care, not considering our own welfare. In this instance, a written contract would have saved a precious life."

Mr. David responded: "In my view, there were other reasons contributing to the despondency. Dr. Sponeyk's separation from his wife, I assume, caused his dissipation with alcohol; the rejection of his just claim by Judge Hoffman was the proverbial final straw that broke the camel's back."

Dr. Fifer had the last word in the argument: "Judge Hoffman's weakness for accepting 'gifts' is well known."

At that moment, a noisy commotion outside the doctor's office interrupted their discussion. The doctor and I stepped out to look and learned that a freight canoe had arrived from Hope, carrying the complete outfit for a blacksmith's forge, including the bellows. As Native helpers were carting the equipment up from the beach, one of them crushed his hand and came to ask for medical assistance. Dr. Fifer found swelling; the skin not being broken, he ruled out a fracture of the metacarpals, the long hand bones; he reassured the crew member.

Checking his timepiece, Dr. Fifer called in to Mr. David. "Jules, it is past 4 p.m.; are you up for another walk?" The two friends strolled down to the beach, now negotiating the undulations of the trail with excessive care, and then checked on the post. Returning to the house, they relocated into the waiting room, resuming their newspaper study, enjoying the warm September sun reflected off the Fraser River through the front window.

Shaking out the *Evening Bulletin*, Mr. David began reading from the heading MISCELLANEOUS: "A female child, the daughter of Thomas McNabb, aged about two months, died very suddenly. It had been very lively and apparently in good health up to the time of its death. It was lying in the cradle, and when the mother went to take it up to nurse, she found it dead. Two medical gentlemen were called to make a post-mortem examination; they found the cause of the death to be effusion of the brain."

Dr. Fifer leaned over to look. "I'd be cautious of that diagnosis. My heart goes out to the mother; however, infant mortality is an indicator of the health and social level of people, including the mother." He conceded, "Every doctor is concerned about the loss of a child from unknown causes; one must not lose sight of possible foul play, of infanticide, or simple neglect." He chose not to mention Sara Allard to Mr. David, nor her mother's grief and accusations against him.

"This table seems to prove your point, Max. A column of figures, prepared by the San Francisco city sexton, John Wallace. Of a total of 1416 deaths last year, 491 were adults, 792 were children under 10, and 133 were stillborn. Considering the general youth and health of the majority of the immigrants, the toll on the children, well over fifteen deaths per 1000 live births, is appalling. Under the rubric "DIED" in the *Alta California* of June 21, 1858, a list of interments for the fortnight. Out of 40 persons buried, 20 are under 1 year of age."

"Yes, Jules, no doubt leaving twenty mothers with the silent sorrow of void laps and the throbbing of engorged breasts, aching to be emptied. Here, this is another misleading caption. WANTED, by a woman with breast milk, desiring a baby to feed. An indication of the high rate of child mortality and stillborns, such advertisements spare the grieving mother the stigma. The toll of the unbridled hedonistic hunt for gold, don't you think, Jules?" The friends had an on-going debate about the central role gold, capital, plays in the lives of individuals.

"I see there has been a price hike of slaves in Brazil." Mr. David seemed to be changing the subject. "Within three years, the price of a likely Negro has increased from $500 to $1,500 and $2,000. As a result of the commodity appreciation, there has been resumption of the highly profitable Mississippi slave trade. A cargo of 700 blacks, imported at a price of between $500 and $1,000 per head, yielded a net gain of $350,000; the cost per slave was $30 steerage. Some slaves had managed to escape to California; the owners are suing for return of their property."

The two friends also had an on-going debate about the ethics of treating slaves to be bought and sold as a commodity. The doctor knew his friend's opinion, that the continued existence of the trade in America, although seen as an economic necessity, was evidence of how far the new world was behind Europe, where the practice has been outlawed for more than a generation. Dr. Fifer feared that this philosophical split in their friendship might soon parallel a more serious quarrel, between brothers, between states, in the great land to the south, where legislators were debating the right of a state to make its own decisions, even if those decisions are wrong.

"A mere forty miles south of us, below the 49th parallel of latitude, they seem to be on the threshold to a conflict, Jules. Mr. Lincoln speaks about the emancipation of the slaves. Here in Yale, we live in a world without subjugation of races. A mere block from my office, Mr. Isaac Dixon, an obscure, Black barber, operates his own shop. Ikey accepted Governor Douglas' invitation for Black men to come to the colony where slavery is outlawed. Most of them settled in Victoria; Ikey Dixon is one of a large group, he's a good talker, and with every shave he keeps his customers aware that somebody in the south raised him to be 'a real good piece of property who saw his mama sold off and his baby sister sold off.' Do you think he loves the folks who did that? I think not. Nevertheless, he cares more about his own fate than about hating them. Here, he's free, and making a life for himself!"

Rather than argue, they rustled the dry pages for news about which they could agree. Lynching of Indians and Negroes. Prison escapes. Duels. Garroting. Corruption of high officials. Tax evasion. Rapes. Lacerations. Alcoholic delirium tremens. Drunk & Disorderly. Addiction. Prostitution. Corrupt coroners removing jewels from the body of a female. Corrupt Branch Mint officials stealing gold. Prussic acid poisoning. Vitriol throwing. Daily inquests. Suicides by drowning. Free sale of poisons. Taking strychnine, arsenic, aconite, cyanuride of potassium. Overdosing on laudanum. Druggists' sloppiness in not marking strong poison bottles. High child mortality. Frequent divorces. Unseaworthy ships causing loss of life. Non-payment of taxes causing lack of fire hoses. Schools refusing black students. Throats being slashed ear to ear. Ballot box stuffing at elections. Horse stealing. Murder trials. Arson. Assault with a deadly weapon. Escaped convicts. Slaves from the South seeking refuge. Chain gangs. Chief of Police Curtis, under arrest for shooting a vagrant while sitting on his horse.

"I see the editorial writers have not changed their opinion—that every man should carry the reference works 'Colt's common law' and 'Bowie's practice', the unquestioned authorities." Dr. Fifer sounded resigned, as if he held no hope of opinion ever changing in the south. As if such tools and simple machines carry more weight than a legal tradition, more authority than wisdom and compassion.

Mr. David turned the page and spotted a story that might brighten their mood. "Here, my friend; I saved this copy not for the ill-boding editorial on knives and revolvers or the sad infant mortality table. Read the front page, Max. An exciting story about a schoolmate of mine from Lyons, Jean Francois Gravelet, who has changed his name to Charles Blondin."

Dr. Fifer read loudly enough for me to hear without straining from my work table in the kitchen: "BLONDIN AT HIS OLD WAYS: Charles Blondin crossed the Niagara River on his rope on 6th June, in presence of a great crowd of spectators, some of whom paid and some of whom did not. A delay in commencing the performance especially exasperated the latter class. The rope was 1,300 feet long; its deflection was sixty feet; its lowest point was 230 feet above the water. On his way back from the Canadian side, the acrobat halted, struck an attitude, and was photographed by an eminent artist. Then the spectators dispersed, inclined to feel wronged because Blondin had not fallen into the torrent."

"Uhm," Dr. Fifer commented, "probably his skill at maintaining equilibrium is no match for you, my friend, balancing your accounts." It seemed to escape Doctor Fifer that Mr. David looked away, as if guilty, avoiding eye contact with his friend, choosing not to comment.

"Here's another, Jules." Dr. Fifer read on: "The report of the board of supervisors of the county hospital. There are a number of persons in the hospital who are not really patients, but rather proper tenants for an alms-house. But as the city does not possess any such institution, they have to be received in the hospital. There is one old Negro slave, Eliza, who is so old that she has forgotten her age. Nothing ails her but old age and an indisposition to do anything. She has remained in the hospital ever since there was one, and evidently considers herself as possessing a vested interest in the institution."

Dr. Fifer chuckled: "Every doctor remembers Eliza."

Dr. Fifer had emptied the dregs of the brandy cask into the sticky decanter; now only a small amber ring remained in the glass bottom as the friends arrived at the end of the roll of newspapers.

Recognizing the last few issues as the *San Francisco Herald*, Dr. Fifer balked. "I never used to read this rag, Jules. The low literary level and the vitriolic content upset me."

Mr. David explained: "I agree, Max. However, I feel you may remember the name of John Nugent, the *Herald's* owner-editor." Dr. Fifer nodded, encouraging Mr. David to go on. "He has strong Democratic convictions, of course, and has maintained his keen opposition to the Vigilance movement. His publication is full of hatred, siding openly with McGowan and his transgressions, spreading extreme propaganda, castigating the general rule of the Vigilance Committee, criticizing their botched executions."

Mr. David pointed out a column headed by a cartoon as one of Nugent's Editorials: "Perhaps it would be as well for the executive of the Vigilance Committee to visit the jail and see to the hanging by the latest and most approved method. They might possibly learn new points in the scientific policy of handling, which might assist them in their future efforts in this humane and Christian-like line of business. At the last execution, the fall was about six feet, and would have been sufficient to break the man's neck instantaneously but that the noose did not slip properly in his descent, and instead of drawing taught behind his ear it caught him around the chin; his decease was slow and painful. During the first five minutes of his suspension the body exhibited repeated convulsions of the arms and legs, together with a stifled gasping for breath."

"Very educational, don't you agree, Mr. David?"

"Very, Doctor Fifer." But Mr. David continued with his Nugent story. "After the *Herald* folded, President Buchanan appointed Mr. Nugent a special envoy to look after the rights and interests of the American miners here in New Caledonia who might be suffering at the hands of the British. This true red, white, and blue American has made it his business to stir up the embittered feelings of the days when the Vigilance Committee was in existence. On the shores of the Fraser River he is raking over the dead embers of the past for a living spark of malice and enkindles it once more into a blaze."

Mr. David made no bones about his personal feelings. "According to the local *Victoria Gazette*, a recent dinner meeting of Nugent with Governor Douglas in Victoria did not go well. His Excellency was quite annoyed at the arrogant speech the American envoy had presented before the Victoria Chamber of Trade, when he openly referred to the English as trans-Atlantic marauders."

Dr. Fifer sat up, his interest piqued. Mr. David continued: "Nugent used stronger language in speaking about the occupation of the disputed San Juan Island: 'A nation guilty of such acts falls below the level of utter barbarism.' In the field of diplomacy, Nugent suggested 'that England copy from the civilization of the Hun Attila.' He boasted: 'The US will never give in to these eel-like slippery tricksters. Abuse of the United States will not settle the argument but it may isolate England, and instead of aiding her, in case she were attacked by a not impossible European combination, we should rather exult at her humiliation or even her disappearance from the map of nations. It will be remembered that under a show of kindness, the American Republic was cajoled out of a large slice of territory in the Oregon dispute in 1846.'

Can you believe the gall, Fifer?"

Mr. David went on. "About the 'pig war,' that recent confrontation over the ownership of San Juan Island, Nugent's patriotism is fanatical: 'Under no circumstances must San Juan Island fall into the hands of these English pig farmers. My mission is to get San Juan Island into US hands. Congress is determined to go to war over the issue.'

"And another time it was: 'I warned the President about the British plan to establish a penal colony on Vancouver's Island. A Devil's Island in our back yard would become a collecting pot, a spittoon for their trash, to the detriment of the United States.'

"As a reward for his patriotic work President Buchanan offered Nugent the position of Ambassador to Ecuador, an unstable country, recently freed from the Spanish by Simon Bolivar. Nugent declined the appointment." Mr. David shook the paper as if to emphasize the indignity of such political appointments, folded it and placed it atop the pile they had completed. He continued:

"You will not believe this, Mr. David. The very celebrity arrived here in Yale. While knocking about the mining spots on Hill's Bar, which was none of his business, Mr. Nugent picked up a couple of wood ticks that crawled up his legs and embedded in his groin. He had consulted Dr. Crane who claimed *arthropod* experience and recommended surgery because the ticks bore serious disease. Then he came to see me, an obscure doctor in a remote region, unaware that I was a Vigilance member and target of his previous newspaper attacks. Mind you, the local ticks carry no serious disease; however, they had to be taken out."

"Did you cut the bloodsuckers out?"

"I removed them painlessly, *in toto*, looping a woman's hair around the *proboscis* and gently easing them out, and Nugent paid the fee for their removal, $16, the equivalent of an ounce of gold."

"Well done, man; well done. I would not have been able to exhibit such restraint myself. It reminds me of a story I heard, on my voyage to Victoria. I had to share a stateroom with the ship's purser. Over drinks, I learned that the English Governor's sagacity can match that of any San Francisco street sharp."

"Go on," Dr. Fifer encouraged.

"One of the American steamer captains recently had an audience with His Excellency, and upon mentioning that he would sail on to Nanaimo for coal, the Governor's secretary handed him a letter, asking that he deliver it to the coal mine's superintendent. At Nanaimo, the captain was surprised to find a steep increase in the coal bill, much higher than on previous refuelings, from 8 dollars per ton to a new price of 12 dollars. He expressed his consternation at the unexpected increase and was advised that the letter he had just delivered contained the order to boost the price. The captain reported the Governor's underhandedness to Mr. Nugent, bringing the acid to his craw."

As the friends had been reminiscing, I had prepared the fresh fish as we do in Guangzhou, cooking it slowly on a grid of skewers over hot coals. When it was ready, I clanged my cleaver on the copper kettle to call the gentlemen to table. I served the salmon as they do here, on a slab of cedar. "Chinook," I said, as I laid the plank along the centre of the table.

"Chinook?" Mr. David repeated: "Do you mean to tell me this fish has swum all the way from China? Chinoise? Chinook?"

Dr. Fifer laughed. The two friends were already in a jolly mood as they set to the meal, anticipating a good long visit in the evening.

"Go ahead, Jules. Ah Chung says the eye is a delicacy saved for honoured guests." But Mr. David declined, preferring a slab of flesh from near the tail.

"Not that I do not trust that you are an honest man, Ah Chung. But this looks delicious, right here." Mr. David was making a joke; he knew how Dr. Fifer had rescued me from San Quentin by convincing the authorities that indeed the shape of my skull confirmed that I "had not a dishonest bone in my body". Dr. Fifer had even taken this teaching aid, pointing out the lines engraved into the human skull and the labels indicating where virtues reside, and proved to the review panel scientifically that I deserved my freedom. Of course, it did not hurt that he vouched to employ me and ensure that poverty would never tempt me into crime as it does many unfortunates.

There was much happiness that evening, three years ago, and ever since, the phrenology skull has rested here on the place of honour, a bookshelf in the examining room, above this very cot upon which Mr. David slept while he had stayed with us in September of 1858. I am tempted to pack the skull and take it with me, but it is part of the estate and must remain.

That evening so long ago, Mr. David was watching me as I served the beans and turned the biscuits in the skillet. "Tell me the story again, Doctor Fifer, about discovering Ah Chung, how you found out. What was the clue?"

"I studied the teachings of Professor Gall and his disciple, Johann Spürzheim. They demonstrated that brain anatomy and personality go closely together. The teachings of phrenology indicate that the seat of talents and behaviour is located in the brain, and the shape of the surrounding skull is the key to these individual characteristics." Dr. Fifer loved to expound on this subject.

"Did you have occasion last year, Mr. David, to attend Professor Pinkham's lectures, in the Phrenological Hall on Clay Street?' There was talk that the skulls he used for demonstration were those of Casey and Cora. That after that abomination of a hanging, by our over-zealous Committee of Vigilance..."

"Revenge was what motivated them, don't you think, Max, for the murder of the newspaper editor, King?" Mr. David interrupted.

"That after the infamous 'strangling' of the gunman and a cellmate, on a jury-rigged gallows, after a push from the window sill, the undertaker sold the heads to science for a good price?"

"And what did the good scientist conclude? Was our vigilante justice appropriate, or did the scientific mumbo-jumbo whitewash the whole mess, Max?"

"You may choose to scoff, Mr. David, but Ah Chung's case confirms the solid foundation of the science. As you know, in San Francisco, I was contracted to examine and treat sick prisoners in the jail at San Quentin Point. One certain inmate, a Chinaman, insisted that he was not guilty of the crime of which he was accused. The poor devil did not know English well enough to convince the judge of his innocence. On examining him and exploring his head, there was no cranioscopic evidence of a criminal disorder. To the contrary, the skull displayed prominences that attested to a high degree of morality, a sense of honour, kindness, the gift of intelligence, and a good memory. I spoke to the warden and to Judge Coon, whereupon they started another investigation into the crime and, indeed, Police Captain Donnellan uncovered the true culprit. As a result, prisoner Ah Chung was vindicated and released."

Dr. Fifer always sounded triumphant at this conclusion.

"Ah Chung is a jewel, Jules; he has been with me since, as a helper and companion, thanks to the modern science of phrenology. Do you see the prominences on the upper part of his head?"

Both men examined me, as I cleared the plates from in front of them, as if they could indeed see the skull beneath my skin.

"Conspicuous. A marked breadth to the upper part of his head. These marks indicate his faculties. Ah Chung is unusually well endowed with the qualities one might want in a person for a companion, an assistant, and a friend. There; you have the story again; I picked him for the bumps on his head; my diagnosis proved correct."

Mr. David smiled at me. We both knew how much Dr. Fifer liked telling that story. But the doctor continued their professional discussion.

"There are now opponents refuting the science, a countryman of yours, Jules. A doctor Paul Broca at the Sorbonne University squabbles about *motor aphasia*, having discovered special centres for senses and nerves deep inside the brain. His ideas do not do justice to the phrenological mapping of the skull surface."

Mr. Jules David, himself a graduate of the Sorbonne, wanted to remain loyal to a fellow student of his *alma mater*; yet, was not Ah Chung *prima facie* evidence that there was proof of Broca's fallacy? We all, including Jules David, laughed at Dr. Broca's absurd idea.

I had made a special effort for this meal, cracking walnuts to stuff into the centre of apples and baking them for a final sweetmeat course. When I brought the heavy skillet out to the table to serve the dessert, sprinkling some cane sugar and ground cinnamon on top, Dr. Fifer retrieved the brandy decanter and poured the remaining drops into the skillet; then he touched a match to it, setting it alight. Blue flames jumped around the pan dancing with the apples. "Aha!"

He got the effect that he wanted. Once the flames died down, I served each apple with a drizzle of the brandy syrup.

Dr. Fifer apologized. "I'm afraid this is the last of the brandy, Jules."

Mr. David looked sad and then he put one finger against his nose and, remembering something, said, "Max, I have a gift for you." He left the table and rummaged around in his luggage. He returned with a small keg under his arm and made a display of placing it before his host. "Your favourite, Max!" he said, sounding both proud and triumphant, as if he had rescued the evening.

Mr. David's special treat, to celebrate their freedom and their reunion, was a keg of wormwood cordial. It was not the cheap bluish brand to which copper sulphate has been added, but the genuine unadulterated opalescent liquor. Absinthe, I have heard others call it. It was indeed Dr. Fifer's favourite. Now they could enjoy a few more drinks in this remote wilderness which was now our home, where, both Dr. Fifer and his friend were convinced, their far-away enemies were no longer a concern.

7

In the happy hours of that reunion, Dr. Fifer and Mr. David took another walk, an evening constitutional to aid their digestion. They felt safe and secure here in Yale. The ever-changing river, the golden light and long shadows of the sun disappearing behind Mount Lincoln created a deceptive calm; everything seemed to glow warmly. By the time they returned, I had tidied the small rooms, cleaned the kitchen, refreshed the glasses, and boiled fresh water for tea.

Dr. Fifer showed the guest to his private withdrawing room and motioned him to the best chair. Having disposed of business and politics, they were happy to settle into a long conversation about those many topics men reserve for discussion among themselves.

"Well, Jules. What is not in the papers? What interesting tidbits have you left to share?"

"Tidbits. Hmm. Yes, Max, much better than 'gossip'. Let me think…" Their conversation continued as if nothing had interrupted. "I attended a few theatre performances, one of them by the infamous Madame Lola Montez."

Dr. Fifer looked up. "Really? Mme. Montez?! I saw her the last time she was in San Francisco. In fact, I escorted Mrs. Fifer to her recital. You knew that, did you not?"

"I believe I had heard that, Max. What did you think, when you saw her? Professionally, I mean. Can a 'dancer' cure a czar?"

"Cure a czar? On 'the great stage of life'? After relationships with

154

Franz Liszt, Alexandre Dumas, Ludwig, King of Bavaria? Liszt was so smitten that he was transformed, like Saul on the road to Damascus. After composing the beautiful Liebestraums, he moved to Rome to take holy orders and became an Abbé of the Papist church. While his former lover is denounced for her passionate lifestyle, as an errant sinner rejecting all sense of morality!"

"Yes, yes; it is a very oriental story, celestial in the way sensuality is seen as the gate to heaven. But did she cure the Czar, Dr. Fifer? I mean physically cure a pathological state?" Mr. David was impatient for details.

Dr. Fifer rubbed his chin, contemplating. "Cure the Czar? You know that I am interested in this topic myself, Jules? You are not fooling me with your 'innocent' questions. I am not the gull of your duplicity. Yes, I do know that Dr. Gustaf Adolf Mandt, a Swedish doctor and personal physician to the Czar, traveled from St. Petersburg to consult Mme. Montez. In fact, the doctor told me so himself, That he confided to Mme. Montez that the Czar was ill, suffering from progressive melancholy. Medical methods—laudanum, homoeopathic strychnine, magnetic sittings, diversion therapy—all failed to improve his condition. The doctor feared that His Highness' malady was likely to kill him; he was bent on ending his life. In the ensuing crisis, the son, a radical prince, had attempted a coup d'état."

"It was that serious?" Ending his life, coup d'état?" Mr. David interrupted.

"A palace revolution was imminent. Dr. Mandt approached Mme. Montez on behalf of the Imperial Court and the Royal family and asked if she would come to St. Petersburg and, by restoring the Czar's health and happiness, preserve the state of the nation."

"What reputable courtesan could turn down such an invitation?" Mr. David inserted, "but, was she successful?"

Undeterred, Dr. Fifer continued. "Upon her arrival at the Summer Palace in Tsaraskoye Syelo, Dr. Mandt took Mme. Lola aside and assured her that she would get along well with His Highness during the interview because he was a pleasant and easy-going person but, although in Russia the Czar is god-like, people in high places can be beset by the same sensuality as ordinary mortals. Doctor Mandt prepared her for a possible confrontation with the Czar's distressing deformities, one of which was a contracture of his fingers. They were curled into the palms as a misbegotten fist and could not be straightened. She also learned of the Emperor's other physical disorder, an unspeakable disease which she suspected to be the true cause of the Czar's melancholy. Bearing the name of the French surgeon De la Peyronie, the deformity of the potentate's male member caused him both pain, failure, and embarrassment, on certain occasions."

"And the doctor told you all this, Max?"

"Strictly in confidence, as one professional to another, Jules. But let me tell you the whole story. The first audience with the Czar went well. After an introduction in the Amber Room, where Mme. Montez was served black tea from the Crimea with honey; the patient and his therapist withdrew to the Czar's boudoir where, over his favorite *Chateau de Calme*, the consultation continued more intimately and Mme. Lola could assess the delicate nature of the other disorder. As her experience in these matters far surpasses a physician's general knowledge, she recognized the emperor's condition to be the result of an imprudent practice in his earlier years, an activity that she amusedly defined as *coitus en postilion*. The female, straddling the male in a certain mode, leans back for her own indulgence, bending and overstraining the *miembro viril* in its delicate brittle state of tumescence, fracturing and tearing the dorsal *tunica albuginea*. As the membrane has no nerve supply, the injury is painless and often goes unnoticed in the fervor of passion. However, healing results in scarring, *fibrosing cavernositis* and *induratio penis plastica*. In practice, Mme. Montez condemns the posture as harmful, indicting the unyielding fulcrum of the female *symphysis pubis*."

Mr. David offered an opinion: "It sounds to me as if Mme. Montez' skills as a consultant parallel her rumoured expertise in her first profession."

"Positive outcomes, Jules, are the best indicator of a person's talents."

A search into the emperor's past medical history confirmed that he had indeed incurred the injury while luxuriating as a young man. The offender, known then as Varinka with the Big Heart, although now a matronly lady of the Czarina's entourage, was banished to Siberia for 'lack of considerateness' for His Highness. The sentence was carried out despite her advanced years and against the Czar's objection, I might add."

"And the patient himself? What of the Czar's treatment, Max?" Mr. David could hardly wait for the conclusion of the account.

"In her plan to heal the Czar, Mme. Lola decided to restore his physical function first, shrewdly assuming, and I concur, that the cause of his melancholy lay with Varinka's mode of entertaining the young prince.

In preparation for the next session, she requested," Dr. Fifer paused for effect, "Mme. Montez requested a pregnant, docile goat with a good udder of milk. After a warm hand bath, Mme. Montez gently pried open the monarch's contracted fingers, wrapped them around the goat's full teats, and taught him to milk. As soon as things worked out, she placed the curved fingers around his own deformed member, to perform a similar milking motion. A most astute woman with a practical, hands-on, attitude, would you not agree, Jules?"

"With experience comes wisdom, assuredly, Max."

"But was her treatment successful, I am sure you wish to know?" Dr. Fifer continued: "The phallus, responding by spontaneous aggrandizement, had to be at least semi-erect for a good milking effect, which works by stroking the blood from the base into the *corpora cavernosa*. The increased volume stretches the capillaries and allows for a greater filling capacity, improving circulation, healing the fibrosis, and correcting the deformity. Voila!"

"Indeed? This is not an 'old wives' tale,' Max?"

"More likely just some good modern advertising for organ enlargement, Jules. But I am not finished. Progress was slow; the cramped hands opened up gradually. As a first modest milestone toward the final goal, the exercise did become effective when the Czar proudly demonstrated (in private, of course), his regained ability to open the front flap of his pantaloons. Throughout the sessions, Mme. insisted on extremely gentle and painless handling of the Romanoff member; to avoid further damage to the tissue, the massage must be delicate yet firm enough to improve circulation,' she cautioned.

In the sessions that followed, Mme. Montez' demands became more complex. The fingers encircling the semi-erect organ learned to milk the blood away from the phallus into the glans, or head, to create a bulging, mushrooming effect. At that precise moment— she instructed her imperial pupil—to tighten the *pubococcygeal* muscles, the anal and bladder sphincters, as though cutting off the stream in mid-urination. By this maneuver, Mme. Lola intended to make his ejaculations more rewarding."

"Ingenious. Teaching him 'to pucker his arse'. The genius of simplicity," Mr. David exclaimed.

"She was an assiduous teacher; Jules; to assess the Czar's compliance, she inserted her larded finger into his rectum and would not withdraw it until she felt the contracting pinch at the critical instant.

As the epitome of success, Mme. disclosed, discretely in Latin terminology, but with great pride, that *intromissio a tergo* had taken place and her pupil had relished the acme of consummation. Moreover, the Czar, after a brief rest, had clamoured for encores. "Success for any man!" Mr. David jested.

Lola Montez had reached the goal of her labours. The Czar had recovered from depression and regained his sanity. Mother Rodina was saved from anarchy. As fee for her service, Mme. Montez received a most generous honorarium—the sum of one thousand gold rubles."

"Not an unreasonable fee, for consultation with a specialist, Max."

"True, Jules. But Mme. uses the award to advance her own standing. She deplores the general lack of appreciation accorded artists of higher repute, the musicians, composers, and conductors, of whom she considers herself to be one. As evidence, she offers the case of the Russian ambassador to Livland who suffered from incurable insomnia. It took Kapellmeister Bach of Leipzig thirty-two pieces of cembalo musick to cure him; whenever the Goldberg Variations, which Bach wrote especially for His Excellency, were played, Count von Keyserling could go to sleep promptly. Yet the one hundred gold doubloons which the count offered J. S. Bach, are in the eyes of Lola Montez a pittance in comparison to the gratification she elicited from her patron, the Czar. *Ergo*, she argues, since the reward was for curing, not for entertaining her patient, the therapeutic value of her 'art' must be ten times greater."

"Wonderful. I like the way this woman thinks, Max!"

"There is more, Jules. The Czar died of natural causes three years later, at the age of thirty-five."

"How do you know all these details, Max? From one of your medical journals?"

"Indeed, no. But perhaps I should write it up and submit it for publication. My information comes first hand, from the self-proclaimed healer herself."

"You have met Mme. Lola Montez?"

"I interviewed her, on the occasion of her first tour of America."

"Go on, Max. Go on."

Dr. Fifer hesitated, knowing that the story of the encounter could bring him into rough personal waters. "A few months after her St. Petersburg debut, Lola Montez stepped off the SS *Orizaba* in San Francisco, a femme fatale, billing herself as a dancer and actor. John Nugent, then editor of the *San Francisco Herald*, commented something to the effect that 'This prominent courtesan is trying to demonstrate to the New World her qualities in the realm of the performing arts, exhausted from bestowing herself on European celebrities.'"

"That's Nugent for you. These American newspapermen can be so 'holier-than-thou'," Mr. David agreed.

"True, to sell copy, they tend to be 'contrarian.' Yet Mme. Montez' performance on stage at the American Theatre was somewhat risqué even by California standards. On that tour, she publicly re-enacted her private affair as the mistress of Ludwig of Bavaria. In the drama, billed as 'Lola Montez in Bavaria', with the role of the King of Bavaria assigned to the actor Mr. McCabe, Mme. Lola performed her celebrated spider dance. I attended the first performance alone, to reconnoitre. The stage was a world of light, luxury, and make-believe. Dancing the *Tarantella,* she expressed the frantic human will to live before inevitable death. I had heard the tale of the Czar's melancholy and miraculous cure, and I wished to assess the ability of this renowned healer, to ascertain whether she might be able to cure Mrs. Fifer's despondency."

When he heard Dr. Fifer mention his own wife, Mr. David set his glass down with a clack, surprised at the personal turn their conversation had taken. "Mrs. Fifer was despondent?"

"She had been melancholic for some time, I am afraid. My preoccupation with Doctor Sponeyk's suicide took my attention from her and our new child. When Margaret did not want to breast feed for fear of flabbiness, she turned to Mrs. Parker, the midwife, who advertised and got us a young married woman with a good breast of milk to provide the baby with lacteal nourishment."

"I have often wondered at those ads, Max."

"Yes, but they offer a necessary service. Since there was no room for a wet-nurse to live in, it was natural that the woman took the baby with her to feed at home. We both adored the child. When a fatal epidemic of putrid sore throat raged through the city, children became very ill and died, and we worried about the baby's health. A Dr. Bouchut had discovered a sure cure for putrid sore throat; he claimed that not in a single case had there been a failure. The treatment consisted in the amputation of the tonsils. Margaret, Mrs. Fifer, demanded surgery immediately; she would not accept the reasoning that the child was too young and went into a state of *postpartum* melancholy about it. The child survived the epidemic without surgery. However, Margaret remained despondent and withdrawn."

"What did you do, my friend?"

"With the baby out of the house, Margaret had a lot of time on her hands and became more ill-humored and glum. It was providence, we thought, that along came a certain Mr. Howe with the eccentric idea of placing the eye of a sewing needle in the needle's point, thus inventing the principle of the sewing machine. Margaret wanted me to buy her one; she had seen one used by Madame Woods, the dress and cloak maker on Sacramento Street. Of course, she did not want a hand-cranked Singer; she wanted only the best money could buy, a treadle-driven Wheeler and Wilson. The machine would do 4000 stitches in one minute, hem, fell, run, lock stitch, chain stitch, seam and bind."

"It seems most unusual to me, Max, but if it works..."

"For a short time, it did work. However, Margaret lost her sartorial enthusiasm and complained that the machine was missing stitches and she had to re-sew dresses every time they came from the wash, whereas the clothes sewn with the new Grower and Baker machines can be worn for two years or longer, she had heard, so we ended up trading the Wheeler and Wilson. The expensive distraction, however, did not improve her despondency."

"It sounds to me as if you were attending to her every whim, Max. What more could you have done?"

"Unfortunately, Jules, I was frantic to find a treatment. Her pregnancy had not been planned. As a doctor, I have seen too many tragic consequences of 'blocked uterus' and complications of pregnancy and childbirth to espouse frivolous unprotected sexual intercourse. Using the rhythm method is an uncertain way because of the contradictory dates. While Dr. Gerry, the local accoucheur in the city, claimed the mid-cycle to be safest, Dr. Lanzsweert, another specialist, warned 'that the date bristles with the wraith of fecundity'".

"Yes, as we used to say in Paris, Max. 'What do you call couples who use the rhythm method?' Answer: 'Parents.'"

"Exactly, Jules. When patients seek my medical advice about birth control, I recommend abstinence, although, with all diligence, the method seemed to have failed in my own marriage. We had pledged to hold off having children but, rather than abstain from marital relations, Mrs. Fifer sought to prevent conception by using a botanical, the berries of *juniperus sabina*, available at Mr. Galen Leipnitz' drug store, under the label of 'Savin Saves'. The dosage is one tablespoonful before retiring; the berries must be crushed to release the active ingredient."

. "I have seen the ads, but does it really work, Max?"

"We had no problem until one morning, over breakfast, Margaret confessed. 'It is strange, Max,' she said, 'I always take my savin berries regularly. Last week, I was very tired and, I think, I went to bed without crushing the berries, and now, I've missed my monthlies.' She seemed heartbroken; I found it strange: due to my preoccupation with the Sponeyk case, there had been no physical contact between us for many weeks, but Nature can play many tricks. Although she conceded to be alert enough to take the berries, she had lacked the presence of mind to crush them. I thought no further of the explanation but accepted the pregnancy as ordained by God and took her to Dr. Straub on Montgomery Street who confirmed the diagnosis and took good care of her. Without complication or tear, he delivered a baby boy, cross-toed but otherwise healthy."

"Are congratulations in order, Max?" Mr. David was again wondering where the story was going.

"Margaret went back on her regime of savin berries afterwards, but she seemed cold to me, not interested in my advances. As a considerate husband, I respected her wishes. I sought the latest information on birth control, thinking a more guaranteed prevention would reduce her anxiety, and permit a resumption of conjugal relations."

Here Mr. David had information to share. "Recently, Capitaine Marcel Yves, a school friend from Lyon, completed his tour of duty on the South Pacific *Îsle du Vent*. On his return home via San Francisco, he stayed with me a few weeks and, being a bachelor, entered into casual companionships with women. He deplored their methods to avoid pregnancy, their cumbersome dependence on tansy syrup, savin, ergot, or Chichester Pills."

"What do they say in Paris today, Jules?"

"Captain Yves extolled on the more reliable method of the Polynesians. He reported to me that, although they cannot suppress Nature's urge, they have long realized that their island can only grow so much taro root to feed so many. To keep the people from starving they have to control the birth rate. Comparable to the ritual of circumcision, they hold a ceremony to induce the adolescent boys into manhood. The shaman chews the anaesthetic leaves of the *noni* plant; with the saliva he lubricates a smooth hardwood stick and slips it into the young male's urethra. Similarly, he anesthetizes the ventral skin of the penis, and with a sharp seashell makes a small, painless nick through the skin against the resistance of the urethral obturator. The incision heals, leaving an opening, a fistula. During intercourse, the male ejaculates the semen through the newly created opening before it can reach the vagina. If the woman desires a pregnancy, she grasps her partner and, like playing a flute, places a finger over the opening, allowing the spermaticules to enter her womb. Naturally, during urination, the male soon learns to keep the opening closed."

Dr. Fifer seemed impressed. "This ancient South Sea method

strikes me as revolutionary and a step toward avoiding a Malthusian catastrophe. It would allow women to space their children and keep down the number of mouths to feed while opening the door to greater female control over her life and her destiny. The method sounds deserving of a place in the Pantheon of great medical discoveries and inventions. However, I am not enthused about my male patients submitting to the procedure. Invasive surgery, even cutting the cords, is not the answer. I have seen men with such congenital defects as *hypospadia*; they are unhappy with their abnormality and seek surgery to close the opening in order to have offspring."

"Yes, I agree. Getting men to participate may be the challenge, Max."

"You mentioned circumcision, Jules. That was another difference of opinion we had, where the child was concerned. Margaret insisted on taking the boy to be circumcised. She actually did so without consulting me or informing me of her plan. I was surprised, but then I thought nothing more of it. I suppose I assumed this was a tradition of her people. Have you heard of the Bible Perfectionists? Mrs. Fifer was raised in a community in northern New York State. I met her in California, of course, and I know only what she has told me of her background."

"I do not believe I have heard of them, Max. Is she a Quaker or a Mormon, or some such group of believers?"

"No, neither of those. But they did have some unconventional attitudes towards marriage of which I was unaware until it was too late."

"Mon Dieu, Max. Whatever do you mean?"

"How can I explain it? The elders of the community believe... Margaret's people were members of a group in Vermont, until they were accused of being a cult and were driven out for their objectionable religious habits. That was when they settled in New York State."

"I'm sure I have never heard of them," Jules David asserted.

"The three hundred members of the community, who called themselves Perfectionists, prospered through their thrift and industry. They were famous for the quality of beaver traps that were all bought up by the Hudson's Bay Company. When fashion changed from beaver to silk hats, they began making excellent silk yarn. They also turned their metalwork skills from the manufacture of animal traps into crafting fine silverware for the tables of the wealthy."

"Of course, Oneida. I have heard of that town."

"Socially," Dr. Fifer continued, "the members of the community felt everyone to be of one family, allowing mutual criticism and free expression of their opinion. In their relation to God, they declared themselves Perfectionists who have attained the state of grace during lifetime. Their assumed freedom from sin through conversion and will power affected their marital habits; they practiced sexual intercourse while maintaining continence, by *coitus reservatus*. Sexual union was a spiritual, intimate experience during which the couple remained motionless until the excitement subsided. Then they would separate. For the husband, there was no need for monastic abstinence or pre-climactic withdrawal; no need for a rubber capot or a full-length sheep's gut baudruche, and he did not suffer loss of energy by seminal spill."

"Mon Dieu, Dr. Fifer! Depravation by self-denial will harm the body more than excess. There are better methods to enjoy life than unnatural suppression of the desires and pleasures our Creator has provided. Does it not make more sense to allow Nature to take her course?"

"Yes, I agree, Mr. David. But there was more to it than denial and deprivation. The women did not depend on the rhythm of the menses, or on the untimely getting out of the warm bed for cold water douching, or on taking rue or Chichester's Pennyroyal Pills, which can make them very ill, sometimes fatally; they were free from the womb veil, the messy Mediterranean toilet sponges, or worse, the use of instruments to relieve a 'blocked uterus.' From the medical point of view, the Perfectionists had a lot going for their method of taming the spermaticules; they were free from the curses of undesirable procreation."

"Yes, I see the advantage, Max."

"Furthermore, Jules, girls coming of age were induced into the system by older, experienced men; conversely, young men were taught to retain continence during the sexual union by elder women beyond the menopause, in case of mishaps. The community practiced selective breeding; the elders decided who should bear a child, and by whom."

"Really?" Mr. David was somewhat skeptical.

"Indeed. Margaret's folks were happy there until their leader, Mr. Humphrey Noyes, changed the rules of marriage from 'simple spousehood' to 'complex marriages'. He decreed that all the women of the community were to be the wives of all the men and all the men to be husbands of all the women. The conflict arose when Margaret was induced by an elder; infatuated, she wanted to be united with him. Her parents rejected the idea and left the community for their daughter's sake because they could not accept the new order of complex marriages. The family followed the beckoning flight of the golden butterfly and settled in San Francisco where I met and married their daughter."

"That's all well and good, my man," Mr. David proclaimed. "So the truth was kept from you? Is that it? I am trying to figure out exactly what the problem was."

"No. It is not that, Jules. I am a realist, and a scientist. I do not equate chastity with morality. It is not that." But Dr. Fifer seemed at a loss, not knowing which tack to take, what to say next.

"You said she was despondent, and that you were burying yourself in your work." Jules David sensed Dr. Fifer's personal conflict, seeming both anxious and at the same time loath to unbosom his grief. "Max, allow me to be frank with you. A trouble shared is a trouble halved. The people here in Yale are under the assumption that you are a widower, yet I sense that your wife stayed behind in California and is still alive, and well, I presume. Is there a burden that I can help you carry? I do not wish to be like a priest who listens for sins but, as a sinner myself, one who listens for his own redemption."

I could tell from the loosening tongue and receding inhibitions that the effect of the opalescent cordial was beginning to show. The doctor nodded to acknowledge Mr. David's encouragement and replied in a slightly heavier voice: "You know, Jules, there is more to marriage than four bare legs in a bed. I have learned my lesson and have kept my troubles to myself; I don't wash my dirty linen in public. This occasion of your visit is auspicious, I feel free here, and able to talk to you about my private affairs."

"Go on then. You were saying that your wife's unconventional and liberal upbringing resulted in some trouble between the two of you?"

"I do not believe I said that exactly. I said that she became depressed after the birth of the child and that we grew estranged."

"Not an uncommon complaint, I should think."

"True. Not uncommon at all. But, as with medicine, a correct diagnosis is a pre-requisite. That was where I failed. I sought to treat the symptoms, without first determining the cause."

"You have lost me again, dear Max. You were going to tell me how you went to Mme. Montez in the hope that she could help your wife in the same way she helped the Czar? With the depression. I assume you are talking about the melancholy?"

"Yes, of course, the depression. I was at my wits' end; I had tried everything I could think, even things I should not have thought of, to try to restore Margaret's *joie de vivre*. I saw the advertisement for Rowe's Pioneer Circus. I tried taking Margaret there, of all things, on the theory that if I could bring back her laughter, things would improve."

"Well, there is a certain logic to that. Did it work, Max?"

"Of course it did not work. I took her to cheer her up, but it is quite a smelly show. Mr. La Rue on his naked horse gave my wife no cheer; finally, we simply left. Another time, we went to a Magnetic Sitting, one Saturday evening. Mr. Girard, using his own daughter as a medium, demonstrated the phenomenon of somnambulism and how in this state of sleep she was singing and dancing. The demonstration put no sunshine into Margaret's heart; she suspected that the sleepwalking was put on, and her assumption was probably correct.

"The Grand Lion and Bear Fight at the Mission Dolores, where a 450-pound grizzly bear defeated a fine California lioness, was a cruel show, not suitable for a woman with emotional trouble. Despite the lively music by the American Theater Band she suffered seeing the brutality and soon was back in melancholy's embrace."

"And that was when you approached Mme. Montez?"

"Yes, Jules. Well, first I spoke to Dr. Mandt, who confirmed that the Czar had openly praised Mme. Montez not only for curing him of depression but also for restoring his male sensuality. That news had been water for the mills of John Nugent who obtained an interview with the artist and asked about the *on-dit*. She dodged his question by asking about his deprecating assessment of her talents in his previous issue of the *Herald*, and about his association with certain infamous political elements."

"Good for her. Do not let that bully take control. She is indeed wise, Max!"

"The *San Francisco Daily Bulletin* fared better, Jules, prudently sending Miss Rolph, their charming female reporter. Mme. Montez confirmed that His Highness had indeed granted her private audiences; she suggested that the reason for the Czar's melancholy was a disorder brought on by unrestrained sensuous practice in his earlier years."

"So, you suspected, on learning of your wife's early years, that such might also be the case with her? Is that it, Max?"

"No. Not at all. I suspected nothing. That was part of the problem.

But the news of Mme. Montez' assessment of the Czar's condition was enough to convince me that a consultation might prove fruitful. However, the fly in the ointment was my inability to match the royal honorarium; at best, I could buy tickets to the premiere of her spider dance. I committed the extravaganza of subscribing to the entire season of performances, offering Margaret a diversion and amends for my frequent absences. Margaret seemed to be very much taken by the show, by the persona of the lover as played by Mr. McCabe, and the life of a woman who so forwardly reveled in her own sensuality. Thus, in a sense, my strategy was working."

"Good. I am glad to hear it, Max."

Dr. Fifer continued: "One evening, on our way home from the performance, I suggested to Margaret that Mme. Montez seemed not as agile as she used to be. It seemed that age was creeping up, and that she must have put on a few pounds. To my astonishment, Margaret took offence and became quite angry, upon which I attempted to explain the facts of life, that gaining weight can be a natural consequence of aging. However, my reasoning did little to assuage my wife's displeasure; her protectiveness for the declining performer was surprising. Nothing more was said about the matter. My practice kept me quite occupied, often through the night, and I thought no further of our dispute; I felt guilty for the many times Margaret had to attend the performances without my company."

"You take so much of the responsibility, Max. Surely, it was not all up to you?"

"I do see that now, Jules. At the time, it had escaped me that Mr. McCabe, the actor, had been paying some attention to my wife. So charmed the rascal seemed with her that he went to Rosenthal and Sornin on Washington Street and bought her a beautiful bracelet, for which he paid three hundred dollars, and had her name engraved upon it. Then, one night when he was taking her to some place of amusement, the trinket got lost. "

"A tragedy!"

"Yes, but that is how I found out. Some honest person came across it and took it to Rosenthal and Sornin's. They at once sent it up to our residence. As Margaret was out, it arrived at my office where I myself received the naughty telltale. It confirmed my suspicions. When she came home, I presented it to her, asking simply that she be more open with me in such matters, whereupon she went into a towering passion and said she would stay not another minute in the same house with me. She slept that night at the Good Cheers Hotel and then moved to the Tahoma permanently. She informed me that she desired to be divorced from bed and board, on the ground of extreme cruelty and incompatibility of temper. I refused to consent on account of the child. I could not imagine how this would end."

"Well, her response does seem somewhat out of proportion to your request, does it not?"

"Out of all proportion. As if I had trod upon a sleeping rattlesnake." Dr. Fifer sat down, holding his head in both hands. "In my profession, I am privy to the matrimonial conflicts of others; I could empathize with her, a young woman whose husband spent most of his time in medicine and surgery, who came home late, and always tired. I felt sorry for her. I finally did consent to a divorce. Since the dissolution of our marriage, she has received religious instructions from Father Gallagher at St. Mary's who converted her to the Papist persuasion and, as you may have read, betrothed her to Nels O'Nedhil."

Jules David comforted Dr. Fifer. "Max, you have my sympathy; however, we are here in Yale, in the British Territories, a thousand miles from your ex-wife. Being divorced is not a disgrace; why do you allow the rumour that you are a widower to circulate?"

Dr. Fifer sighed: "I would have forgiven her the affair with McCabe, but there is more to it. This was only the first act." He hesitated, noticing that Jules did not follow his reasoning. Finally, Dr. Fifer broke down; tears filled his eyes and he cried openly. "It's more serious than you can imagine. A blot that all the water of the River Lethe cannot wash out. Her affair was not with Mr. McCabe. He was only the delivery boy. The bracelet was paid for by Lola Montez."

Jules David stood and attempted to console his friend, commiserating with him the shock of the dismal outcome of his good-intentioned plan to treat his wife's depression. He poured the last of the absinthe into Dr. Fifer's glass and ordered him to 'drink up', murmuring something about the benefits of oblivion and the arms of Morpheus. Then he called me in to assist Dr. Fifer to get to bed. Immediately, I shouldered his languid body, his burdened mind, and assisted him up the steps to his sleeping loft; I removed his shoes, jacket, shirt, and trousers, and rested his head on the pillow. I went down and retrieved from the office a receptacle and placed it next to the head of the bed, in the faint hope that should he vomit the absinthe, he might aim at the vessel.

I went back down to assure that Mr. David was settled comfortably into the doctor's office which we had converted to a temporary guest room. The examining table sufficed as a cot, surrounded by the shelves of basic medical instruments, a cabinet containing a supply of drugs; the Spanish sampler hung beside the eye chart on the wall. Another shelf above the desk was stacked with patient charts, Ramsbottom's Textbook of Medicine, and the phrenology skull; Dr. Fifer had left the rest of the skeleton behind in San Francisco. "Talk about your skeletons in the proverbial closet," he had said to Mr. David when he showed him the room; both men had laughed.

I repaired to my own cot by the pantry near the stove and felt happy that Dr. Fifer had been able to relax so well with a friend, and that he had been able to unburden himself to Mr. David. I knew that the memory of his failed marriage distressed him, that indeed he and his wife had dreamed different dreams in the same bed. But he never spoke of his despair. I was about to doze off, expecting a well-deserved rest. However, I was premature to think that the evening was over.

"Die! Die, you bastard. Arrgh!" The harsh words woke me; they seemed to come from the street. I got up to look out the window;

Mr. David joined me, having been disturbed also. But we saw no movement. The darkness was complete; the streets seemed empty. Then we heard a thumping from above, and we both feared, at the same moment, that Dr. Fifer was being attacked. We crashed into each other, trying to mount the ladder as quickly as possible. But when my head poked into the sleeping loft, I saw only the white sheets in a tumble and Dr. Fifer still asleep but flailing about as if trying to escape the bonds of night. I moved aside to admit Mr. David who whispered "He is safe; it is merely a troubled sleep; it is dangerous to wake someone from such a state," and he held his hand to my shoulder, to prevent me from going to the doctor.

At that moment, the doctor sat upright, his eyes wide but vacant. He raised his arms, fists together as if gripping something, and repeated the scream we had heard earlier: "Die, you bastard. Die!" I noticed that he swung in his fists the pestle I had placed under the bed when I set the vessel down for him, and I could see that in his dreadful nightmare, he was smashing the pestle, as if it were a club or a sword, into his own knees and thighs. Mr. David recognized the danger of self-injury at the same moment, and we both rushed forward. Mr. David grabbed the tool; I touched Dr. Fifer's shoulders as gently as I could, hoping to awaken him without startling him or turning his violent intentions towards us.

"What? Ah Chung? David? What is wrong?"

"Nothing is wrong, sir. You were dreaming," I said, at the same time as Mr. David responded: "Absinthe is hallucinogenic, Max! We heard your screams, and feared you were in danger."

"Screams? I was screaming? Dreaming?" He was still partially asleep and trying to assimilate our presence into the drama which was quickly fleeing from his head. "O'Nedhil. I was dreaming about O'Nedhil."

"Your wife's fiancé?"

"The very same, Mr. David. But I fear my distraction is my own fault. I fear I have not been honest with you. I have taken advantage

172

of your friendship and have won your sympathy, but I have withheld the truth; I have not told you the whole story."

"The whole story? What more could there be?" Mr. David pulled up the chair over which I had lain Dr. Fifer's clothing, and prepared to listen further. I went down to brew a pot of tea, but I could follow the gist of the doctor's confession.

"O'Nedhil is a man known to me. Originally from Philadelphia, he came west with the gold seekers. He has many friends in San Francisco. Perhaps you even had dealings with him yourself, when he was the chief of police?"

"Not Nelson Victor O'Nedhil? A name not untainted by gossip, surely, Max."

"True. But I learned that too late. At one time, he was a welcome guest in my home. He passed himself off as my friend. He even consulted me on matters of intimate health concerns. O, foul. Foul." The memory seemed to make the doctor want to reach for the handy vessel.

"He knew about Mme. Montez and said nothing?"

"No. Nothing like that. He betrayed our friendship in a much more infamous manner. And I never even suspected."

"What happened, old man?"

"I was at work, during office hours…"

"There seems to be a recurring thread here, Max."

"Yes. It is true. In this case, my work life melded with my personal life in a way no one could have predicted. A patient named Evelyn came to see me. She worked as a chambermaid in a hotel. She had given birth out of wedlock to a child. A child with the same cross-toed feet as my own child, she was anxious to tell me. I felt she sought someone who could sympathize with her sad story. However, her child had died, and her lover, a married man, had failed to live up to his promises to her. She was angry and distraught."

"A chambermaid named Evelyn?" Mr. David was trying to concentrate.

"Yes, named Evelyn. Although I was not clear why she had come to consult me, I permitted her to talk, just as you have encouraged me this evening, knowing that to share the burden lessens our load. Evelyn wanted to talk about her daemon lover. During their long affair, he had spent many hours with her. To amuse themselves and in response to her curiosity and constant questions—-he probably tried to seduce her—-he told her about the ladies who had been intimate with him. And confided that the one he enjoyed best was the wife of a well-known local physician. It did not cross my mind to wonder whether I knew this couple, although Evelyn seemed obsessed with the details."

"Her rival was a doctor's wife?"

"Yes. According to Evelyn, this other woman had become so infatuated with her lover, or so the man claimed, that she wanted a child by him, and the two contrived her conception behind her husband's, the doctor's, back. At the age of thirty-five, this Lothario raved, she was paradise, as tight as a virgin. The doctor's wife had been so infatuated with his prodigious member, she craved it even when they were not together. The affair was a lark and a prank, a practical joke, the gigolo boasted; if the jerk of a cuckold doctor only knew what a good friend and protector he had in Officer O'Nedhil. The braggart!"

"Surely, a scoundrel through and through."

"Yes, and Evelyn who had listened to O'Nedhil's salacious tale, begged him to tell her the woman's name. Tempering the wind to the lamb he intended to shear, he relented and told her the name of the woman who had a child by him, a boy."

"No discretion!'

"No, but the risk, the titillating pillow talk, excited Evelyn, making her good and ready for her part of the *quid pro quo*. Alas, poor O'Nedhil! At the very moment, about to make his debut, his *miembro viril* let him down; it went limp, loosing its tumescence. The malfunction did not upset him; it occurred often while with the doctor's wife, who would overcome his flaccidness by intricate oral stimulation. Should

174

all else fail, she would resort to a jar of salve in her purse, lifted from the doctor's office. Her husband used Seidlitz's Nitro Glycerine ointment to restore the circulation in old sourdoughs' limbs. While the good doctor searched his office in vain for the precious balm to save a foot from gangrene, his wife was frivolously applying it to O'Nedhil's flabby member, prodding it back to a state of readiness. During the ensuing intimacy, the couple enjoyed the drug's tingling sensation."

"Seidlitz's Nitro Glycerine is a common remedy, if I remember correctly," Mr. David probed.

"True, Jules, although the procedure of rubbing it in may have a greater restoring effect than the drug itself. At the time, I thought only that the man must know his business. However, Evelyn talked on, explaining how, in contrast to the sexual astuteness of her rival, she lacked experience and the knowledge of discriminate lovemaking. To be intimate with a stranger and finding him impotent mortified her. O'Nedhil, expecting the customary therapeutic lathering-up, lacking the restoring salve, seeing his part of the bargain shrink away, impatiently gripped her by the hair, brought her mouth down over his shrunken mollusc, and forced her head up and down, and up and down, until she had successfully restored his manhood."

"He is no gentleman, surely, Max?"

But Dr. Fifer continued: "During the intercourse, the lover ejaculated prematurely without climaxing, which augurs declining vigour. He was angry, blaming the malfunction on the lack of nitro glycerin salve. Unhappy, with a piggish grunt, he withdrew, got off the bed, and closed the flap of his breeches over his flaccid slippery member, the scant, sticky semen drying on the cloth of his well-pressed police uniform."

"Trust a cleaning woman to notice such details, Max." Mr. David was attempting to lighten the mood.

"Indeed, Jules. What does one expect from a pig but a grunt, but I chose not to speak the words which had arisen in my head. Nor could I share with Evelyn any confidential details of my own professional consultation with the very man—venereal warts propagated during intercourse. However, Evelyn's story went on. She had paid the price to satisfy her curiosity."

"You mean, as payment for the entertaining pillow talk, she paid with her body?"

"Exactly, Jules. Evelyn did not think of the consequences; she went through the transformation of a pregnancy. Her face assumed a dark tan, *cloasma*, and grew fine hair, *lanugo*. She craved raw carrots and exotic foods; more than that, her personality changed to that of a jealous, possessive mother-to-be. She wanted the father of her child for herself; she did not want to share him with another woman's *nullius filius*, whether she was the wife of a lawyer, doctor, groom, or charcoal burner."

"Did she confront the rival?" Mr. David was anxious to hear of a violent confrontation.

"No, Jules. She chose instead to confront the rival's husband."

"No!'

"Indeed, yes. And that was the reason for her appointment with me. O'Nedhil had confessed that the rival woman was Mrs. Margaret Fifer, the wife of Dr. Fifer on Washington Street."

"Did you say 'Fifer?' No! Your own wife! My friend, is it true?"

"You know, Jules, it never crossed my mind not to believe her. Yet her disclosure, her defiant provocation, spilling the beans about my wife and her illegitimate offspring, was a revelation of seismic proportion, toppling the cosmic order of my world as surely as the earthquake razed Lisbon, as Mount Vesuvius destroyed Pompeii. At the same time it was as if everything had fallen into place. Instantly I recognized Margaret's depression as that of an abandoned woman, one who has loved unwisely and whose lover has disappointed her, just as O'Nedhil had failed Evelyn."

"No, surely not, Max!"

"Instantly, Jules, I concluded that there is no reasonable God, no just, all-good Creator. My mind was chaos; I could listen no further and escorted Evelyn to the door even before she could ask me for money or other assistance. Immediately I was searching to understand where I had gone wrong. What had possessed Margaret to commit such a perfidious act of infidelity? I was never disagreeable, violent, dissipated by drink; I never kept another woman. There were no quarrels, except for her one-time mysterious accusation of spending good money on alimony for some imaginary illegitimate child. I assured her that the only children I would ever have to support would be those I would have with her. My answer seemed to settle her; our relationship improved, and even more so during the time of O'Nedhil's friendship and his visits to our home. If my marriage had been in jeopardy, would not the best friend of the family have noticed and alerted me?"

"You trusted the man, Max. You had no reason not to."

"Not until Evelyn's scandalous hearsay had opened my eyes: the pair had played a Machiavellian charade in which I was the cuckold. The houseguest, pretending to be my friend, had no intention to warn me of my crumbling marriage. The greater the marital discord, the easier and more enjoyable would be his consorting with the mistress of the house, with the doctor standing by as an unwitting dumb-bell."

"You are too hard on yourself, my friend."

"Like aftershocks, my mind continued to be shaken, Jules. Under Margaret's clever goading, O'Nedhil, the opportunistic gigolo, had not stopped at the sacredness of marriage or the purity of friendship. The cuckoo bird had laid his egg; Margaret's body was the Trojan horse to implant into our family an alien, a human parasite who did not belong and to whom I had no relation. I could no longer even look at the infant, so angry did his brown skin, his deformed toes, make me."

"Yes, I can understand."

"And O'Nedhil, Jules. The scoundrel was anything but a good friend; he had destroyed the purpose of my life. Like a vague *déja* vu experience, the puzzling changes in our marital relationship I could now see in a different light. Margaret's perceived loss of sexual interest, her abrupt change to a lascivious libido with a repulsive lust to feel my penis rise in her mouth, now had deceitful origins. What possessed this woman to assume the role of O'Nedhil's sex servant? What would happen in the event of an unexpected ejaculation? Would she swallow the semen? Had she swallowed his semen? Was this not sodomy? There is no comparable behaviour observed in the animal kingdom. The members of the Bible Perfectionists do not advocate oral sex. I find no reference to it in the Scripture. Had I unknowingly married a nymphomaniac, a woman obsessed, with pathologically abnormal sexual desire?"

"Max. Max. You cannot let yourself filibuster like this. You will make yourself crazy."

But Dr. Fifer was not hearing his friend's reassurances. "I wanted the man dead, Jules. Dead. The gigolo had not merely betrayed our friendship, taken advantage of my hospitality, befouled my nest. He was a threat to society. His cavorting, his irresponsibility, had to be stopped. Only I was aware of his unforgivable sins; only I could save humanity; destiny had ordained that I act. It was a moral imperative. Only I knew the simple solution—a bullet behind the ear, the location of amativeness, the source of sexual excess."

"You were not yourself, Max! It is understandable, surely."

"True. I was not myself. What doctor uses his knowledge to take a life? What doctor sets himself as jury and executioner? Yet my dream was lucid. I pack my doctor's satchel—lancet, scarifier, linen bandages, my new flexible binaural stethoscope. A hand mirror in a velvet sheath and a wad of eider down plumage, *someteria mollissima*, for establishing official death. A flask of strong-smelling Spirits of Hartshorn, and wrapped in a sound-muffling cloth, a loaded Derringer pistol. In the streets of San Francisco, crime is rampant.

"I knock at his front door but no one answers. I let myself in, having been there before. I make my way to the parlour; a big bluebottle fly, *calliphora vomitaria*, buzzes drunkenly into my face. O'Nedhil is there, stretched out on the chaise lounge, his oversized brogans off his feet. I notice an odd medicinal odour. I notice his pale, slightly jaundiced colour, his sunken eyes, half closed, the white of the eyeballs visible. At his side, a phial containing a thick brown fluid. Laudanum. Not a good drug to administer to patients with jaundice or diseases of the liver.

"Here is an easy solution in the palm of my hand. A drop or two more and no one will question a conclusion of suicide by overdose as the cause of death. But I am not satisfied. I want to wake him, to make him regain consciousness, to ensure that he is aware of his evildoing and its consequences. The Spirits of Hartshorn have no effect. I can detect no audible heartbeat. I can feel no pulse of blood at the carotid artery. The mirror is too warm; no vapour of breath will precipitate. No respiration stirs the down of eider. I pull back the eyelids to check the pupils' response to light; they are wide and remain rigid in the light; the miotic morphine effect has worn off hours ago.

"Foiled. I am unable to fulfill my calling. As I repack my bag and move towards the exit, the bluebottle continues to feast off the morphine-laced drool trickling from the corpse's mouth."

"A man cannot be hanged for his dreams, Max. You were disturbed. Your sleep was disturbed. This is not you."

"You are kind, my friend. And I suspect you are suggesting what I already know—the dangers of self-medicating. But what kind of doctor dreams murder? What kind of man thinks himself God's emissary, above his fellow sinners? It is madness, surely."

Sitting there in the dark, the rumbled bedclothes, three men in nightdress like characters in one of Mr. Dickens' stories, two of us having just rescued the third from cries of 'Die, you bastard, die!', Mr. David's prediction seemed more of a reality than a figure of speech. We can make ourselves crazy.

"Yet still, it is true, I often dream of disturbing his grave, and piercing his heart with a stake, as our ancestors did in the superstitious past."

"He may have deserved to die, Max, but you do not deserve to sacrifice your own life for one so scurrilous and despicable. You have much to offer; you are a healer and a prophet, the shining monument known as Camelot; you have started a new life for yourself."

"Thank you, my friend. Indeed, I do get your reference, and your drift. 'Don't be the Fool, Fifer. Am I right? Don't be the Fool."

8

Woo. Woo. Woo. WooOOoo. The paddlewheeler's steam whistle. Does it bring Governor Douglas' response? Will Reverend Crickmer's petition be successful? Has the condemned man been able to rest in his death cell, or are his eyes wide in terror, his sleep disturbed the same way mine has been, awaiting the dawn of this fateful day? Will his sentence be commuted? Yea or Nay? Life or death? Mercy or retribution?

Alone here, chained in my own way to an empty house, I steam myself some rice as the river outside carries the past into this sad present. The past of that fateful morning, three years ago, our distinguished visitor ready-packed, about to return to Victoria, the ship's whistle calling, we all were unaware of his Nemesis lurking outside the door. After such a full day of entertaining and reminiscing, of long conversation and too many tumblers of wormwood cordial, after that night of so many confessions and painful memories, I had feared that we might all three sleep in. We might not be awake in time for Mr. David to embark on the *Umatilla* to return to Victoria. However, I was already up and about when the ship announced its arrival, warning us to be prepared for its imminent departure. Disembarking passengers, unloading freight, loading firewood, loading freight, and then boarding passengers usually took less than an hour. I had coffee, fried biscuits, and bacon ready as both Dr. Fifer and Mr. David shuffled in, rumpled and tired looking, but awake, up and out of bed.

All three of us were less talkative than the previous day, subdued by the agonizing throbbing of the two friends' heads. Mr. David had packed and placed his valise at the door before sitting down for his breakfast. He avoided the bacon, preferring the blandness of flour and water flapjacks and several hydrating cups of coffee. He was generous with his thanks to me, and somewhat raucous, manly with a "Buck up!" shoulder-slapping attitude towards Dr. Fifer, not wanting the intimacy of the darkness to shadow their friendship.

Dr. Fifer stood to accompany Mr. David as he picked up his valise, but the banker waved him off. "Stay! Relax, Max! Surely I know my way by now," and the doctor did not seem to mind being excused. After saying good-bye with an awkward hug and a handshake, he sat back down with another cup of coffee and dumped the uneaten bacon on to his own plate. However, the intent to eat it would never materialize.

"Die, Strangler, die!" and "Die, David, die!" reached our ears from the front door before it closed.

"No. Help. Murder! Max, help me!" came Mr. David's voice loud but shrill, shaking with fear. "Fifer, help me!"

Dr. Fifer and I both dashed to the door. We could see Mr. David, his valise split open where it had fallen, the knees of his city trousers in the grass by the footpath, his forearms raised, attempting to deflect blows which continued to rain down upon his head, his back and shoulders. The man wielding the gnarled wooden bat I recognized immediately from San Francisco. I had not seen him before in Yale, but his red hair and moustache were now a dirty white, as if he had washed his head in rusty water; it was the same face—that of the "ubiquitous" Ned McGowan, voice of the Law and Order Party, sworn enemy of the Vigilance Committee. With each new blow to Mr. David's head, McGowan was spitting an insult.

"Don't think your little fifer friend can save you from this drumming!" Whack. "You'll be the first Jew to die like a dog on Her Majesty's precious streets." Whack. "Now who's an able guy, Strangler?" Whack. McGowan had lain in wait for his prey, pounced, struck, chased him down the street, and beat him senseless; it was assault with a deadly weapon, planned and executed. That took place three years ago, in 1858, and I remember every word that was uttered.

Ned McGowan's name had been splashed in the newspapers even more than the doctor's when we all lived in California. Before we left, Ned had been arrested for libel, convicted of multiple crimes and sentenced to transportation, to be hanged if he were ever to set foot back in California. Before that, he had run away and evaded a conviction for his part in inciting Casey to murder the newspaper editor Mr. King. Indeed the evidence suggested that McGowan had manipulated the situation which resulted in the two deaths—the murder of King and the hanging of Casey—by releasing Casey's criminal record to the newspaper editor and then by providing Casey the weapon with which he took his revenge.

The criminal's assault on poor Mr. David continued even as we tried to intervene. The number of witnesses increased as everyone rushed to gawk but all were reluctant to step forward. Dr. Fifer himself grabbed the club and ripped it from the assailant's hands, passing it to me as he rushed to his friend.

McGowan seemed unconcerned about arrest or capture; he made no effort to flee after being disarmed. He was staring at his victim, ignoring the doctor's ineffectual efforts to assist Mr. David to his feet. Swift as an eagle, McGowan scooped something, a blood-stained rag-like object, from the ground. Raising it above his head like a trophy, he crowed: "My first scalp in British territory." Some in the watching crowd chuckled. "Nothing remains but the wig," McGowan added, playing to the crowd. Indeed, Mr. David's distinguished head was now bald; McGowan had captured an expensive toupee. But there was nothing to soften the blows; his naked pate was bleeding profusely, the blood running down Mr. David's forehead and face saturating his white shirt collar. The once-elegant businessman was disoriented and in considerable pain.

Dr. Fifer yelled at me to bring the ladder and once I had returned with the steps to his loft, we lifted the injured man onto our makeshift litter and carried him back into the surgery, on to the cot which he had so recently vacated. There the doctor attended to the patient, applying styptic to staunch the bleeding, daubing the cuts and abrasions, reducing and slinging the dislocated shoulder, and administering laudanum for the pain. He bandaged the head and covered it with one of his own hats and, together, we helped our woozy guest to the dock. The doctor waited with Mr. David while I went to retrieve Police Chief Donnellan who took the victim's statement before the *Umatilla's* departure.

The attacker, McGowan, had disappeared, by canoe down to Hill's Bar, some of the bystanders pointed. Chief Donnellan knew us all from San Francisco—the doctor, the banker, McGowan, and me. He also knew Hill's Bar by reputation and chose not to pursue the assailant into another jurisdiction.

When Governor Douglas heard about the attack, he issued a warrant for McGowan's arrest. Ned issued a counter-bulletin declaring that it was his intent not to be taken, and that was that. He knew that he was safe from both Donnellan and Perrier, the magistrate on Hill's Bar "who values my judicial experience and my friendship."

This vicious assault was indeed the first transgression we had seen of the infamous "Ubiquitous," Ned McGowan, actually here on British territory in Yale, although word of his imminent arrival had been swirling, snow-balling, for weeks: he landed in Victoria on the Fifth of July, to a gun salute orchestrated by himself when he and his friend Dolan commandeered the *Pacific's* gun and used it to celebrate; he was accosted on the streets of Victoria by Myers Truett, a former member of the Vigilance Committee; he was in Whatcom; he was on the steamboat, at the mouth of the Harrison River, hassling Governor Douglas; he was in Fort Hope; he was on Cornish Bar. Finally, his arrival had been confirmed with the almost fatal assault on Dr. Fifer's business manager and friend.

One of Ned McGowan's victims was Charles Cook, an ex-San Francisco policeman, who was assaulted by Ned McGowan in front of the Hudson's Bay Company store in Fort Hope.

Charles Cook: "The steamboat had just docked and passengers were straggling up the riverbank to the Hudson's Bay post, Fort Hope. I was standing in front of the store when I spotted a fellow known to me, a man I arrested once in San Francisco, the man who calls himself Ubiquitous. Here on British soil, we are equals, but McGowan is famous for his long memory, and his many promises to get his revenge on any member of the Vigilance Committee. In no time, he and his men had me down on the ground, under his boot, cursing, yelling 'Confess, you dog, before I kill you!'

"What choice did I have? I used one of his own favourite tactics; I tried to distract him by talking. 'I joined the Vigilance Committee on the second day after the shooting of James King. They could not register me on the first day, the crowd was so great. My reason for signing up was to unite with something that would put down the shooting in the streets, the robbing, thieving, swindling and all that sort of thing, which the courts could not or would not stop or punish. I did not know how long the vigilance organization was to continue, I only hoped it would last till the end, until the great evil under which we all laboured would be corrected.'

"McGowan got his revenge against me alright. They had to take me to Dr. Bradshaw who said I had a ruptured spleen; I was unable to work my claim for weeks. It all dates back to San Francisco. I delivered that man McGowan to the foot of the gallows, but he's slippery as an eel, slithery as a snake; he's made me pay for doing my duty."

Miner Mike Dooley was threatened by McGowan who attempted to run him off his claim on Cornish Bar, just below Hope.

Mike Dooley: "I was workin' my claim on Cornish Bar, wot's also called Murderer's Bar on account of som'thin' that happened there before my time. I was hard at work panning out gold at the rate of from five to ten dollars a day. It was early September, when the water was at its lowest, and the prospects, of course, are richest.

"McGowan and his men stood around and watched me for a while. Then Ned sez, quite casual like, 'Hey, Dooley, you's got more land than ye need; we's here to help.' I sez 'I don't need no help, Ned,' then they threatened me, and kept threatening me, and then I sez 'This is my claim. I've recorded it; it belongs to me by law, and God save the Quane!'

" 'Jist say that again and I'll have ya buried alive!', Ned swears.

" 'God save the Quane!' I sez, an' I looks him in the eye.

" 'Dig a trench and bury the blasted beggar!' Ned sez, an' he wanders off looking for other claims and t' see what he could do with their owners.

"His men bound me hand and foot and proceeded t' dig a deep trench in the sand. When it was deep enough t' suit them, they threw me in and begun t' cover me up.

" 'What do you say now?' they inquired.

"God save the Quane!

"They covered me t' my neck and axsed, 'Will you say that again?'

"I spat the sand from my mouth and promptly replied, 'God save the Quane!'

"Then Ned, he comes back. Only my mouth and eyes were showin'. McGowan kneels down, and looks int' the pit, and axs 'Now what do you say?'

" 'God save the Quane!' I squeezes the words out, the sand pressing my chest like that.

" 'Oh, pull the beggar out and let him go!' sez Ned. It's not that he show'd me any mercy; it's jist, men like him, ye can't back down; he'll make ya dig yer own grave an' then he'll push ya in hisself."

Miner Bloody Edwards was harassed by McGowan and his crew

on Hill's Bar.

Bloody Edwards: "Whenever Ned and his cronies got to feelin' jolly over a fresh arrival of the juice of the barley, they tried to make an American citizen out of me. They bullied me; they applied one of Ned's favourite cruelties, rolling me into a ditch and covering me with sand. But all their efforts got them nowhere. I told them: 'I'm content to be a bloody good Englishman' and every time we argued, I'd end with 'three bloody good cheers for the Queen'.

"I opened a trading post on Hill's Bar; amongst my stock, of course, was whisky. One evening the boys collected at my store and were enjoying themselves as usual when someone questioned my bravery. You could not let such things pass; not with that bunch. I went to the back of the store; I had to prove my grit. I held a lighted candle at arm's length; some of the boys stood at the front end and commenced to fire shots at the candle from their revolvers. Fortunately, a few sober men were present, among them Dr. Fifer here, from Yale, who had attended to a gunshot wound. The doctor, seeing the danger and not wanting another patient just then, proposed that all hands take a drink, which they did. So ended the shooting; the doctor here probably saved my life. "

In spite of his professional credo, in his very heart, Dr. Fifer despised Ned McGowan; he detested everything Ned represented. Whenever the name was mentioned, he pushed the wire of his spectacles up the bridge of his nose and shook his head in disbelief. He had despised Ned McGowan when we lived in San Francisco, and he despised Ned McGowan here in Yale. The unprovoked attack on Mr. David only confirmed what the doctor already felt about the man he considered to be his only enemy. Well, almost, with the exception of that other slime, O'Nedhil, as I realized during his wormwood hallucination that dark morning. Sometimes I suspected that Dr. Fifer confused the two men, both from Philadelphia, both two-faced, dishonest, disloyal, untrustworthy, often choosing to work behind scenes, using the agency of innocent others to inflict unbearable pain. Crows everywhere are equally black.

As a domestic, I know only the vague outline of the history of the enmity between the doctor and Mr. McGowan in San Francisco. Some of this I overheard in conversations with Mr. David; some I heard after meetings in San Francisco, of the Vigilance Committee. Some I overheard as the doctor attempted to warn Mr. Allard to beware McGowan's insinuating himself into his family. "Beware of being too trusting, Allard. Don't be fooled by phony Irish charm! A man can smile and smile and still be a villain."

Dr. Fifer struggled to separate his own feelings about Edward "Ned" McGowan from the facts as they were documented in the press: born and raised in Philadelphia, of Irish descent; trained as a lawyer; elected as a member of the state legislature; expelled for assault with a knife on another member; appointed, through political connections, as chief of police in the city; accused by an incarcerated felon of using inside information about security procedures to plan and organize bank robberies; fled to California with a warrant outstanding for his arrest, found Not Guilty *in absentia* because the witness was not credible; carried his acquittal papers with him and produced them whenever officials in each new jurisdiction attempted to arrest him.

"Some of us came here in service to our country, willing to risk our lives and to live in great discomfort until our mission was accomplished," the doctor used to say, referring to his arrival in California as a member of the New York volunteer regiment. "Others came later, as exiles, fugitives, expelled from other jurisdictions and seeking a new start where their schemes and scams would go undetected, at least until someone from their past spread the word. You know me, Ah Chung. I'm all for giving anyone a second chance. But the onus is on them, to make the most of their good fortune."

In San Francisco, Ned McGowan did not belong to the businessmen's association. He seemed to be one of those men who believed that knowing the right people would get him appointed to a good government position. He did have legal training, and experience in elected office. But the elections on which he worked were suspect; rumours always hovered of stuffed or false-bottomed ballot boxes. Ingenious, Ned was,. in the ways he could come up with to fool the voters, subvert the system, shaft the opposition. Newspapers referred to him as "the harpist," the one who plucks one thousand strings. It was as if he took personal pleasure in creating chaos. Wherever he stood, a maelstrom circled him like a dust devil in the desert, like the dead man's eddy at the entrance to the canyon.

McGowan's opposition to the Vigilance Committee in San Francisco had been partisan and political. The businessmen wanted law and order to ensure security for their investments; the opposition wanted power for its own ends, to be able to control political appointments and collect graft. Ned McGowan had the gift of the gab. "That man has licked the Blarney Stone," I heard more than one Englishman comment. He could rally men by his speeches; the letters he wrote to the editors of the partisan newspapers, signing himself Caliban and Ubiquitous, were constantly calling people down and stirring things up. Dr. Fifer called him a contrary, and when I asked him what he meant, he said something like "a man who opposes everything that anyone else proposes, whose first instinct is No, and whose second instinct is Do it my way. One who stands for nothing and against everything."

After the newspapers stopped publishing his diatribes, McGowan started his own broadsheets to attack the opposition. He manipulated weaker men to write, speak, or act according to his wishes; Ned McGowan provided the weapon by which a rival newspaperman was assassinated; some even said he spun the assassin around and stopped him when he was pointed in the right direction, towards the intended victim. Witnesses saw McGowan fleeing the scene of the shooting.

Ned McGowan left town, hiding out in California and Mexico, to evade a warrant for his arrest. By turning himself in at Sacramento, he manipulated a change of venue. By playing up the debate about whether King died from a gunshot wound or from poor medical treatment of the injury, he created enough doubt that he was found Not Guilty of ordering the hit, not guilty of conspiracy to commit murder. Ned McGowan was found guilty of libel and sentenced to transportation, with hanging to result should he defy the order of banishment. He hid but was arrested as he attempted to board a ship for Victoria. A friendly judge released him; Ned McGowan stowed aboard a friend's ship, a government customs vessel, in order to escape San Francisco.

Ned McGowan made his way to Yale to join cronies from San Francisco, including the exiled Martin Gallagher and other "boatmen" at Hill's Bar. He bragged about having travelled up river on the same steamboat as Governor Douglas, en route to assess the situation of the miners' war against the Indians. Ned claimed to have roused the governor from a too long lie-in as he encamped on shore near the confluence of the Harrison and Fraser rivers. I do believe he liked to trumpet such tales as evidence that he held Englishmen and all colonial or government officials in nothing but contempt.

Ned McGowan is like many of the bullies I encountered when I worked selling drinking water on the docks in San Francisco. They all seem to misinterpret the American ideal of "freedom" as freedom to dominate and intimidate, to take advantage of others, especially those they consider to be of an "inferior" race.

Thus, Ned McGowan's assault on Mr. David signalled the criminal's arrival in Yale. However, the doctor's efforts to warn his townsmen of the risk McGowan posed fell on deaf ears. "Judge him by his actions, Mr. Allard," I heard Dr. Fifer urge more than once. "Don't listen to his silver tongue; the man has kissed the Blarney Stone; he could charm the devil back to heaven. But, trust me, there is something wrong with the head of any man who will say and do anything to get his own way. Such men cannot be trusted. Do not trust them around your daughters, Ovid."

Why did Mr. Allard not listen to Dr. Fifer's warnings? I suspect that Ovid Allard thought that Dr. Fifer was sweet on Miss Lucy himself, and was simply trying to discredit a romantic rival. Had Mr. Allard not said to me that they had no professionals here before the gold rush? Neither had they met such a villain; they did not recognize McGowan for what he was—a man without a conscience who enjoyed causing trouble; a man who cared about nothing except himself.

On the other hand, it is also true that Mr. Allard is often underestimated, because he does not seek attention or self-promotion. Or perhaps it is on account of his accent; I heard him say that French-speakers did not get promoted in the Hudson's Bay Company, but I have no knowledge of their business. However, I do know that many men who speak only English, listening to those of us who struggle with their language, mistakenly assume that we struggle also with thinking, that our brains are somehow deficient. But there is no explaining it to them.

I have long suspected that treating the visitors to his home with his good Hudson's Bay brandy, is Mr. Allard's way of ensuring that he knows everything that is happening or is going to happen. Along with hospitality as his way of collecting information and forming alliances, Mr. Allard also subscribes to the new convention of the gold fields—that a person's past is nobody's business. Regardless of the errors they may have committed previously, once accepted by the community, everyone enjoys its protection.

Indeed, did he not go along with Dr. Fifer when they saved Charles Gregory, who, it was discovered, had embezzled money from his New York employer? Saved him from the duplicitous scheming of Mr. Merrill, a detective, a bounty hunter incognito, who was attempting to lure Gregory back across the border in order to arrest him?

Did Mr. Allard not tolerate the presence on the Fraser gold fields of the infamous Martin Gallagher? Peddling drinking water on the San Francisco docks, I had witnessed Gallagher's deportation myself, as he and his compatriots were marched, chained and shackled, up the gangplank for transportation to the Sandwich Islands, under sentence of death, were he to set foot on American soil again. Gallagher turned around, showing up in Victoria as a deck hand on the brig Glencoe, and disembarked in British territory. Within days of his making his way up river, two men were found dead on New York Bar, just across the river, and Gallagher was the new boss.

Mr. Allard conceded that these deaths were no accident. The two were murdered in cold blood because, rumor had it, they refused to give up their mining claims to the new "chief" who was now ruling New York Bar. Martin Gallagher's name had been in the local newspaper already, for raping a Native woman, and for taking out thirteen pounds of gold on August 11th, from his new claim on Hill's Bar.

"Why did you let him get away with it?" Dr. Fifer had asked Mr. Allard, referring to the murders, shortly after we arrived.

"Mais, mon ami, what could we do? No one at New York Bar was going to say anything; the gang at Hill's Bar is all Americans, ex-convicts and murderers. They call themselves "the Boatmen" as if it is some badge of pride. In reality, they outnumber us here; at least, they outnumber those of us who are interested in good order, rather than merely in good pay dirt."

"But this cannot continue, surely, Mr. Allard," the doctor insisted. "How do you expect decent people to stay, if these scoundrels are calling the shots?"

"Oui, mon docteur, that's it in a nutshell. We look to Chief Factor Douglas, our old chief factor, I mean. Douglas looks to London, not to tell him what to do, but to authorize him to do what he knows to be right for these circumstances. But he lives in the real world. It takes six months for an answer to his epistles."

Those were the unfortunate conditions, in the first few months of our move here. Every one of us was holding our breath, trying not to disturb the Americans, not to give them any sort of reason to pick a fight, to provoke them into calling on the American army to come in and defend their 'rights', to make good on their boast of "Fifty-four Forty or Fight". Decent people were waiting for word from London, awaiting the creation of a colony, the appointment of a governor and other public officials, the arrival of military forces. There was no real local authority to investigate or order an inquest in the early weeks when Martin Gallagher arrived. The Yale magistrate and his policemen were helpless without real authority or a realistic back-up force; the townspeople prudently kept quiet lest the boatmen would cross the river and make more trouble.

From Hill's Bar, Martin Gallagher had written his friend Ned McGowan in California and invited him to join their "boatmen of San Francisco" community. "I enjoy my freedom here, no one is after me. My claims here on New York Bar and Hill's Bar yield better than $50 a day. Come and pick up your share of the gold." The letter must have been music to the fugitive McGowan's ears.

Mr. Allard had also accepted Mr. Donnellan, appointed by Governor Douglas as Chief of Police, although Dr. Fifer knew the man had been forced to leave a similar position in San Francisco because of too aggressive interrogation methods. He also knew that Donnellan had left a lucrative association with the madam of a house on Commercial Street. The woman with whom Mr. Donnellan had been consorting was indeed the same who had accompanied her new "husband", Mr. Abel Guy, to see Mr. Jules David off at San Francisco's Pacific Wharf. Did Chief of Police Donnellan perhaps have reasons of his own to revel in Mr. David's humiliation?

Mr. Donnellan lasted only a few months in Yale before he was fired for extorting $500 from a prisoner, George Harrison Jones, awaiting trial for murder. But during those few months, Donnellan "cut quite a swath" as the doctor said, seducing Miss Lucy with his urbane ways and sexual experience, and leaving town before her condition became common knowledge.

Mr. Allard's door is open to them all; he shares his brandy with everyone. He does a brisk business in the store; he gets along with the "Boston men" and defends them against the claim they are nothing but a set of ignorant navvies (though many are the refuse and rowdies of the Californian mines). Morally perhaps, many are bad, but mentally, some are as sharp as a Fox razor, he claims. Indeed, many are educated men, and not a few of them left their positions as lawyers, doctors, schoolmasters and ministers of Christ, their mania for the "Gold of Columbia" turning them to the nomadic life of adventurers.

Such were the diverse attitudes faced by Dr. Fifer. What more could he do but continue to feed his friend Mr. Allard with facts? But even here, his motives were suspect, confused with his reputed interest in Lucy, who was gentle-mannered like her Cowichan mother and, at the same time, endowed with the charm and vivaciousness inherited from her French-speaking father.

Indeed, Lucy had fallen for the seductions of Police Chief Donnellan while receiving attention from yet a third caller, "Judge" Ned McGowan, after he had established himself safely on Hill's Bar. In his crude courting, Ned had bought her a rather gaudy new dress with hoops sewn into the underskirt. When Mr. Allard was away on business, McGowan insisted on taking both Lucy and her mother to a ball at Campbell's dance hall.

In San Francisco, Dr. Fifer knew, McGowan had fire-bombed the home of Mrs. Perrier, his former mistress, after their affair ended. "Not the type of man one wants to be calling on one's daughter," he hinted again to his friend Allard. The doctor tried to offer proof of how untrustworthy McGowan was by reciting details of his previous political activity. "He chose to oppose the order that the businessmen of San Francisco worked to create, before the infrastructure of the new state government was put into place. Of course, it was in our own self-interest, to establish law and order, to ensure that criminal elements did not destroy the opportunities that endeared the newly acquired territory to us. But men like McGowan, not keen to work, used to being appointed to positions by their connections or elected with the help of party loyalties, took a contrarian position, opposing everything our Vigilance Committee attempted."

"But why does he call you a 'strangler'?" Mr. Allard asked.

The doctor tried to explain without making himself or his committee look bad. "We did make mistakes," he said. "We felt that justice had to be swift; we felt that hanging one would teach a lesson to one hundred. Such is not the case; men like this do not learn lessons. However, we sentenced a murderer, Casey, to hang. Along with another incarcerated criminal, Cora. Casey's victim, the newspaper editor Mr. King, had lingered at the graves' edge after being shot. The city had held its breath, and as soon as word reached us that Mr. King had died, the breath was let out and the hanging was demanded. The execution was rushed, and a certain Mr. Hale..."

"Do you mean Jehil Hoadley Hale, the carpenter?" Mr. Allard interrupted.

"The very same, Allard. Hale had the contract to build the gallows. A lucrative contract. With Casey's hurried execution, he had no time to build a proper structure. The attempt to hang the two convicts from the upper level windows of the building that was committee headquarters turned out to be an unfortunate decision. The push from the sill proved to be not enough force to snap the neck; both men strangled; the crowd below watched and cheered as the men dangled and jerked in the air."

"So, 'strangler' is true then?' Mr. Allard prompted.

Dr. Fifer nodded perfunctorily; he had to agree. "Unfortunately, there is a grain of truth to the accusation. In our desire to do right, to establish the order of law in an unorganized territory, after the turmoil of the gold rush, to accept responsibility as citizens of a democracy, to make the difficult decisions, we may have been somewhat too enthusiastic. Too quick to judge. Too harsh in our sentencing. Eager, yet unschooled in law, mistaking swiftness for justice."

"I have heard," Mr. Allard inserted, "that Americans love their 'lynch law'. Is that what your committee was doing?"

"Lynching? I suppose it could look like that, but we did insist on arrest, imprisonment, trial, evidence, conviction, a jury or judge passing sentence. It is not exactly a 'lynching', yet perhaps in our haste, in our carelessness about the defense, in our refusal to consider the possibility of appeal, perhaps these actions would qualify as a 'judicial lynching'. In the sense that the outcomes were predictable, inevitable, once an accused was arrested."

"Checks and balances? That's what Americans boast about, isn't it?" Mr. Allard added.

"Exactly, Ovid. Checks and balances are in the Constitution, but where the authority of the people is unchecked, unquestioned, no doubt abuses have occurred. And continue to occur."

"And do not the voices of the strangled and the oppressed haunt you now?"

Dr. Fifer pondered, as if he did not like to admit it. "The strangled, gasping? Yes. It should never have happened that way. The oppressed? It is true. Opportunities are there, but not for everyone."

"Then you came here," Mr. Allard offered, "to try again? To establish a new country, and get it right this time?"

Dr. Fifer admitted to his friend that he hadn't thought of it that way, but perhaps it is so. "Yet a colony is not a new country. In a colony, the system of laws has already been devised, and it is just a matter of building the infrastructure, transposing the successful system to a new place. It should be easier," he mused.

But Mr. Allard liked to challenge the doctor's belief that the British system applied here would preclude the mistakes of California. He asked, "But Dr. Fifer, Britain is full of Englishmen. Here there are men from everywhere in the world. What makes you think they will accept the British system?"

Dr. Fifer agreed that that was a challenge. He suggested that it was up to men like them, the leaders in the community, to make the advantages known, to lead by example, and to communicate their reasoning to the members of the community, whether they were citizens eligible to vote or not.

Mr. Allard pulled out a copy of the New York Times, many months old, which he had come across in a bundle of wrapping paper; it contained an article about the conclusions a judge had drawn with respect to the crimes attributed to various ethnic groups. "Murders, riots and violent assaults were the work of Irishmen," his article said. "Daring burglaries and highway robberies are assigned to Englishmen; while Germans commit petty thefts and larcenies. Skilful forgeries and obtaining goods under false pretence are strictly American offences."

I wondered if this means that the skulls of these diverse groups reveal their different virtues and vices. I noticed that "Celestials" were not included in his list. I am not sure why Mr. Allard focused on this article. Perhaps he wished to suggest that the variety of origins of men here in the British territory would result in a greater variety, or perhaps a greater quantity, of crime?

Mr. Allard had no prejudice, he assured us, in comparing the manners of the "Boston Men" against those of "King George Men", the men from England showed him, a Hudson's Bay Company representative, more of the respect he felt he deserved. Not one had ever accused him, the Company's trader, of fraud.

It is true, Mr. Allard felt himself a cornerstone of Yale society, and Dr. Fifer saw himself as another. The concept of "service" was ingrained in him, he once told me, from a family which had always served their kings with loyalty and pride. "I was born in an orphanage," I heard him proclaim once, but he had gone on to explain how his parents worked there—a public appointment to compensate his father who had lost a leg in the war against Napoleon. "We answer the call when we are needed; our loyalty has always been rewarded when we in turn need assistance."

That is why the doctor was eager to work with Mr. Allard and others on the town council. That was why, when Governor Douglas' replacement for Chief Donnellan, an Australian named Kirby, was also weak, and when the new local magistrate, Peter Blundon Whannell, also from Australia, behaved like a madman, Dr. Fifer stepped in to do what he could. Whannell, who had also stopped in San Francisco before reaching Yale, used to put on his fancy uniform with the Vigilance Committee's white ribbon on his lapel and wander the streets flaying his sabre at the air, thrusting at anything that moved. He threw so many men into the new jail that they had to sleep standing up. Many were incarcerated only because they were witnesses to a crime, or could not afford to pay bail. Judge Begbie said later of Mr. Whannell that he could not believe how one man could cause such a mess. Dr. Fifer and Mr. Allard tried to prevent the bizarre Mr. Whannell from being duped by Ned McGowan into starting a war.

So much happened so quickly back then. The town was holding its breath; the Hudson's Bay Company's trading monopoly was due to expire and no formal structure had yet been set up to deal with the influx of miners and future settlers. James Douglas, governor of the Colony of Vancouver Island, was the acting administrator on the mainland until official word could be received from Whitehall. On November 19, Judge Begbie, newly-arrived from London, was sworn in at Fort Langley. He immediately read the proclamation creating the Colony of British Columbia and then in turn swore in James Douglas as the new colony's first Governor. It was the season of heavy rains; we did not attend the ceremony, but the news spread quickly by handbills, the newspaper, and word of mouth.

With the change to colonial status, Governor Douglas' earlier acting appointees were re-evaluated; some, including the first Chief of Police and the first Commissioner of Lands, Richard Hicks, had to be replaced. It was the unfortunate choices of some of the Governor's early appointments, ineffective, incompetent, corrupt officials, around which Ned McGowan rallied opposition that first year. "How could the miners obey Her Majesty's laws when she was represented by such asses?" Hicks was known to be "skimming", Donnellan had robbed a prisoner in his charge, and Whannell's flamboyant deficiencies, ignorance, combined with pomposity, were obvious to everyone.

Although Yale was the largest community while the miners were present here, both Fort Hope and Hill's Bar also had their own local administrations. The pool of qualified applicants was limited as appointees had to be British subjects. The Chief Justice on Hill's Bar, Georges Perrier, had the necessary qualifications for Governor Douglas' purposes; for Ned McGowan's sinister ambitions, the malleable Perrier was also very suitable. Relying on McGowan's superior training in law (albeit American), Perrier did whatever Ned recommended. Perhaps they felt as close as "in-laws", having both lived with the same woman. Whether Perrier knew of the terror McGowan had used against the woman, fire-bombing her house before she fled to France, I do not know.

Dr. Fifer's War

As our first Christmas in Yale approached, we could feel the anticipation. Dr. Fifer had been selected as chairman of the Yale town council; in this mayoral position, he instigated plans for a community Christmas party, the first ever in the new colony, to be held in one of the gambling halls. Dr. Fifer and his friends went around collecting funds; everyone contributed. They all had great ambitions for Fort Yale; they had sent invitations to prominent citizens and newspapers as far away as Victoria.

However, I have noticed, the winter holiday partying and drinking often result in unhappiness. A few days before Christmas, Ikey Dixon, the Negro barber, was assaulted. Farrell, a Hill's Bar resident, had argued with Ikey over the price of a bottle of hair oil in the barber shop. Farrell's friend Burns came to his aid; the struggle moved outside; Ikey was pistol-whipped and left lying in the street.

Of course, some people blamed Ikey for calling retaliation upon himself. The assault on him may have been racially motivated. It may also have been part of a deliberate plan to cause trouble. Or it may have been a simple attempt to shut him up, to get even for his repeatedly telling of an earlier confrontation, a garrulousness which annoyed many "Boatmen." Ikey himself was known to like to talk; he had a 'mischief-making tongue in his head', some said. Tom O'Neil, another rough from Hill's Bar, had gone in for a shave and had threatened the barber. Dixon of course was the hero of his own story:

"Barber," O'Neil said, "I want yer to shave me."

"Yeth, sah," I sez, "take a seat."

"And, barber," continued Tom, drawing a revolver and placing it across his knees, "if yer draw so little as one drop of blood, I'll shoot yer."

"I did na' nick the customer," Ikey bragged, "but if I'd a cut that man ever so little, I made up my mind that I'd cut his throat from 'year to 'year. It would ha' been my life or his'n, and I was shore it wouldn't ha' been mine."

After the attack, Ikey Dixon went to Judge Whannell and laid a complaint against the two men who had assaulted him. Judge Whannell issued a warrant for the arrest of Farrell and Burns. The two accused men turned themselves in, not to the Yale magistrate, but to authorities on Hill's Bar who refused to turn the suspects over to the authorities at Yale. "We'll try them here," they insisted, and summonsed Dixon to appear as a witness. It was a good ploy based on knowing the advantages of a change of venue. McGowan had managed to manipulate an acquittal in California after turning himself in at Sacramento, thus getting the venue changed from San Francisco. He had been found Not Guilty on the 'conspiracy to murder' charge although evidence showed that he had provided the pistol which became the murder weapon and he had been seen fleeing the scene of the crime.

The Dixon assault grew into a power play between two administrations. Hill's Bar held the two accuseds; Yale had the victim laying the charge and was the scene of the crime. Both sides ignored the rules for determining who had jurisdiction which rests in the territory where the crime occurs unless and until legally changed. But before the wrangling could be settled, another crime occurred.

On Christmas Eve, a man was shot outside the very same gambling hall where the town celebration was being set up. The miner, Bernard Rice, had ordered a drink and refused to pay; the bartender, Foster, shot him. The body lay for hours in the street before it was moved inside and laid out on one of the banquet tables. Dr. Fifer was called to complete a post-mortem examination. The accused, Foster, escaped and was suspected of hiding out at Hill's Bar. The mood of festive anticipation changed to feelings of apprehension.

Judge Whannell called the Yale citizens to an emergency meeting in the Courthouse. Resolved: that Magistrate Whannell arrest the gamblers and others from across the river who had been infesting the town. Resolved: that all the gambling houses in Yale be shut down and their licences revoked. Resolved: that the Christmas party be cancelled.

Judge Whannell issued a warrant for Foster's arrest and, fearing trouble, should the Hill's Bar authorities refuse to comply, swore in forty or fifty special constables. He was interviewing witnesses to the murder, throwing some in jail, when proceedings were interrupted by a delegation from Hill's Bar with their Constable, Henry Hickson, as spokesman.

Hickson demanded that Ikey Dixon accompany them back to Hill's Bar as a witness in the trial of Farrell and Burns. Judge Whannell refused the request, saying that Farrell and Burns would be tried in Yale. Whannell then threw Hickson in jail for contempt, allegedly for using foul language and interrupting the earlier proceedings.

When news of the affront reached Hill's Bar, fifty or so of Hickson's most loyal supporters crossed the river and invaded Yale, liberated their constable, and "arrested" Judge Whannell in his own courtroom (although he later called it a kidnapping), removing him against his will, escorting him down to a waiting canoe. Placed into custody on Hill's Bar, Whannell was accused of "contempt of court" and scheduled to appear before their magistrate on the charge. Dr. Fifer insisted on accompanying Judge Whannell, riding with him in the canoe. Ikey Dixon, also from Yale, was to appear as a witness in the case against Farrell and Burns.

I was working in the kitchen in our first little house on Front Street when I witnessed a procession marching in a straggly file towards the beach. The bowler hat, the wire spectacles of Dr. Fifer crossed in front of my eyes and I dashed outside to find out what was happening. I followed them down to the beach and watched as they found enough spaces in enough canoes to take the group downriver, across to Hill's Bar.

I confess that seeing the group of men marching with prisoners took me back immediately to San Quentin, and I feared that I would never see Dr. Fifer again. I paced my kitchen all that night, and spent many hours walking the beach the next day, watching for any sign of canoes, of life, rounding Sawmill Point, the big bend below town.

To the people of Fort Yale, Hill's Bar was the snake pit. Although the duly appointed authorities had jurisdiction on their side of the river, the defiant attitude of the "Boatmen" towards Her Majesty and her laws made their neighbours suspicious. Most of the Americans on Hill's Bar favoured the oppression of the Negro race, legalized slavery, and the right of the southern states of the Union to make their own laws. Such racist attitudes made the likelihood of Ikey Dixon's receiving justice dubious at best. Furthermore, Dr. Fifer feared that Ned McGowan may have wanted to instigate a battle that could explode into a war at this time, before British troops could be deployed effectively. For these and other reasons, including Judge Whannell's limitations, Dr. Fifer decided to attend the Hill's Bar proceedings.

Although a fearful Dixon was unable to identify his attackers, Farrell and Burns were convicted and fined $75 each. Judge Whannell was convicted of contempt and fined $50, which Dr. Fifer paid with the Christmas party fund.

I have heard Judge Begbie refer to the confrontation as "Ned McGowan's war" but to me it will always be Dr. Fifer's war. He was the brave one who insisted on accompanying Dixon and Whannell, riding along in the canoe downriver into the Hill's Bar lions' den. Dr. Fifer was the one who paid the fine to satisfy McGowan and his puppet, the Hill's Bar Chief Justice Perrier, allowing Whannell to return to Yale. It was the doctor who kept the volatility to a manageable level until Judge Begbie and Colonel Moody and Captain Grant could get their Royal Engineers and Marines into place in case a show of force should prove necessary.

Back in Yale, Dr. Fifer called another emergency meeting on New Year's Eve, to decide what steps to take next to protect the town. The Hill's Bar gang under Perrier, with McGowan whispering into his ear, had committed a flagrant violation of the law; the citizens of Yale were very disturbed and did not know what to do. Judge Whannell was still shaken from the ordeal of being abducted and incarcerated. Dr. Fifer persuaded him to attend the meeting and give an account of the treatment he received at the hands of Perrier and McGowan.

Judge Whannell: "I was in Yale, presiding in court, hearing evidence on the murder of Barney Rice by William Foster, when a gang of twenty well-armed toughs, disregarding the inviolability of the court in session, barged in, shouted down the proceedings, and claimed that they themselves were the law. McGowan had them take me off the judge's bench and drag me to the beach. Dr. Fifer insisted that he come along."

Whannell struggled to recall the details: "They pushed me into one of their canoes. The Stars and Stripes were hoisted on the stern. I commented to my abductors: 'I see you are going to make a national affair out of this,' to which McGowan replied, 'Never mind,' grinning like a Cheshire cat."

Whannell's statement was an outcry of indignation: "My kidnappers took me across the river and threw me into the Hill's Bar jail. I was made to appear before their court and was perplexed to find McGowan sharing the Judge's bench as his advisor. Perrier humbled me by making me stand and lecturing me about tyrannous and illegal acts. I tried my best to explain and justify my action, but Perrier was inexorable. He listened impatiently to my defense and sentenced me as guilty of contempt of court. I was fined $50 and costs, to remain committed in jail until the judgment was complied with."

Whannell was grateful; he thanked the doctor for standing beside him. "Dr. Fifer paid the fine. Perrier took the money and retired with his friends to Paddy Martin's "Deadfall", the drinking place at Hill's Bar, where they spent the Yale Christmas fund on 'drinks all 'round'."

The crowd attending the meeting began to murmur, discussing the magistrate's report amongst themselves. The apprehension of Judge Whannell was a serious offence which could not be allowed to pass. It was defiance of the rule of law. It was flagrant disrespect, treating Her Majesty's official representative in such a way. If it could happen to the magistrate, none of them were safe. Resolved: that a courier with an account of the outrage inflicted on British sovereignty be dispatched to Victoria, "begging His Excellency to afford prompt aid." They were confident Governor Douglas would agree, and would deploy Colonel Moody and his Royal Engineers whose ship had docked in Esquimalt on Christmas Day.

Ned McGowan, it was said, prepared to defend Hill's Bar while making strategic plans to take Fort Yale and Fort Hope, and then to retreat into Washington territory. From the safety of the United States, he would clamour for annexation of the gold fields, up to the 54th parallel, the Alaskan border, Russian territory.

Her Majesty to the Rescue.

Colonel Moody mobilized twenty-two of his sappers. Accompanied by Judge Begbie, Dr. Mitchell, a military doctor, and Captain Grant of the Royal Engineers, the sappers proceeded on the *Enterprise*, through snow, sleet, and ice, as far as Fort Hope. Here they paused, waiting for further reports from the trouble spot, Yale. Rumours swirled: that the situation had worsened; that the Hill's Bar mob had murdered Whannell and his constable; that the colony would be invaded.

Colonel Moody decided on a cautious approach. Leaving his troops behind at Hope and proceeding to Yale by himself, demonstrating considerable personal courage, he arrived in Yale on a Sunday morning with plans to pour oil on troubled waters. After holding morning church service in the courthouse, after a benediction of "God bless us every one!", the colonel proceeded to Hill's Bar where he managed to turn McGowan's animosity into a party of "brandy and cigars." Perrier he fired on the spot, for "straining a point of legal dignity."

The mastermind behind the kidnapping had been Ned McGowan who had had Perrier appoint him a Special Constable and had used that position to take down another of "the stranglers." To many of the rowdy Hill's Bar residents, the abduction of Whannell was a practical joke, an entertainment, even part of the rivalry between two small towns. Ned McGowan gloated; they had goaded the law. He was surprised by and resented the sympathy and support the Yale people showed for their judge who, in Ned's eyes, had only received his just deserts. McGowan was sore also at Dr. Fifer, for calling and presiding at the town meetings. He attempted to undermine the local elected authorities by misconstruing their activities, by labeling it as a revival of vigilantism, this time on British soil. However, the arrival of a British military force, with a colonel backing the townspeople, put everything in a new light.

On January 16, 1859, a Sunday, Ned McGowan crossed the

Fraser River to Yale. He walked up the beach and stopped in at Ovid Allard's, perhaps for a New Year's drop of brandy, perhaps for a smile and a wink from the beautiful Miss Lucy.

Ned McGowan opened the door to Allard's store only to be faced by his sworn rival, Dr. Fifer. Conversation stopped abruptly; the doctor stepped aside to allow McGowan to pass. Miss Lucy interceded, pulling McGowan to her side.

Lucy Allard: "Mr. McGowan dislikes Dr. Fifer and is suspicious of everything he does. 'That black'ard is bad-mouthing me, I can tell!' he whispered. I answered 'They have been talking about you. The doctor says you were defying the law; he called you a thief and a murderer; he says you organized the kidnapping of Judge Whannell.' Hearing these allegations from my lips, I think, forced Mr. McGowan to take a stand. He could not, in front of me, allow this insult to pass. He puffed up; his buttons nearly burst in anger. Pretending self-control, he said icily to the doctor, 'Please step outside.' He was pretending to be courteous; he opened the door and Dr. Max passed in front of him. I wanted to scream, 'Max, don't. Please, don't go!' but I was afraid and could say nothing. I followed them out the door."

"And what did you see, Miss Lucy, outside your father's store?"

"Once outside the house, on the street, they faced each other. Both wore revolvers, but neither attempted to draw. Out in the open, for everyone to hear, Ned, Mr. McGowan, yelled loudly. 'You, sir, are slandering me, without any cause. My patience is at an end. I am pissed off with you, Fifer. You are nothing but a second-rate hospital orderly, masquerading as a medical doctor.' Then he grabbed Max, Doctor Fifer, and knocked him around. He spit in his face and then beat him up. Other witnesses were watching on the street; someone said they were going to run and get Colonel Moody."

Colonel Moody: "To me, McGowan's assault upon Fifer was a serious transgression. Here was a known outlaw from the United States brazenly attacking a Yale resident on British territory. This was no longer a practical joke; this was a challenge, showing contempt of British authority and of me, its military commanding officer, in the full knowledge that I was practically next door, and that twenty of my sappers were standing by at Fort Hope. I realized I had been too soft with this troublemaker during our first palaver. From here on, I determined to proceed more formally."

"And what did 'more formally' entail, Sir?"

"It was a Sunday evening. I dispatched Lieutenant Mayne who had accompanied me, in a canoe manned by Natives, down the river to Hope, in the dark, through slabs of floating ice. Their boat passed the flickering lights of Hill's Bar unseen. I suspect every man was in the 'Deadfall.' They had not posted sentries. At Hope, Lieutenant Mayne passed my message to Captain Grant who made his way back up the river with his men that same night. In the late daylight of January 17, the miners of Hill's Bar wakened to a company of very efficient soldiers, tired but quite prepared for action, lined up in their muddy street with rifles and fixed bayonets. I had sent word downriver for further reinforcements of sappers and bluejackets to be mobilized from Fort Langley."

"And, was your show of force successful, Colonel Moody?"

"Ay. We made our point. No shots were fired. The next day, McGowan and his associates were brought before Judge Begbie in Fort Yale on two charges. To the accusations of 'jail break' and 'assault on Judge Whannell,' Mr. McGowan argued that he had merely executed a warrant while properly appointed as special constable under the authority of Chief Justice (since dismissed) Perrier. Judge Begbie and I concurred that he had us there. The charges were dismissed. For the second indictment, 'assault and battery' on Dr. Max Fifer, citizen of Yale, there was no defense. McGowan pleaded guilty and was duly fined. One of his cronies paid the fine."

"Well, Sir, was this the end of the hostilities?"

"Yes, so it seems. Mr. McGowan did attempt to make me a gift of a keg of brandy after his court proceedings. However, with an eye to the appearance of conflict of interest, I returned the keg but accepted an invitation to christen it with him the next day, on Hill's Bar."

"And did you do that, Sir?"

"Share the brandy with him? I regret, the next day I seemed to have contracted the ague, or the influenza. However, Judge Begbie accepted the invitation and expressed my regrets. He asked that our appointment be rescheduled, to which Mr. McGowan agreed."

"Did anything further come of your showdown with the 'ubiquitous' Ned McGowan?"

"I believe the most significant bit of information came to me by way of Judge Begbie upon his return from the Hill's Bar festivities the next day. He had indeed joined in the libations, but could by no means keep up with McGowan and his friends. After consuming more than could be healthy for any man, McGowan felt at ease enough on his home territory, you might say, to let the judge in on how clever he really was. Perhaps sly is the better word.

"'Yer know, Jedge, ya almost had me there, when ya offered to make me a subject of Her Majesty right then and there. Called m' bluff, ya could say. I was trying to turn around midstream without tipping my canoe. All m' blustering about being loyal to Her Majesty and respecting Her Majesty's laws was so much hot air, blowing it out m' arse. If you'd a made me a subject then and there, I'd have no credibility left, here, with m' boys, m' American and Irish-American compatriots here on Hill's Bar.'

"The man admitted to the judge's face, that his profession of loyalty had just been a line, saying what he had to say in that situation. The man actually bragged to the Judge that he had lied to us! Judge Begbie reported to me that we had been duped, that McGowan indeed was a scoundrel whose silver tongue was forked."

Thus, although it took some months, Dr. Fifer's dire warnings were heeded, and the newcomers at least began to see Ned McGowan for the bully he truly is. Perhaps Dr. Fifer felt that this sacrifice—his drawing McGowan's fire, being victimized himself—was worth it. I did my best to assist that day, swabbing the abrasions on his hands and face, cleaning the stains from his coat; mending the tear in his trousers, and trying to straighten the wire frames of his spectacles. In the days following the assault, while his face was still one giant plum-coloured bruise, the doctor stayed close to the house, avoiding the stares and the miners' rude ribbing. Although he did continue to see patients and to attend the evening council meetings, he did not return to full practice until the swelling had faded and the yellowing had almost disappeared.

The Final Confrontation

It was after the trial for McGowan's assault on the doctor that Judge Begbie placed Chartres Brew in charge of the police, to better the security in Yale. To Mr. Brew, McGowan was "a bad fellow who can only be restrained by fear."

In this conflict between outlaw Americans and the British Crown, Dr. Fifer was both a player and, involuntarily, a sacrificial pawn. It was to the credit of Colonel Moody's *suaviter in modo, fortiter in re*, his initially conciliatory but later decisive action, that the colony did not burst into open hostilities.

The shaky peace lasted all of four weeks. Violence broke out again at the George Washington birthday celebration. Ned McGowan, perhaps in an effort to patch up relations with the Yale citizens who had missed out on their Christmas party, who had funded "drinks on the house at Hill's Bar" with the $50 fine, Ned organized another opportunity to celebrate. George Washington's Birthday, February 22, is an American holiday. Old Ned and his Hill's Bar cronies decided to host a banquet and dance in Yale.

While he was seated at the head table in one of the gambling houses in Yale, as the townspeople were filing in to enjoy a feast and dance, one of the younger miners taunted McGowan. "Hey,

Old Man, don't' you think you're getting too old to reel in the young ladies?" McGowan replied in his usual manner, his impulse swifter perhaps because of the whisky. He pulled out his pistol and fired. The younger man ducked most of the bullet, diving for cover behind a tipped table. The hall emptied quickly; the magistrate was nowhere to be found, although poor Mrs. Whannell was standing straight in terror, alone, in the far corner of the hall. Dr. Fifer attended the patient who was wounded only slightly.

After a frantic search, Judge Whannell was found cowering beneath his wife's enormous skirts. It is said that he never fully recovered from his abduction to Hill's Bar. However, it is also said that Mrs. Whannell, defending her man, claimed that "His Worship's" erratic behaviour was a result of a sabre blow to the head which Mr. Whannell had received during the Crimean War.

Some say this last public display gave Police Chief Brew the ammunition he needed to hassle Ned McGowan out of town. Perhaps it was the legal technicality, that Ned had breached his recognizance, his promise to Judge Begbie to respect the Queen's laws and keep her peace. That is possible, but there is also a less public possibility.

One evening that first winter (after the trial, but I cannot remember whether it was before or after the George Washington dance), after dark, I opened the door to Chief Inspector Brew in the company of another man, obviously in pain. I led the two men to the examining room and went to fetch Dr. Fifer. The patient was Edward McGowan. Poor Ned had been in distress since the early morning, in a most embarrassing pain. By noon he could hardly walk. With Chief Brew's moral and physical support (by this point Ned did not care who would ease his pain, be he friend or foe) they sought Dr. Fifer's help.

Dr. Fifer took a few minutes for the *diagnostic*. He inspected the patient's painful area and saw a diffuse bulging mass below the umbilicus, above the symphysis pubis. Palpation of the abdomen confirmed extreme suprapubic tenderness, and percussion, tapping the finger against it, revealed the dull resonance of a very full bladder, near the point of bursting. McGowan had contracted an infection of the urethra, resulting in a stricture. He was unable to pass water; immediate release of the pressure was required, or the bladder would rupture, with fatal consequences.

To relieve the symptom, Dr. Fifer carefully probed the urethra with a blunt, soft silver wire until he felt resistance, noting that the obstruction was in the distal urethra. He advanced the probe gently past the stricture and then left it in place. For lack of a catheter, he used a quill, softened in a strong solution of potash, which he threaded over the guide wire, advancing it through the narrowed urethra, past the *stenosis*, the point of constriction, until he felt the gratifying trickle of warm urine running over his hands. The patient, initially a suffering human in submissive misery, expressed his relief from the near-mortal pain and regained his imperious composure.

The doctor advised McGowan that the stricture, the consequence of social disease, would require further stretching, dilatation, in order to allow urine to pass freely. McGowan, who must have realized that he could have died, from a burst bladder or from the infection, had he not submitted to the treatment by Dr. Fifer, his enemy, one of 'the stranglers', was nothing but grateful. The payment he offered Dr. Fifer was courteously declined. The two old enemies parted with a handshake witnessed by Police Inspector Brew. Dr. Fifer laughed when he heard later how Brew had claimed to the Governor that he was responsible for the momentous act of reconciliation of the two arch-adversaries: "I made McGowan apologize and shake hands with Dr. Fifer."

I think it was after this appointment, which was obviously viewed differently by all three men involved, that Ned McGowan knew he had been bested. In spite of all the wrongs, the personal affronts, the assaults on himself and his friends, Dr. Fifer was still able to maintain his professional objectivity and treat an enemy as a patient, with the same care as anyone else. McGowan realized that his violent and libellous attacks would never succeed in bringing the doctor down to his own lawyer level. Soon we heard that Ned McGowan had sold off his claim and was planning to leave the colony.

Others say that it was the hard work on the claims, and the cold of that first winter, and the violation of his promise to keep the peace that led to Ned's departure. On February 26, 1859, he sold his claim for $500, saying he wanted to join his son in Mexico. He left Hill's Bar on March 4, in the company of his assistant, "Major" Tom Dolan. Banta, and a fourth partner, Raines accompanied them.

On their way south, McGowan and his entourage stopped at Fort Hope, taking Colonel Moody up on his promise to share the brandy. Their trip downriver, to Fort Langley, to stopping houses en route, was shadowed by rumours of Jules David's threatened revenge. It is said that Ned McGowan continued to brag as he departed the colony: "Fifty-two years old. Carrying $4700 cash. Not bad for an old man."

When I suggested to Dr. Fifer some time later that his own professional attitude had won out, that McGowan knew he had been defeated, the doctor expressed skepticism. "I think you are being too generous, Ah Chung. Men like McGowan see goodness only as weakness. He is a man without a conscience, and no doctor can cure that. As they used to say of him back in San Francisco: 'The only thing good about Ned McGowan is his horse.'"

Another time Dr. Fifer confessed that meeting men like McGowan had changed his mind about democracy. "Ned made me realize that there are some men not motivated by goodwill, or by doing what is best for the greatest number. Our system must protect us, the good people, from selfish self-interest and the machinations of criminal minds like McGowan's. Good laws are our only protection against such evil." I think that was later though, after we moved to this house. Maybe even after Lady Franklin's visit, which seemed to upset him so much.

These ghosts of yesteryears have appeared and reappeared as if I myself were Mr. Scrooge of the Christmas Carol Dr. Fifer read to me every year. Spending so much time alone here, lost in the dusty past, my dreams too are troubled. Last night, it was the specter of my own grandfather, wearing curious bent-wire spectacles, chiding me with one of his unending supply of adages: "He who seeks revenge, Ah Chung, should dig two graves." Then, the shade of Ned McGowan, still grinning, laughing, wafted in. Deliberately refusing the warning of the proverb, Old Ned responded: "That, sir, can be arranged."

9

CLIPPINGS

September 18.—This day, about eight o'clock, the body of a man floating in the Fraser River was found by two Indians and towed to a sand bar, situated at a point 4 miles above. These facts were made known to Mr. E.C. Johnson, agent of Ballou's Express at Yale and recently appointed by Governor Douglas as deputy collector of licences at 5% commission with expenses.

Johnson at once proceeded to the place indicated above, usurping the prerogative of a coroner, he empanelled a jury with J.W. Rebe, foreman, R.B. Lovejoy, John Miers, J.J. Riley, James Enid, Matthew Hontis, Carl Dean, A. Warner, Thomas Blackburn, A.H. Sargent, E. Champlain, and T. Van Vechtan, to investigate the facts into the cause of death.

The autopsy report completed by Dr. M. W. Fifer, the well-known San Francisco physician, recently arrived in Yale, confirmed death by unnatural causes, based on the following findings:

In consideration of the sodden condition of the skin on the palms and soles, the body had been in the water for about ten days, he was naked from the waist up and had on a torn pair of pantaloons. On his right arm was marked, in India ink, J & I, and underneath a cross on a pedestal, and on the left arm a representation, worked in India ink, of Eve's temptation in the Garden of Eden. Estimated height 5 feet 8 inches; age, 40 years.

Judging from the external appearance of a wound between his eyes, the deceased came to his death from a bullet, discharged from a gun or pistol in the hands of some unknown party. He was dead before disposed in the river; the body was in an advanced state of putrification in spite of the low water temperature of the Fraser River.

The jury confirmed that the person had come to his death by unnatural causes.

The Daily Alta California Dec 3, 1857, City Items: "Using Obscene Language. -The Jackson Street offenders are in constant fear, through the vigilance of that indefatigable officer, Mr. Clarke, who never suffers one of them to indulge in a horse race or in a buggy ride, without arresting them for furious riding or driving, and who never hears one of them speak loud, or use a vulgar epithet, but like a faithful guardian of the rustic peace and morals, he seizes the offender and brings him or her before that terror of evildoers, Judge Coon. Yesterday, Clarke brought before the Court a notorious woman named Johanna Maguire, who, it appeared, had been guilty of very indecent language upon the public street, in their presence and hearing of sundry persons passing. Judge Coon fined her ten Dollars."

A scrap of paper, found tacked to the side wall of the Hudson's Bay store at Hope:

"henery fawler, Tomus Brumfield, Fat Charley and Crab Ware hev gon tu Fort Yale with doc Fifer."

"The usual method of separating the mercury from the gold is to press the amalgam in a piece of linen cloth doubled, whereby most of the quicksilver that has entered into the amalgam escapes. The mass remaining in the cloth is put into a frying pan and heated, and the mercury passes off in a vapour. A little mercury is lost in this way, but the loss is so small as not to be cared for now, but the time will come when the miners will be more economical. The mercury is generally driven off in the cabins, and over the fire where the cooking is done. This appears imprudent to me, for the mercury condenses as soon as it gets cold, and in consequence of that it must collect about the chimney, and whenever a strange fire is made it is liable to be volatile again, thus keeping up kind of a mercurial atmosphere. It is to such imprudence that most of the numerous cases of sore eyes in the mines are to be attributed."

The *Victoria Gazette* "Almost a shooting.- Yesterday, Myers P. Truett and McGowan met outside Bailey's Hotel. McGowan shouted: 'There goes one of the bloody stranglers', at the same time drawing his revolver. Truett drew his; a large crowd instantly collected, the Vigilantes, largely in the majority, sided with Truett. High words took place, but there was no shooting; mutual friends interfered, parting the combatants."

Truett, Vigilance Committee executive, president of the Victoria Hook and Ladder Fire Department: "On my return from Fraser River I was informed that Edward McGowan had arrived in Victoria about the 5th. That he had used disrespectful language towards me, 'that he would take the life of the strangler,' or words to that effect. During the evening, near Bailey's Hotel, as I was passing, I saw Edward McGowan. I stepped up to him and asked if he had made such remark, or threats; He replied, "that he had not." On my approach towards him, he, thinking that I was going to attack him, as I have been informed, drew his pistol, muzzle down and by his side; thus the affair ended."

Alta California, Sep 26, 1858: - "Governor Douglas is still up the river, making arrangements for winter operations. On his way up in the steamer he had for fellow passengers, among others, Ned McGowan and some of his confreres. Opposite the mouth of Harrison River, night came on, and the steamer was detained until the next morning, owing to the dangerous navigation. There being a small station there, His Excellency went ashore to sleep, and just before his departure, on being informed that the boat would start at six in the morning, he intimated that he could not get up, eat breakfast, and be ready before nine. The captain did not think it proper to enforce punctuality, and the boat was to have been detained. Early next morning McGowan and his friends went on shore and the former entering his Excellency's tent, aroused him with something like the following familiar address: "Hallo Gov'! Steam's up, and the boiler's a humming old fellow. O-h Gov! Wake up here," & c., & c., until the Governor, not choosing to notice the insult, arose and proceeded on board the boat, when the trip was continued. Several gentlemen, who were along, as a suite, were justly indignant at the proceeding, but the number of McGowan's par prevented any retaliation. The arrival in the interior, of such a party, will scarcely tend to improve the social aspect there."

Received: from the Yale Town Council: *Victoria Gazette* to attend. The newspaper, in the edition of 23 December 1858, acknowledged:
"Christmas Ball at Fort Yale.
We acknowledge receipt of an invitation to attend a ball to be

given in the Court House of Fort Yale, on Christmas Eve, from the Committee of the Arrangements: Capt. J.B. Whannell, Hugh Nelson, M.W. Fifer, MD, and John Kurtz."

Victoria *British Colonist* "through the kindness of Mr. Tennent: "On the 24th of December, Christmas Eve, Bernard (Barney) Rice, "a stalwart young Irishman" from a short distance above Fort Yale, was shot by William Foster in front of his saloon. Rice had entered Bennett's saloon and called for a drink. When served, he refused to pay and walked out. The barkeeper, one Foster, followed him and as the miner moved off, shot him dead in cold blood. The body fell on the snow in the street and lay there for some hours. This was a dreadful murder, thought to be the culmination of the iniquity, which the criminals had been heaping up for many months, and there were calls for the forming of a vigilance committee, San Francisco style, to take charge of the town and drive the evildoers out. A great excitement arose and the magistrate, issued a warrant for Foster and swore in 40 or 50 constables. Foster escaped and has not since been located.

The *British Colonist* of January 8. 1859, reported: "At Yale, an unprovoked attack on a coloured person was made by two gamblers from Hill's Bar who after snapping their pistols at him, beat him unmercifully and then absconded to their settlement across the river. This outrage caused great excitement, and at a meeting the local citizens decided to assist the law in keeping the gamblers out and close all gambling establishments. When the Hill's Bar gang learned of the measures, they took offence and promptly retaliated. Like a bombshell, they arrived unexpectedly in Yale with their constable, Henry Hickson, who openly confronted the Judge, using very foul language. Whannell, with the backing of his people, took action and promptly had the constable arrested. Within an hour, a party of 45 men from Hill's Bar, many of them hard cases, previously sentenced to transportation by the Vigilante Committee in San Francisco, crossed the river, climbed up the beach to Front Street, broke into the jail and liberated Constable Hickson. The intruders then entered the courtroom, interrupted a murder trial in session, seized Judge Whannell, and abducted him to Hill's Bar. The next day he was made to appear before the Hill's Bar court presided over by Justice Perrier, with the notorious Ned McGowan at his side. After hearing Constable Hickson's testimony the court fined Whannell $50 and costs which was paid. He was then permitted to return to Yale."

Henry Hickson's rebuttal of the newspaper report: "Not so, piped Henry Hickson, the Hill's Bar constable, in his letter to the editor of the newspaper, "the statements are untrue. On the twenty-first of December a man named Farrell from Hill's Bar went into a barbershop in Fort Yale, kept by a coloured man named Isaac Dixon, to purchase a bottle of hair oil. Some angry words passed between Farrell and Dixon; they afterwards began to fight when a man named Burns, a friend of Farrell's, came to fetch him. The coloured man got pistol-beaten but no shot was fired and no pistol hammer was snapped."

"A complaint was made by Dixon, the barber, against Farrell and Burns before Justice Whannell. The Justice issued a warrant for their arrest."

"Whannell's officer was not able to make the arrest. Then the warrant was endorsed by Mr. Perrier, the Justice at Hill's Bar, and passed on to me to make the arrest. In the mean time Farrell and Burns gave themselves up to me at Hill's Bar and were taken before Justice Perrier. I went to Fort Yale with a summons from Justice Perrier for Dixon, the barber, to appear as witness to prosecute Farrell and Burns. On arriving at Fort Yale, I asked permission from Justice

Whannell to take Dixon to Hill's Bar which was refused, and Justice Whannell requested that I bring the two prisoners to Yale to be tried before him. He refused to acknowledge Justice Perrier's summons for Dixon. Mr. Whannell stated that it would be my duty to bring the prisoners before him."

"Whannell then asked me did I not consider him, a Justice of Peace, my superior? I told him that I did not, upon which Whannell had me placed in prison for contempt of court. Whereupon my Justice Perrier at Hill's Bar issued a warrant for the arrest of his brother justice Whannell at Yale for contempt of his court, for having arrested his constable. The warrant for Whannell's arrest was given to a man named Francis Kelly.

Whannell complied with the warrant and went along quietly to Hill's Bar, not having been bullied or dragged out of the court house as stated by clerk Tennent. The next day I went to Yale for the barber Dixon and took him to Hill's Bar to charge Farrell and Burns. They were fined $75, including costs, for striking Dixon with a pistol on the head. Dixon was not able to identify his attackers and the matter was acquitted. Thus, Mr. Editor, ended the great storm in a teapot. Very likely the difficulty would not have occurred had it not been for Whannell's overbearing manner which together with his want of legal knowledge and gentlemanly deportment, makes him totally unfit for the office he has been appointed to, being more fit for a constable than a magistrate at Yale." Signed - "Henry Hickson, Constable at Hill's Bar."

"Almost a shooting.- Yesterday, Myers P. Truett and McGowan met outside Bailey's Hotel. McGowan shouted: 'There goes one of the bloody stranglers', at the same time drawing his revolver. Truett drew his; a large crowd instantly collected, the Vigilantes, largely in the majority, sided with Truett. High words took place, but there was no shooting; mutual friends interfered, parting the combatants."

Truett, previously a member of the San Francisco Vigilance Committee executive, was recently appointed president of the Victoria Hook and Ladder Fire Department. Out of concern for his good name in the community, he published a denouement of the affair with McGowan: "On my return from Fraser River I was informed that Edward McGowan had arrived in Victoria about the 5th. That he had used disrespectful language towards me, 'that he would take the life of the strangler,' or words to that effect. During the evening, near Bailey's Hotel, as I was passing, I saw Edward McGowan. I stepped up to him and asked if he had made such remark, or threats; He replied, "that he had not." On my approach towards him, he, thinking that I was going to attack him, as I have been informed, drew his pistol, muzzle down and by his side; thus the affair ended."

Fort Hope: the Hudson's Bay post, in front of the store. Ex-policeman Charles Cook from San Francisco, Vigilance member number 1875, the very fellow who had arrested and delivered McGowan to the henchmen. Here, on British soil, they were equals, and he would get even with this ball squeezer. In no time they had Cook down on the ground, under his boot. Obligingly, the "strangler" spilled the whole story about his Vigilance membership: "I joined on the second day after the shooting of James King. I could not get registered on the first day, the crowd was so great. My reason for signing up was to unite with something that would put down the shooting in the streets, the robbing, thieving, swindling and all that sort of thing, which the courts could not or would not stop or punish. I did not know how long the organization was to continue, I only hoped it would last till the great evil, under which they all laboured, would be corrected."

The *London Times* published a regular column about Yale. The paper reported that on the whole, there has not been much crime in the mines. A few murders which were promptly taken cognizance of, and the murderer punished; another man charged with a similar offence is now about to be tried by due course of law. Insufficient as the legal machinery is, no punishment takes place except by its agency.

Of the newspapers covering the 1858 Gold Rush, the *London Times* had superbly kept up-to-date and even despatched a special correspondent, Donald Fraser, to the scene. His report, dated 21 August of that year, made the headlines; the article, fresh out of Fort Yale, the epicentre of the action, garnered the better part of the *Times* front page:

"I arrived at this place nearly two weeks ago, and a steamer being about to leave for Victoria, I have only time to write a few lines to catch the mail which leaves for San Francisco and Europe on the 5th proximo. My letter of July last described the troubles between the gold-seekers and the Indians. Firearms and firewater fed the flames of incipient trouble, and soon the natives became so threatening that the whites were forced to flee for their lives from the canyons. Some, who were unable to escape, were killed, and their bodies, in some instances scalped, even decapitated, were seen floating down the turbulent river. The local Hudson's Bay manager, Allard, has no news and believes that the reports are exaggerated since the local Indians here are a peaceful people, but the American gold-diggers became impatient and a band of private US militia, about twenty men, are expected here, to move north for a punitive expedition to the Rancherias between Lytton and Boston Bar to teach the natives a lesson, as one of them expressed it, that "the only good Indians are the dead ones."

"Friday last was unusually cold, with a sprinkling of snow on the mountains. While the local Hudson's Bay clerk had retired, his wife and a visitor, the local doctor, were sitting with their very sick child, when a crowd of black guards (Capt. Snyder's), had proceeded to the Hudson's Bay post, noisily hammered at the door and demanded arms and ammunition to go and fight the Indians. Allard got out of bed, went to the door and told them he would not admit a mob into his house, neither would he give arms or anything else, under threats such as were being made by the enlightened "deputation," that if they broke into the house they would do so at their own peril; but that, as both he and his guest, the doctor, a veteran of the Mexican war, were armed, the first man who entered, and likely enough the second, would be shot; that as the doctor was attending to a very sick child in the house, with his wife alarmed and other children disturbed, he begged they would make less noise. He added that if they retired and sent a reasonable deputation of their number, say two or three, he would admit it and see what could be done. This suggestion was adopted and Allard counted out a number of rifles - which wouldn't go off and be a flash in the pan at best, as he candidly told them. Taking a receipt for a total of twenty muskets, he closed the door and joined his wife and the doctor in their bedside vigil."

"I may write more fully and be in time to catch the same mail, which will take this letter from San Francisco.

Your obedient Servant,

Donald Fraser,

Special correspondent."

NY Times Oct 1858: "Governor Douglas returned from his trip up river, having had no difficulties with miners or gamblers, simply because he made no issue with them. A little inquiry satisfied him that it would be useless to attempt to punish. The gamblers kept quiet while he was at Fort Yale, and the governor winked at their iniquities. Soon as he had left, however, everything went on just as before, and the gamblers and the rum sellers had affairs their own way."

Governor Douglas had the Provincial Secretary Mr. Young write to the Yale town Council, proposing steps for an easier way to get to Yale. He stated "that he was interested in the cutting of a road from Hope to Yale."

(*Victoria Gazette* of 7 September 1858: "Gov. D. arrived in Fort Hope on Wednesday night. It is said that the Governor was busying himself and taking a lively interest in the cutting of a trail from Fort Hope to Fort Yale.")

Captain Welch of the steamer *Wilson G. Hunt* received an interesting letter, signed by Thomas Yorke of Yale. The Captain wasted no time in taking it to the *Victoria Colonist* who promptly, on the next day, 29 May 1860, published that Doctor Fifer of Yale had been challenged to a duel with a McSerly of Hill's Bar, previously a member of the Law and Order party in San Francisco, that during the duel, at a distance of thirty paces; with the first fire McSerly received a ball through his hat, and the doctor was shot in the neck. McSerly was said to have escaped across the river, back to Hill's Bar.

Dr. Fifer demanded a prompt retraction and the *Colonist* printed a refutation; the June 9, 1860 issue reported that the information was without the least foundation of truth.

The adverse publicity against the doctor was Thomas Yorke's attempt to slight his good name. Regardless, Fifer continued unshaken in his role of doctor and councilor of the town of Yale, caring for the well being of the community.

British Colonist: "Terrible Catastrophe." Flags in Victoria were lowered to half-mast at the news. An eyewitness on the shore, Magistrate Peter O'Reilly, gave an account of the disaster:

"On April 14, taking advantage of an adequate water level, the S.S. *Yale* was on her way up to Yale. In full splendour, to the chagrin of the people of Hope, she had departed after taking on passengers at Hope at 4:30 of Easter Sunday, when half an hour later a loud report was heard which, together with the crash, resembled a heavy blow upon a sharp sounding Chinese gong. Her boiler burst as the steamer was going over Union Bar Riffle, about one half mile above Hope. The wreck became buried in the silt and sand of the river, some miles below Hope."

Mr. McFie, a passenger on the *Yale*, described the incident: "A succession of rapids is the most signal impediment offered to the navigation of the brief interval between Forts Hope and Yale. In illustration of the strength of the current to be overcome, it may be noticed that, while it takes but half an hour to descend to Hope, six hours are occupied in ascending by high-pressure steamers thence to Yale. Our steamer happened to be the first that attempted the passage beyond Hope that year. The struggle was so intense on our reaching the gurgle of the rapids that, with a pressure of steam greatly beyond that allowed by law, for twenty minutes no ascending motion was perceptible. The captain, a reckless American, with other men on board betting, became intensely excited (under the influence of liquor) as to the issue of the dangerous experiment. Some were foolhardy enough to lay a wager that an explosion would take place, he cooly discussed the experience they would have when blown into the air. At the critical moment, while the question remained undecided as to whether the rapid or the steamer would win, a pipe connected with the boiler burst, and was regarded as the infallible precursor of our common destruction. The cabin floor raised and then fell in, at the same time, the hurricane roof fell upon us, cutting our heads more or less, and blocking up all means of escape towards the forward of the dinner table. All quickly made for the windows and doors in the after part of the cabin, and got to the roof of the hurricane house, and there beheld a scene that baffles all descriptions, and such as I trust I may never witness again."

Those killed were Joseph Growler, Joel Osburn, fireman, and a coloured person, name unascertained. Samuel Powers, a blacksmith of Hope, was blown up in the air against a rock, gashing his brains out, and when found the body was perfectly naked. The body of the cook, although seen in the cookhouse, was not recovered. There was a report that seven Chinamen were aboard and six lost. Others say there were only three aboard and one of them was saved.

Of the passengers, Messrs. Langley, Stevens, and several others were cut in the head and face and bled freely. Some of the injured crew were James Ellison, boatman of Hope, who was carried up into the air to a great height and then plummeted into the water. Engineer McGreary who was in the engine room injured his arm. Mr. Smith, the mate, was standing on the guards by the side of the boiler and was blown over board. Thomas King, a deck hand, was blown into the water and lost his leg below the knee. He afterwards had the stump of bone sawed off by Dr. Bradshaw of Hope, assisted by Dr. Oliver, a fellow passenger. It is feared, however, that King will die."

10

CORRESPONDENCE

Draft

M. W. Fifer, M.D.

to Governor James Douglas, Fort Victoria, Vancouver Island

RE: Medical Services to Indigent Patients

1859

Proposed:

"The Undersigned, being aware of the fact that no proper provisions have been made by Her Majesty's Government, for the medical care of indigent sick in this district, would respectfully submit the following proposal, viz:

- to take medical charge, in all cases of sickness or injury, on all such persons that may become chargeable to Her Majesty's Government
- to furnish the necessary drugs and medicines
- to hold all postmortem examinations within the close environs of Yale,
- for a monthly salary of one hundred dollars (or twenty pounds Sterling)."

"In connection the Undersigned would respectfully state, that he is 36 years of age, and has been in active practice of medicine and surgery for the past 14 years, and is well and favorably known in the city of San Francisco (California) and to members of the inhabitants of this district."

"All of which is herewith respectfully submitted."

Annotation:

Acknowledged: by provincial secretary, Mr. W.A.G. Young, "the proposition will meet with due consideration"

Notes

25 August 1860

Yale Town Council Special Meeting, Reverend Burton Crickmer, Doctor Max William Fifer:

RE: the abuse of liquor and its catastrophic after effects.
- the destructive result of alcohol inebriation
- concern for the health and the social life of the Natives
- Governor Douglas' Liquor Bill had been introduced in the legislature and passed unanimously
- the proclamation "forbidding the sale or gift of intoxicants to Natives" posted conspicuously at the Gold Commissioner's office
- enforcing the law is another problem entirely

Conflicts between the local immigrants and the neighbouring Yale Indian Reserve detail all the evils flowing therefrom to the detriment of the morals of the white inhabitants' families with children we wish to encourage the influx of more.

We wish broad vice and immorality to be banished from the daily, yes, hourly, sight of the offspring of their race.

This close neighbourhood of the Indians to us has been of manifold evil to the Natives themselves. The women have become more vile and depraved than heretofore.

The men,. with a view to gratifying their desire for liquor, often yield their wives' and daughters' virtue to the seducer.

Already the prey of a filthy disease that will leave its traces on future generations.

For the sake of humanity and Christianity We beseech Your Excellency to give us a hand "aid in saving these unfortunate beings from their otherwise inevitable disgrace and ruination."

Recommendations:

1) the Natives' removal to a suitable point below Yale, for winter quarters

2) the Town Council's introduction of a curfew restricting the Indians from visiting the town after certain hours of the day.

Precedents:

1) At Fort Hope, the Indians occupying the north part of the town agreed to resettlement and compensation in form of land

2) They moved to the Chawathl Indian Reserve, eight miles down river, on the opposite bank of the Fraser.

3) On the shore of the inner Victoria Harbour,

4) Governor Douglas leased the land to individual parties and applied the proceeds to the general benefit of the Natives involved.

We, the Yale Town Council, expect a similar solution of the problems in Yale.

Annotation:

Governor Douglas's Response: "The presence of Indians near the town is a 'public inconvenience,' but their violent removal would be neither just nor politic. The government is bound by the faith of a solemn agreement to protect them in the enjoyment of their village sites and cultivated fields."

1859

Max William Fifer, M.D

To Colonel Richard Moody, Royal Engineers, New Westminster, British Columbia

RE: Medical Services to Royal Engineers

I advised Sergeant Major Conn to return private Colston who was yesterday accidentally injured, to the care of Dr. Seddall, R.E.

I forwarded some time ago my account for medical services and medicines - in the case of Private Sturtridge - to Dr. Seddall and have not even received a notice of the receipt of the same.

I must confess that under the circumstances, it was with some hesitation on my part, that I answered to the call yesterday. I admit that I have done very little in these cases; I have not amputated part of a finger that ought to be amputated. But had there been other than cases of injury requiring some little attention at the time of occurrence, I should not have answered to the calls. As I will not attend, for I get not common courtesy in return for my services. I address this line to you, Sir, solely for the motive of defining my position.

With high regards for you and your family.

July, 1859

Yale Town Council

Governor James Douglas, Fort Victoria, Vancouver Island

RE: Road Navigation, South

The Town Council has taken His Excellency the Governor's recommendation into consideration, and would respectfully submit:

We concede: That a road from Fort Hope to Yale would be of individual benefit to the inhabitants of Yale; but it would not in the least benefit the inhabitants of the Colony above Yale.

The Council therefore respectfully recommends to His Excellency that for the present only such roads be constructed, as will be conducive to the highest welfare of the Colony, by promoting the best interests of the largest number of its inhabitants, viz: the miners.

Notes:

Yale Town Council

Governor James Douglas, Fort Victoria, Vancouver Island

RE: Government Contract, ferry services at Spuzzum common knowledge—price gouging, improper business practices

- Frank Way making barrels of money by gouging the miners with high tolls for taking them and their effects across Fraser River.
- Like Charon, Frank Way, for two dollars instead of the lawfully set fee of fifty cents a head, takes the ignorant miners across the Fraser into the uncertain promises of the gold fields.

• immoral exploitation of Orinda Hicks

Earlier this month, at the request of Governor Douglas, the council contracted Frank Way for another job: to explore, inspect and report on a practicable alternative trail from Yale to Boston Bar.

The expedition was a failure, the fault of Franklin Way who ignored the Council's request "to take along as a guide Spintlum, the Indian Chief from Spuzzum."

No personal animosity because of Way's failure: "now the Yale council has to send another party of which Mr. Way is not going to be one".

Max Fifer, M.D., private correspondence

Governor James Douglas, Fort Victoria, Vancouver Island, personal concern over a matter of near-national importance

"I trust you will pardon the liberty I take in writing a private communication to you. The provisional Town Council of Yale is without a quorum at present. Messrs. Power and McRoberts (the road contractors) are away, and Mr. Allard and myself are the only members in town; it is therefore impossible to get the council to bring the subject of this communication before Your Excellency's notice, and believing the matter of most importance to the prosperity of the Colony and its inhabitants, I thought proper to bring the same to your attention."

"I understand from Mr. Saunders, Justice of Peace, that the ferry licence of Mr. F. Way of Spuzzum expires on or about the 4th of December, and a new licence has to be granted after that date. It is a general complaint that the charge of Mr. Way of $2.00 per animal is too high and imposes one cent on each pound of provision, which is consumed on the route above Spuzzum. I cannot help thinking but that the complaint is a just one."

"The question would be, if Your Excellency think it proper to make an alteration in the toll fee at Spuzzum and how the same could be effected."

"I beg to state in this connection that I am on the most friendly and intimate terms with Mr. Way and that I sincerely hope he may be the successful applicant for the said ferry privilege. At the same time it does not prevent me from bringing this public matter before Your Excellency's attention, and I trust that you may in good time consider the same."

"Your Excellency will no doubt be pleased to hear the many flattering accounts from the Cariboo Diggings, and I can assure you that I have seen many returned miners with large amounts of gold from that region."

With high consideration,

Your most obedient servant,

M. Wm. Fifer, M.D".

Yale Town Council

Governor James Douglas, Fort Victoria, Vancouver Island

RE: Road Navigation — North

(Your request of June 1859 to explore the Canyon above Yale for the location of a wagon road along the river; your appropriation of funds for the survey.)

"In June, 1860, Yale Town Council contracted the initial survey with Messrs. Way and Barnard; the result proved entirely impractical. The Council took it upon ourselves (and they hope to receive your approval) to send another party, viz. Messrs. McRobert and Barnard along with the Indian chief (Spintlum) from Spuzzum whom Mr. Way had neglected to take, to find a suitable trail.

"The second party, consisting of McRobert and Barnard, together with the Indian chief from Spuzzum, were on route five days, and went first on the other side of the river and returned on this side. They found the only suitable trail for a mule and a wagon road on the other side, skirting within 200 or 300 yards of the river. The only impediment they found was at a "saddle of a mountain" near Nicaragua slide, where they think it necessary to tunnel. The distance is one hundred yards or less, I enclose herewith a copy of a map as furnished by Mr. Barnard, which may serve to illustrate the difference of the proposed trails."

With high regards,

Your Most Obedient Servant

M. Wm. Fifer, M.D, Chairman of Town Council

Notes:

Yale Town Council

Governor James Douglas

RE: Road Toll

- To balance the economic equation
- Yale must look to the North
- A better road between Yale and the interior must be built if the town is to prosper
- Funding for such a project can come from one source only, road toll.
- The higher the tax revenue the sooner we can expect

construction.

- The council explored all possible avenues of raising the tax.

- We propose an amendment to the original road tax petition of one half of one per cent per pound levied upon all goods passing from Yale to Lytton.

- The residents of Yale and vicinity request that the levy be extended to all goods sent by river in canoes.

- "By this we trust Your Excellency will be enabled to prosecute with renewed assurance the great work already commenced, and already assuming its position as one of the most important and practicable trails to the interior.

And as in duty bound your petitioners will ever pray..."

Yale Town Council

Governor James Douglas

RE: Location of Road Tax Collection

- Further to your suggestion that it would be more economical to collect the tax not at Yale, but at the initial point of water transportation, in New Westminster the charge would be on a per tonnage basis.

- "In answer to Your Excellency's suggestion in regard to the impost of additional tonnage of $7.00, seven dollars, at New Westminster, in lieu of the one half of one percent per pound, on the roads, we are perfectly convinced that the same is preferable to the annoyance of having so many officials on the various roads, whose salaries would consume half the revenue."

"We prefer not to bring this matter before the public at present, but assume the entire responsibility as elected representatives, preferring this to the agitation of any new or changed imposts, during the present repressed state of trade; and in view of the length of time which must necessarily elapse before the same can be imposed, viz. (videlicet) after the roads shall have been completed".

Yale Town Council

Governor James Douglas, Fort Victoria, Vancouver Island

RE: Tax Collection

Goal: to see a wagon road built along the Fraser Canyon

Suggestion:

- include the "Celestials" in the taxation scheme
- suppress their incentive
- "We would also beg to bring before your Excellency's notice the large influx of Chinamen, and a few cogent reasons why they should be made to bear more equally with us, than theretofore, and share the expenses. They, the Celestials, are fast settling in the country, getting acquisition of all the bars, benches and water privileges, and only paying miners' licences, and only so when they have good paying claims. Their principal articles are brought direct from China, consigned to China houses, distributed through the country to Branch houses. With the exception of opium and brandy, they use none other of the luxuries from which the principal portion of the revenue is derived. For instance our tobacco cost us in addition to first cost and freight 12 cent per pound duty, our cigars $1.00 per box.

"Now, the first of their luxuries, opium, could not be successfully taxed, as the bulk of a valuable invoice is so small, their facilities for smuggling wide, wide trousers, etc., so great, that no revenue could be derived from that source. The second article, brandy, is a vile concoction, manufactured here expressly for them."

"We would therefore suggest specific duty on all articles imported for the exclusive use of the Chinese, embracing such articles as opium, rice, dried fish, oil, etc, together with many other articles too numerous to mention.

"Taxing the Celestials is a subject which has already elicited considerable discussion, but any direct tax on them to the exclusion of all other foreigners would appear unjust; but just an indirect tax as we have suggested would not only be just and equitable but prove a source of revenue to the Colony, from a now barren and unprofitable soil."

Yale Town Council

Governor James Douglas, Fort Victoria, Vancouver Island

RE: River Navigation—clearing the rock obstacles

"We would state that we ourselves are unable to ascertain the cost of the work, for removing some rocks at Hill's Bar, Sawmill Point and Emory's Bar, which is necessary to the safe navigation between here and Hope, and would respectfully call your attention to our communication of August 11, 1860, bearing on the subject."

Suggestion:

- have engineers measure the obstacles and come to an estimate of the cost of their removal.
- to engage the Royal Engineers, their sappers and miners with power to employ civilians, this latter would probably prove the best, as the sappers now engaged at the

point, will have finished just at the time when the river will admit of blasting operations, and having with them their implements and the choice of civilians from experience, could do the work most economically, and the profits which all contractors expect to make, would revert to the government.

June 25, 1861

Yale Town Council

Governor James Douglas, Fort Victoria, Vancouver Island

RE: River Navigation

"The Town Council of Yale, B.C., would most respectfully request that as the steamers *Colonel Moody, Hope*, and *Fort Yale* (not the perished *"Yale"*), have of late made their several successful trips to this place and as it is now an undisputed fact that this can be done with perfect care and safety to this place at certain stages of the River. Yet it cannot be denied that to run a steamer to this place without improvement to the river at Emory's Bar and other points will be risky if not entirely impracticable. Your Excellency will well understand how much the interest of the Colony will be benefited if steamer communication can be carried to this place during the entire year. We would therefore most respectfully urge the importance of the necessary improvements to be made at Emory's Bar and other points between Hope and Yale during the winter, the most favourable season for the accomplishment of such work".

Annotation:

Governor Douglas' Reply: "I feel the great importance of the proposal for improving the navigation of Fraser River at Emory Creek and other points between Hope and Yale and beg the Town Council may have those places examined by competent miners and estimates prepared of the cost of such work".

May 31, 1861

Yale Town Council (copy)

Governor James Douglas, c/o A.G. Young, Esq., Colonial Secretary

Plea for Customs Relief

Dear Sir:

I am requested by the merchants whose names are attached to the enclosed certificates to beg your assistance in being allowed to pass through Her Majesty's Customs for British Columbia duty free indelible goods such as were lost or made valueless by the late disaster of Steamer Fort Yale on Fraser River.

Enclosed please find correct memorandum of goods lost with the Consignees' names attached the certificates.

By giving this request attention you will greatly oblige the parties as well as

Your very obedient Servant,

Wm. T. Ballou

11

Clipping. Correspondence.Correspondence. Clipping. Epistles to M. W. Fifer, the doctor; petitions and appeals to M. W. Fifer, the mayor.

Pounds and pounds of paper, now sorted into three files I have named Patient Treatment, Newspaper Clippings, Correspondence. This desk is almost cleaned up.

These shelves are almost empty. Alas, poor Yorick, my sole companion; your vacant sockets stare, piercing my conscience. I remain in your debt, yet I leave you behind; I am told: "The phrenology skull must remain, as part of the medical practice, along with Dr. Fifer's diagnostic and surgical tools." This room is almost empty. I will take this framed needlework sampler—*doctor, prophet, fool,* with me. And the mortar and pestle, mine since I began using them in the kitchen, will perhaps help me establish a new life. What will I do? What can I do? Where will I go? Victoria? San Francisco? Hong Kong? Guangzhou? I'm undecided,

Where shall I file this piece of paper? Under Clipping or under Correspondence? Personal or Council? Have I been too hasty in taking the Council Correspondence file to Mr. Allard? A business calling card: 'Alexander Rattray, M.D., Edin., R.N., Surgeon;' on the back, in hand-written letters, "p.p.c." (*pour prendre conge*), one corner folded courteously, I took the card to Doctor Fifer when Doctor Rattray departed. Yes. The all-knowing doctor who was travelling with Lady Franklin.

Initially, Doctor Fifer had dutifully written out the town coucil's invitation, requesting the wife of the missing explorer Sir John Franklin to extend her travels from Victoria and New Westminster up river as far as Fort Yale. How excited everyone was when, on Friday, March 8, 1861, a canoe from Fort Hope brought the message—Lady Franklin and her attendants were due to arrive in Yale on board the *Maria*.

Lady Franklin, the wife of the eminent Arctic pioneer, has been travelling the world on her own ever since her husband and his ships disappeared in July, 1845, after leaving England for the Arctic on their quest for the illusive Northwest Passage to China. Sir John's wife refuses to consider herself a widow, insisting that, without proof to the contrary, she prefers to believe that her husband and his men are still alive. True, their ships may have been frozen in ice and destroyed, but it is possible that the men have survived, or have abandoned ship and been rescued by the *Esquimaux*. She refuses to give up hope until she can see the coffin, a saying which makes me suspect that her travels have included stops in the homeland of my ancestors.

Bringing paddlewheel steamers all the way to Yale is hazardous at low water, and March is a month of low water levels. However, using modern steamers under experienced captains, the Council concluded, no major naval disaster was likely to occur on the river between Hope and Yale. The captain, who had originally intended to come only as far as Hill's Bar, decided that he would bring the *Maria* all the way up. To the surprise of the townspeople, albeit without apprising Lady Franklin of the danger, the captain succeeded. The businessmen, who had already formed their venture company for a regular year-round steamship run, welcomed this accomplishment as a splendid opportunity to profit from the celebrity traveler's visit, publicizing Yale as the natural head of navigation on Fraser's River.

As a member of her escort, Dr. Rattray lauded Lady Jane for her bravery, for her determination to act, to do something about the missing ships and men. On her tours she speaks to crowds and raises money to finance searches and to shame the British admiralty into offering a reward to anyone who can bring back proof of the expedition's fate. Some in town, including Dr. Fifer, who had been outvoted on council (he confided to me), originally objected to the invitation. They feared that Lady Franklin's attitude towards Americans might cause offence. Her famous words, chastising their boastfulness, seem to epitomize the British attitude of superiority towards colonies and former colonies. Others felt the bad luck of a black widow would descend upon their town. Still others held Lady Franklin next in esteem to Queen Victoria herself and treated her as a *de facto* representative of the monarch and the motherland.

I suspect that the unhappy woman, who has neither children nor worries about money, is simply distracting herself with travel, of which she has done a great deal. Indeed, she first arrived in New York in 1846, the same year Dr. Fifer arrived, although he disembarked a few weeks later, and in less auspicious circumstances. On that first visit, Lady Franklin toured hospitals, schools, factories, and a deaf-and-blind institution. She offered her views freely about the value of the Oregon Treaty, the virtue of the Mexican War, and about whether the United States of America should seize California. Without qualms, on that first visit she told the mayor of Boston her frank opinion of Yankee manners and customs: "The reason for not thinking as highly of the Americans as they deserve is owing to their own bragging."

Thus, Lady Franklin's reputation preceded her, and the council had debated the pros and cons of inviting her, but when they heard that she wished to check up-river, as far into the interior of the continent as she could go, literally in search of her husband or of her missing husband's bones, they felt that her quest meshed nicely with their own—to plant into the brains of investors and decision-makers in Victoria and New Westminster that Yale is the logical head of navigation, and the logical place to begin any land access to the interior.

At sixty-nine years of age, Lady Franklin's hair is gray; her eyes are still keen. She is, as the doctor quoted, "more attractive than beautiful," a description from fifteen years ago which still applies today. She leaves an impression of tirelessness—indefatigable, Dr. Fifer said, although he could tell that she was in far from robust health.

Of her several eccentricities, Lady Franklin brought with her to Yale her own iron bedstead, with linen bedding and eiderdown comforter, which the council accommodated to be set up in the courthouse, with space for her travelling companion Miss Cracroft available in the loft. This same iron bedstead had accompanied Lady Jane to the Sandwich Islands, on two voyages up the Nile, through the Holy Land where she nearly broke her neck ascending Mount Sinai. It was with her as she inspected the Seven Churches of Asia, rode up Mount Olympus, and visited the battlefield of Troy. By her reputation, this woman has the energy of a dowager empress; yet when I caught a glimpse of her in person, I saw a gentle shy lady whose eyes behind her spectacles reminded me of Dr. Fifer's own—the eyes of a compassionate person who has lost something very dear.

Although the weather was warm for March, to the arriving passengers, world travellers, Yale must have looked rather dreary and impermanent, with its tents and shacks and wooden buildings, with nothing but a few foundation walls built of stone. The March streets were "sop and mud." We all assembled down at the beach, and after the ship was made fast, Reverend Crickmer, shepherd of St. John the Divine's Church of England flock, appropriated the privilege, by his spiritual connection, to be the first one to go aboard and invite the prominent guest and her companions to his house, where, he assured them, everything was prepared. As they followed him down the gangplank towards Front Street, they observed the sandy beach ringed with tents, even a futile attempt at diggings and miners' flumes within the town. Lady Franklin declared Reverend and Mrs. Crickmer's house (our first house in Yale, which Dr. Fifer had rented to the Crickmers) "a very fair house." They had furnished one of the two sitting rooms very well and also used two more rooms upstairs.

Anxious to show his standing, Reverend Crickmer had invited the most prominent people of Yale for tea to ensure that everyone could meet the guest of honour. Benches were put up and twenty-five or thirty of Yale's most distinguished citizens went to pay their respects. It was at that first gathering that Dr. Fifer was introduced to Dr. Alexander Rattray, R.N., medical officer on the *Topaz*, presently in Esquimalt Harbour, and assigned to Lady Franklin's retinue.

Dr. Fifer always enjoyed meeting other medical men, swapping stories, discussing medications, surgery, and natural sciences, and hearing about scientific advances which had not yet reached the San Francisco or Victoria newspapers. Sitting there side by side, deep in conversation, the two physicians were oblivious to the circle around Lady Jane and Miss Cracroft as they recounted their tales of travelling to Niagara Falls and touring Toronto with the Prince of Wales. Instead, Doctor Rattray, who sensed in his colleague a receptive, sympathetic, and travelled listener and debater, brought to Doctor Fifer's attention a recent London bestseller, an account of the unusual observations of an explorer and "natural philosopher" who had journeyed around the Still Ocean. "Four hundred and ninety pages!" Dr. Rattray claimed, describing the hefty volume which had kept him enthralled the entire several months of his voyage out.

Being quite eager to discuss the author's exciting theory with another intellectual, Dr. Rattray expounded, "In The Origin of Species, Charles Darwin expresses a grandiose idea–natural selection, survival of the fittest, and evolution of species through adaptation to the environment. Darwin credits Thomas Malthus and his Essay on the Principle of Population as it effects the future Improvement of Society, as the spark which ignited his evolutionary imagination."

"Yes, I have read Malthus," Dr. Fifer added. "Quite frankly, I have tried to apply his observations here in Yale, to our local dealings with the unfortunate native population. Without much success so far, I must admit."

"Well done, Doctor Fifer, using your own backyard right here, an ideal opportunity to observe in miniature the struggle for dominance, the competing traits in different peoples, the ability of different groups to co-exist, to create a new and better world. A perfect crucible, so-to-speak, Doctor Fifer. You have addressed the Malthusian question—whether the human race can transform the world into a paradise."

"Or whether the human race could transform a paradise into a cesspool," Dr. Fifer added, remembering our arrival and first night on the beach.

"Perhaps," Dr. Rattray continued, "but Malthus thinks that we will not recreate Eden. In his simple and most convincing contention, Malthus describes the 'surplus of mouths over loaves; he points out that 'while the number of mouths increases geometrically (by a common ratio, as 2, 4, 8, 16), the number of loaves only grows arithmetically (by a constant quantity, as 2, 4, 6, 8, 10). Consequently, the human population increases faster than its food supply, causing a struggle for existence. By simple calculation, he ends up with the 'Malthusian Disaster'."

Dr. Fifer nodded, "the outcome is obvious. Without enough food, the Horsemen of the Apocalypse pay a call. Homo sapiens will perish in the same way as did the dodo bird."

"True," Dr. Rattray agrees, "but at this point, enter Charles Darwin, *deus ex machina*, offering hope. He applies the Malthusian principle to the whole world of organic life. He argues that the struggle for existence under varying environmental conditions induces adaptive changes in the organism to ensure its survival. Durability of a species attests to the success of adaptation. Relationships and environments are constantly changing and those conforming and adjusting with them will survive better. The weak and unfit will be eliminated. Those with the best endowment for any given environment will be 'selected' naturally to be the parents for the next generation."

"Well, it seems almost obvious, when you explain it that way, Dr. Rattray."

"The crux is that Darwin's argument," Dr. Rattray explained to Dr. Fifer, "offers an answer to the age-old question 'Where does it all come from?'"

"Ah, hence, 'The Origin of Species'?"

"Exactly! And, Dr. Fifer, many facts which have been known before Darwin," Dr. Rattray continued, "have not been recognized as parts of a single scheme. Variation, inheritance of variations, selective breeding of domestic plants and animals, the struggle for existence—all fall suddenly into place, explained as natural selection, according to Darwin's theory."

"So you are saying that his theory is nothing new? That it just helps us see things in a new light, Dr. Rattray?"

"Quite logical, Dr. Fifer. Nothing new at all," and with this lapidary conclusion they parted for the night.

At home later, when I prepared the evening meal, Dr. Fifer was telling me of this conversation, but he stopped talking at this point. I sensed that he needed time to let the ideas sink in. I also feared that, as a scientist, he had connected 'adaptation' with 'mutation' and that he was seeing the crossed toes of his erstwhile offspring.

As Lady Franklin's visit lasted three days, the two doctors met again. For the second discussion, Dr. Fifer had prepared his arguments, or his questions, as he liked to think of them. "Dr. Rattray, I am a Christian myself, although a Methodist, not one of our friend Crickmer's flock. How do you reconcile the Book of Genesis with Mr. Darwin's writings? To me, the complex systems of our natural world appear very unlikely to be the product of numerous, successive, slight modifications. Had not Archdeacon Paley argued fifty years earlier that finding both a stone and a watch while crossing the heath, we would regard the stone as a simple part of nature, while no one would question that the watch is an artifact, designed for the purpose of telling time. Paley then proposed that objects of nature, such as the human eye, indicate to be of similar contrivances, produced by natural processes. We assume an intelligence, a Divine Creator, is responsible for the design, do we not?"

"Science is tolerant to ambiguity. Some of our Creator's species could have perished through bad luck, or unique periodic catastrophes in the history of our planet—a giant comet striking the earth, plagues, ice ages, global overheating, earthquakes, floods, or volcanic eruptions, could they not, Doctor Rattray?"

"I know, Fifer. It is hard to grasp. The London magazines are rife with satire and cartoons—'Well, I'll be a monkey's uncle!' is everyman's quip of disbelief, although to be fair, Mr. Darwin does not single out the species homo sapiens. But think about it. Darwin claims that each new species is produced and maintained by having some advantage over those with whom it comes into competition. This conflict, he claims, is almost inevitably followed by the gradual extinction of less favoured forms."

"New species. Natural selection. Inevitable extinction. These are not words I read in the Bible, sir, but it tells us of the Flood."

"Indeed, Dr. Fifer. True. But to me, I think it is a matter of reading the Good Book differently. Not literally, like the story of Little Nell. But rather, metaphorically, like the story of Mr. Scrooge."

Dr. Fifer poured himself a fresh cup of China tea and took a sip: "Instead of disputing literature, I wanted to ask Doctor Rattray whether he had any children, but he turned to someone to his left who began to tell him about our plans for next year's Great Exhibition. It is probably all for the better. You and I know that if I had asked, I would also have had to admit that the Fifer line is without descendants, doomed to cease to exist." Doctor Fifer did not want to think that the survival of the misbegot O'Nedhil line indicated in any way superiority over his own.

For the final day of her visit, the people of the Indian village arranged to take Lady Franklin in their dugout canoes across the narrowest stretch of the Fraser, over to the flats on the south bank. The processional progressed from town, through the Indian settlement, and down to the canoes at their landing. Others of their officials walked up this side, to the cliffs above the island that splits the river and causes all the eddies. Where they maintain permanent fish drying racks which in summer are festooned with the red swags of scarified salmon, from the tallest rack which has the look of a permanent but rather unplumb scaffolding, they had attached a long streamer. The other end of the fabric they had tied to a tall pole which they erected like a mast in the centre of a canoe which was then paddled ceremoniously out into the current. When Lady Franklin's canoe rounded the curve of the shore, skirting the sandbar that rises in low water, she glimpsed their carefully-crafted surprise—a long banner, a pennant ribboning from the cliff face towards the island, with lettering proclaiming Lady Franklin Pass. They were naming their sacred fishing site in her honour. Some of the townspeople speculated later that they mistook her for the Queen.

It was strange, the way Dr. Fifer reacted to the Indians' honouring Lady Franklin. Perhaps he felt that their enthusiasm made his council's somewhat lukewarm reception seem tedious. Perhaps it had something to do with the irony. "Irony, Ah Chung. When you say one thing and it comes out the opposite to what you intend." He went on to explain in more detail. "Lady Franklin's Pass is no pass at all. It is as far as she will ever get, into the interior, into the belly of the land which has swallowed her husband and refuses to spit him out. In reality, it must indeed mark the line where her dream dies. She will never see Sir John again."

Perhaps it was the hooded cape she wore as she sat in the middle of the dugout canoe in the middle of the roiling river, or perhaps it was simply the gentleness in her voice, but seeing this English lady buoyed me. Just as crows everywhere are equally black, wisdom and mercy, the spirit of the goose goddess, is found in every yard.

That afternoon, the steamer's whistle summoned the entourage and the host party to return to the *Maria*, putting an end to Dr. Fifer's sad musings. The visitors were requested to go into the ship's salon where about twenty inhabitants of Yale assembled for the farewell address to Lady Jane Franklin. Dr. Fifer, as mayor, attended, of course. On his way in, he inspected Lady Franklin's legendary bed lashed to the hurricane deck because it was too big to go through the door of her stateroom. "From what I saw of the contraption, it appeared to be an ordinary iron bedstead, Ah Chung, with paint chipped off where it's been knocked about and rusty spots where its age is showing. Yet the very fact that the Lady has made the effort to have the contrivance lugged up the Fraser River has accorded our town of Yale a place in line with the other world attractions she has visited." I could tell he was searching for positive attributes in a visitation which seemed to have made him very sad.

Or perhaps it was just Reverend Crickmer's smooth-spoken farewell:

"May it please your ladyship. We, the inhabitants of Yale, here presenting well and nigh every nation under heaven, esteem the presence as the proudest monument in the annals of our country, and in the existence of our town—for today is our town of Yale forever linked in history with the name of one, the memorial of whose abundant kindness and wifely devotion will never die, and whose immortal veneration princes bow down to and kings and queens of the earth may envy but never win. From the bottom of our hearts do we pray God to bless your ladyship with many happy days and when called by God's good providence from the holy church militant to join the heroic in the church triumphant, may the grave be transmuted, by the touch of a living faith, into the gates of ever-lasting life, and a glory more lasting than the perishing laws of earth, forever crown the double brows of the noble pair whom the whole civilized world of Christendom delighted to honour."

Dr. Rattray, also an amateur naturalist, had been taking copious notes on the journey. He plans to write an account of his visit to the colonies of British Columbia and Vancouver's Island and has prepared sketches of Yale and Hope to be included as lithograph illustrations. As they parted, the two doctors shook hands; Dr. Rattray handed him this card and promised Dr. Fifer a copy upon publication of his book. They bowed to each other and said good-bye. The salon was cleared of visitors. Amid cheers and a local salute of volleys fired from various rifles and handguns pointed towards the sky, the ship steamed off the bank, and, in perfect weather, chugged downriver towards Hope, taking with it the excitement of the three days.

Treatment Files. Clippings. Correspondence (Personal). I should have checked these lower drawers sooner.

Where do I put this? A receipt, the bill of sale, for the vacant lot Dr. Fifer sold this spring to Hope magistrate Peter O'Reilly, soon after the Yale catastrophe on Easter Sunday. All his savings gone in one fiery explosion. "Beware the fireworks," hadn't the soothsayer said? But Dr. Fifer refused to believe that our lives, our ends, are predetermined. "This is the joy of the New World, Ah Chung. We can make our own destiny. Are not we both evidence of this new reality?"

Yes and No, I thought, but we never argued; we never debated. After the explosion, he had talked about moving on, with the miners, north to the Forks or the Cariboo. The gold-bearing sandbars here are mostly played out; dredges and hydraulics are replacing the men; the number of patients had plummeted along with property values. Should we move on to Cayoosh where the encampment was larger, and a doctor was needed? Or back to Victoria? Or San Francisco? He had asked me himself: "Should we move on, Ah Chung? Should we go back?" But neither of us wished to go back, without funds, to a city where business was still depressed. Perhaps the animosity against former Vigilance Committee members had cooled, but many of the doctor's old friends were gone. Jules David a fugitive; Dr. Wierzbicki dead of consumption, last Christmas; Dr.

250

Manrow, San Francisco vigilante prosecutor, dead by his own hand. Dr. Manrow had become half insane with the conviction that his home was haunted by the spirits of those he had committed to the noose; suicide was his escape route.

Neither of us wanted to go back to California. War fever had replaced gold fever and was affecting everyone, since the bombardment of Fort Sumter in Charleston Harbour on the very day the steamship Yale exploded. The dream of liberty was becoming a nightmare; even in California, citizens were taking sides, lining up for the North or the South. Neither of us wanted to go back. Yet war seems inevitable, and even here, we are unable to escape it. The men still mining Hill's Bar make their allegiances obvious.

Yet neither of us wanted to move forward; to go north to the Thompson or Cayoosh on the Fraser, or the Cariboo; that would be more of the same, without all he had achieved here in Yale. The sale of the lot to Mr. O'Reilly brought a slight profit and tided us over to the summer months. We didn't have to decide. We stayed, hung in, and hoped for business to improve while old enemies retreated and old grudges seemed to fade into obscurity. There were bigger issues to debate—freedom or slavery; independent thinking versus toeing a party line; states' rights or federal authority; the old ways, or a new world order.

All this seems contemplative philosophy and although I liked reading it, perhaps it's a bit too long.

What shall I do with this? File it as Clipping or Correspondence? A program for the performance by The Robinson Dramatic Troupe, a group of itinerant players. The Town Council invited them to appear, and offered the Yale Courthouse as a venue for their performance. The doctor sent me to help the wives ready and decorate the building. The empty jail cells served as change rooms for the two actresses and four actors. I was able to watch from the back of the room. The audience, mostly miners, was most impressed by the pantomime and applauded loudly.

"The Clown Outwitted," a burlesque, featured Mr. J. B. Robinson and his daughter, Susan, a most attractive young lady. In the play, the clown, seated in full enjoyment of bread, cheese and a bottle of ale, was outwitted by the fairy (Susan) coming behind and stealing the glass, which he had filled by his side. The fun was that the astounded clown attributed the theft to someone in front of the stage. The first time the ale was gone, the clown pitched upon a man in the first row, and amidst absurd gesticulations, drew himself off to the other corner of the stage and began afresh, evidently in the hope of finishing his beer and cheese in peace. The fairy having a second time drunk it off, the clown fixed upon Dr. Fifer, who was seated just opposite him, as the thief. The clown then renewed his gestures, pantomiming as he moved off once more to a safer place. The audience laughed as much as they ever did in their life. All enjoyed this trick hitting on their own esteemed mayor.

This clipping from the *British Columbian*, March 14, 1861, is an enjoyable account of the exact show, performed in the Victoria Pioneer Theatre. Perhaps this is what Dr. Fifer took to his council to spark their invitation to the troupe. Perhaps I should have included it with the Council Correspondence. Yes. Reverend Crickmer had proposed a May Day celebration, or a Queen of the May Maypole, or something "flagrantly English."

It would be nice to see a trial at balancing against the overwhelmingly American celebrations of Washington's birthday and the Fourth of July in a British Country. I remember, Mr. Allard described it, and Dr. Fifer supported his friend, objecting, as a non-Anglican, to the clandestine pagan symbol which he claimed the maypole represented, and offered instead to invite the travelling Thespians to help Yale celebrate the Queen's birthday.

Afterwards, although he and Mr. Allard were proud that their proposal had been so well received, Dr. Fifer was quiet and brooding. "No fun?" I asked him.

"No fun, being the thief, Ah Chung. After the pantomime, I

couldn't get it out of my head. Remember how it said in the paper 'Thief'? That San Francisco newspaper citing Mr. David as a thief, with a warrant out for his arrest, for absconding from Abel Guy's bank with the alms gathered for the widow King and her family?"

I remembered; I remember how he shook his head in disbelief; how he called out for me to come from the kitchen; how he read the news aloud to me as was our habit.

"Jules David, a thief!" Dr. Fifer could not believe it. At first he suggested that there must be some mistake. Then he suggested that Mr. David must still not be himself, after McGowan's terrible beating. He had been so discombobulated, the doctor recalled, that a concussion must be assumed, and brain damage certainly a possibility. But then he had to admit, that if indeed the theft had happened, it had occurred before Mr. David's visit here. That it probably explained all the cash Mr. David had spent in Victoria before his trip to Yale, purchasing the freshwater spring, renting offices, placing expensive advertisements in the local papers. "How can we know the hearts of others, Ah Chung?" He did not expect me to answer. It was his way of saying that the news had pierced his own heart. And that the pantomime had re-opened that wound.

What shall I do with this? Is it Clipping or Correspondence? A poster. A broadsheet, Dr. Fifer called it, announcing the American Independence Day celebrations, the Fourth of July, 1861. The Town Council had debated the proposal and voted to permit it, but the residents of Hill's Bar were the organizers. Most businesses, except for the gambling and drinking establishments, closed for the festivities. Everyone was invited to attend. Salutes at Sunrise, at Noon, and at Sunset. Horse races. Dancing. Fireworks. I have almost forgotten this day, because of what happened the day after.

Although we had heard for several weeks that Robert Wall was threatening harm to Dr. Fifer, the doctor refused to let such madness force him to change his plans. He would perform his mayoral duties "rumours be damned," he said. And since McGowan's departure two years ago, the temperament at Hill's Bar had remained patriotically American but compliant. The moment to take advantage of British weakness had passed; the Royal Engineers were making their presence felt in positive contributions to the communities of the new colony they were assigned to—Fort Langley, New Westminster, Harrison River, Port Douglas, Fort Hope, Fort Yale.

It did raise some eyebrows, on the morning of the Fourth of July, when we, the people of Yale, saw the American secession flag, a blue St. Andrew's cross on a red ground, with thirteen stars on the blue crossbars, one for each seceding state. The battle flag of the South was flying over the Land and Fleming sawmill across the river, challenging those other American citizens whose hearts were with the northern states.

People who regard thirteen as an unlucky number predicted that the rebel flag presaged the failure of the Confederacy. Others replied that the thirteen original colonies that fought for independence from the British Crown in 1776 had won their war. It is a poor rule that will not work both ways.

The horse races over the course on Douglas Street were run in the afternoon. The red, white, and blue bunting, the beribboned grandstand, the large crowd, including many ladies, in their best dresses and hoops and parasols against the summer sun, all contributed to the festive spirit. Dr. Fifer's quiet manner, the able way he settled all disputes, contributed to the smooth running of events. The day passed in the most agreeable manner.

Mr. Oppenheimer, Mr. Commeline, Messrs. Dietz and Kimball, and Mr. Martin sponsored three races—The President's Plate, The Queen's Cup, and The Douglas Street Stakes. Clipping or Correspondence? I think this must be one of the judge's slips, marking the placing of horses securely on paper for the runner boy to dash across to the master of ceremonies for the official announcement.

1: Stalk Away (L. Commeline)

2: Tipperary Boy (W. Powers)

3: McLean (O. Allard)

4: Mary Hawk (R. Gardner)

5: Dick (Dietz and Kimball)

After dining out that evening, Dr. Fifer and his councillors waited for darkness to fall, for the sun to drop behind Mount Lincoln and shadow our valley enough to make the fireworks even more impressive. I believe they had ordered in supplies from San Francisco, to surprise the townsfolk with a sound and light show. Red. White. Blue. Rockets and Stars. Candles and Flowers. Streaks and Willow Trees. As beautiful as any I remember from childhood. But the biggest surprise was not ordered in. Who in the grandstand even expected its arrival, sitting as they were high above the Fraser, watching the lights in the sky and again as their fire was repeated in the shimmer of water below?

Someone from the beach noticed it first, as it came in the opposite direction from the river. People pointed; the watchers in the grandstand twisted their necks, their backs, to catch what was attracting attention. It was silent, but bigger and brighter than anything we had watched being ignited on the sand. Brighter than Haley's comet, bigger and more splendid than Donati's comet which we had watched over Victoria in 1858, our celestial visitor was (I think it was Reverend Crickmer who knew) Tebbutt's comet, "of a magnitude zero and a tail of 100 degrees. It is unusually bright; I must make a note of its appearance; over Yale on July 4th, 1861," the reverend proclaimed.

I was almost upset; I could not believe how these celestial omens seemed to be tracking us. But Dr. Fifer remained calm and seemed unperturbed. He was silent, almost brooding, I remember now. At the time he just shrugged and said: "Perhaps some unseen forces are smiling on our simple display."

Dr. Fifer refused to be pushed into fear or negativity; he refused to believe that he was being stalked by misfortune. Nor would he condone a reading of foreboding or apocalypse. However, neither did he repeat his assertions from three years ago, that with a comet comes the music of the spheres and good comet wine; no longer did he take the astral appearance frivolously. Did he feel that the arrival of Tebbut's comet was omen of a dramatic event? Did he feel the icy hand of eternity on his shoulder? Did he have a premonition, a dream moment that with hindsight may seem precognitive? If he did, he did not say.

Among Dr. Fifer's friends, the pessimists saw the comet as a spectre and portent of evil things to come, but the doctor was determined to be optimistic and undisturbed. He always scoffed at superstition, old wives' tales, even proverbs and legends. "The cat will mew and the dog will have his day, and so shall comets. They come, wag their tails for a while, and then they pass and we move on to the next novelty."

Perhaps he was a bit too blasé; then again, what difference did it make? What could any of us have done differently?

Early the next morning, the morning of the fifth of July, the sky took on a peculiar yellowish hue as the light dimmed. "The sun was so weak that morning that I had to light candles to illuminate the pulpit for the seven o'clock matins service," Reverend Crickmer reported later. "There were murmurs and speculation about the astral visitor the night before. It was different from their reaction to a recent sun eclipse, when people had wondered at the creator's ingenuity, to make the moon just large enough to cover the sun. The unusual sky continued even on into the night, with strong luminosity not unlike an aurora. Perhaps, someone suggested, the Earth was passing through the comet's tail." Reverend Crickmer did not use it, but "eerie" is the only word to describe the light that day. The fifth of July, 1861.

Is this a Clipping or Correspondence? This seems to be both. A draft of the council's request for an expression of interest, clipped to an advertisement for Francis George Claudet, Landscape Photographer, New Westminster. "Further to our decision to prepare a professional photography display to accompany our submission to the 1862 London Exhibition, you are invited to submit a proposal outlining suggested content and your fee for consideration of the Yale Town Council."

I have heard that Mr. Claudet did intend to submit a proposal. Does, perhaps, still intend to participate. That he had come to prospect locations, that first week of July. That he had set up his camera on the beach that very day. That he had captured in his camera's eye the very canoe that brought Robert Wall to Yale, the very canoe that waited for him to return, in which he effected his escape downriver. This I heard at the courthouse; I have not seen the photograph, and Mr. Claudet did not attend the coroner's inquest. He submitted a written statement.

What shall I do with this? A folded newspaper, July 4, 1861. Somewhat crumpled, with a smeared brown stain?

Robert Wall had been a patient; Dr. Fifer had successfully treated him, cured him of a sexual obsession the previous spring. His medical bill is still outstanding. We had heard that Wall had abandoned his prospecting claim and had become a vagabond, loafing about New Westminster, Fort Langley, Hope, and Yale. He had become bitter and vindictive, alleging that the doctor's treatment had harmed him and exposed him to the jests of Native women as an impotent, no good, *cultus* man. Many witnesses had heard him express his yearning for revenge against Dr. Fifer.

At about six o'clock in the evening, the fifth of July, that day of eerie light, a man approached our drug store and inquired for Dr. Fifer. Mr. Davis, a visitor who had been sitting on the bench outside the store for most of that afternoon, informed the man that the doctor was in his office, in the back room. I was busy at the mortar and did not look up; the man rushed past me without speaking. At the door to the examining room, he called out to the doctor, who came towards him. The man was neatly dressed in a suit jacket; his hair was cut and combed. He had his right hand concealed from view in the bosom of his shirt, making us suspect that the arm might be injured and need medical attention.

Dr. Fifer approached, squinting at the patient through the glasses on his nose, but failing to recognize him as the scruffy deranged miner he had treated several months before.

The man held out his left hand which was gripping this newspaper, partly folded, and said: "Doctor Fifer, look at this."

The doctor took the paper from the man, and bent his neck towards it. Quick as thought, the man drew a small derringer pistol from his bosom and fired.

Dr. Fifer stopped, still gripping the paper, and stared down at the front of his white shirt where a red flower was growing. He looked surprised, quizzical, then staggered, then turned partially around and leaned against the side of the room. Then he sank down slowly, awkwardly, into the corner of the room.

Without a groan, Dr. Fifer died instantly, there on the wooden floor planks, wedged into the corner of his examining room. I could see that the bullet had entered his left breast and passed directly into his heart. At such close quarters, it had soiled his white shirt with residue which darkened the stain around the hole where the large ball had entered. His gold spectacles, still on, had slid a bit down his nose; his head was leaning slightly forward, but otherwise he sat erect, propped, with this newspaper, crumpled, clutched to his chest.

12

A crumpled newspaper, smeared with dried blood. Do I need such a souvenir? It is neither Correspondence nor Clipping; it was not even considered to be evidence. I should toss it into the fire and close the door.

My life closed too, that July evening, in Dr. Fifer's examining room, back of our drug store. An explosion. Shock. Horror. The next hours were a flurry—running to fetch the chief of police, waiting for the coroner, moving the body on to the examining table, remaining outside the door as Mr. Dietz assisted Dr. Bradshaw with the statutory examination of the corpse. Two ladies helped me lay him out; Mr. Allard and three others bedded him into the coffin. Reverend Crickmer shared with Reverend Browning the funeral service. I sat with Mrs. Crickmer in the front row; the crowd overflowed the meeting house, out the door, down the steps, on to the street below.

All the White inhabitants of Yale, with one exception, attended the funeral. Rumour has it that Dr. Silas Crane lay in his room in the Hotel California, drunk, comatose. Some take his absence as proof of his responsibility, that he incited the murder by playing into Robert Wall's paranoia, by alleging Dr. Fifer had made Wall's unfortunate condition worse.

In the procession to the cemetery, I walked alone behind the pallbearers; there is no next of kin. I threw a fistful of dirt into the grave, before the men with shovels covered the box. I barely remember any other details of those three days; I moved as if in a daze, in a dream, a nightmare from which I have not yet been able to wake. A nightmare of fog and forgetting. I am lost in that fog. Someone is forgetting me, someone who has walked on ahead and left me, lost in a forest. Wait. Wait for me.

I am not alone, though, in my feelings of shock and disbelief. Every person in Yale seems to need to recount where they were, and what they did at the time of the disaster, and how they heard the terrible news.

Mr. John Davis of Victoria, who, with several other gentlemen, had been seated on a bench outside of the drug store: "We heard an explosion inside. As it sounded just like more fireworks, we paid no attention to it. The murderer stood there at the door for a moment, looking in, surveying the corpse, but we did not realize it at the time, and then he walked out of the store, quietly, leisurely. I followed as he proceeded down the street toward the beach and jumped into a waiting canoe, manned by a white man and two Indians. The canoe then shoved off, the paddlers pulling it down stream at a rapid rate, disappearing behind Sawmill Point, where the rebel flag was still flying after yesterday's festivities. We realized something terrible had happened."

Mr. Ballou, of "Ballou's Express", who had tried to intervene: "I heard of Wall's threats against the doctor. Not half an hour before he was killed, I cautioned the deceased, telling him that Robert Wall was coming up the river with the avowed intention of murdering him. The doctor, it seems, took no precautions, and hence his melancholy and untimely end. Indeed, he thanked me and said that he had already heard the threats, but he did not intend to run or hide."

Mrs. Sophia Crickmer, Reverend Crickmer's wife, speculates: "At about five o'clock on the day of the murder, I saw the doctor, a short, stout man, wearing spectacles, passing our door. I knew him well as our landlord, and in his capacity as mayor of our town. On that day, his head seemed to be hanging, and the swing of his arms left such a suggestion of sadness that I remarked so to Mr. Crickmer at that time. Had the doctor some vague presentiment that he was walking straight to his doom?"

The Reverend Arthur Browning, of the Methodist Church, reported his own involvement: "On arriving at Fort Yale, I was welcomed by my friend Doctor Fifer. I entered his store, sat down in his consulting room, and conversed for about half an hour. Immediately after leaving I heard what I concluded to be the explosion of a Chinese firecracker, but was almost immediately undeceived by being informed that the doctor was shot. I hurried back to witness only his last breath, the bullet having perforated the heart of the man I had left so strong and healthy a few moments before. The murderer had, like myself, come up the river, I having noticed the canoe most distinctly. He had watched the house until I had left, and then committed the murder."

Reverend Browning is proud of the fact that Dr. Fifer was a Methodist. "The doctor was an attendant on our ministry, and one from whom I had ever experienced kindness, and whose death I sincerely regret. At the funeral, as also at the service the subsequent Sabbath, touching the sad event, I had the privilege of addressing almost the entire population of Yale."

Even visitors were requested to document what they may have witnessed: "I, Francis George Claudet, Ambrotype photographer from Queensborough, New Westminster, in the Colony of British Columbia, travelled to Fort Yale the first week of July, 1861, at the request of the town council. Deputy Sheriff and postmaster Henry Commeline had written to invite me to take photographs of the Fort Yale area for inclusion in the Colony's display at the 1862 Industrial Exhibition, planned for next year, in London. It was four o'clock in the afternoon of Friday, the fifth of July, my assistant and I had set up a darkroom tent and a tripod overlooking Yale's riverbank.

"As on the day before, light conditions were unusual, created by the comet's appearance. The sunlight was diffused, coming from the side, but offering good contrast of light and shadows. We had taken a number of scenic pictures that morning; one last unexposed plate was left for the afternoon, a view of Yale and the Fraser River. To my chagrin, I saw the bucolic scene about to be disrupted by a canoe with four occupants which was rounding Sawmill Point, entering and disrupting the peaceful composition.

"The canoe's progress was slow against the strong current; I determined that it would take some time before it would be out of the picture. By then, the light would have faded and my plan would be spoiled. Rather than dismantle the equipment and waste the unexposed plate, I decided to make the best of the situation. Covering the camera box and my head under a black cloth to exclude daylight interference, I focused the lens to optimal sharpness on the screen. Opening the camera's iris diaphragm to full aperture, I waited until I saw the vessel's inverted image in the centre of the ground glass plate. I inserted the silver iodide cassette and removed the lens cap for one brief moment of exposure time, thereby producing an action picture.

"While I was occupied taking down the equipment, the canoe continued its course and pulled up on the sandy beach below. Two of the four occupants disembarked and walked towards town. The two others remained in the canoe as if waiting.

"After completing our shoot, we dismantled the camera, the collapsible tripod, and the darkroom tent; we stowed the precious glass plates safely in the satchel, stopped on Front Street for a bite to eat and had a celebratory drink or two. Upon returning to Mr. Commeline's house, we learned from his Chinaman that while we were taking pictures, the sheriff was called out to apprehend a criminal who had just shot the local doctor. Everyone seemed upset. I thought it best to take the next canoe to Hope and return to New Westminster via Langley on the *Enterprise*.

"At home, I developed the negatives and pencil marked each plate with the date, the location, and a name of the occasion. I marked the plate taken last, for lack of a better designation, as what I assumed it to be: 'The 4 o'clock mails at Yale.' A print is enclosed."

Within an hour of Dr. Fifer's death, while I sat with his body, a manhunt had begun. Deputy Sheriff Commeline immediately sent men in pursuit of the departing canoe; three canoes followed the fugitive and his accomplices. At Hope, the posse was informed that Wall had left the canoe a short time before and had taken the river trail for Old Langley. One of the pursuing canoes proceeded five miles further down the river and encamped for the night, and before the morning Wall made his appearance at the camp. He was fired upon and fled to the woods where all trace was lost. The white man who was in the canoe with Wall was arrested the same evening, half a mile back of Hope, a young man, an American, aged about twenty-four years, who denied knowing the object of Wall's visit to Yale.

On the Monday following, Wall was seen at Old Langley and was arrested on the next day by a posse of police from New Westminster, on the trail between Langley and Semiahmoo, while making his way towards American territory. He surrendered at once. He was taken to New Westminster and lodged in jail.

With Sheriff Commeline's permission, on July 8, I attended the coroner's inquest into Dr. Fifer's death. Dr. Bradshaw, who was first to testify, took the stand and was sworn in, stating his full name and occupation: "Dr. John Armstrong Bradshaw. I am a physician and surgeon, practising at Fort Hope."

The presiding coroner questioned him: "Did you identify the body before you examined it?"

Dr. Bradshaw replied: "Sir, I recognized the unfortunate deceased as my colleague. A few months ago, when the steamer Yale exploded near Hope, and one Thomas King, a deck hand from Hope, was blown into the water, losing his leg below the knee, I was ably assisted by the late Dr. Fifer when I requird help with the amputation." (Dr. Bradshaw omitted any mention of the animus between Yale and

Hope; he chose not to mention that Dr. Fifer's arrival had not been particularly welcome.)

"What were your findings at the autopsy of Doctor Fifer?"

Dr. Bradshaw reported: "I was assisted by Mr. George Dietz of Yale. We found that a single bullet, a .48 calibre, fired at close range, had entered the left chest cavity between the fourth and fifth ribs. The skin surrounding the wound was darkened by a black powder tattoo, a sign that the shot was fired at close range, probably from less than twelve inches away. Around the entry wound we found a ring-like bruise." ·

The coroner asked for an explanation, and Dr. Bradshaw complied: "When a bullet enters, it stretches and scrapes the skin and leaves a bruise around the hole. The abrasion, in this case, was circular, evidence of a straight, frontal shot. If the bullet had struck at an angle, the bruise would be elliptical. The bullet continued its course into the left ventricle of the heart and caused mediastinal haemorrhage and death from *cardiac tamponade* due to *haemopericardium*."

The coroner reacted immediately: "Not so fast, Doctor, the jury cannot understand what you're saying. Please explain your statement or put it in layman's terms."

Dr. Bradshaw elaborated: "The human heart is a remarkable organ. Despite the bullet hole in its wall, it can continue to pump. But it is fighting a losing battle. With each heartbeat, a portion of the circulating blood leaks into the pericardium, the wrapper around the heart. Stroke by stroke, the outside pressure increases until the heart is choked off. Furthermore, the blood in the pericardium is lost to the circulation, and the victim will ultimately die from the internal haemorrhage."

The coroner probed further: "Will you tell the court, Doctor, if such an injury is always fatal, or is there medical help? Could anyone have saved this man's life?"

Dr. Bradshaw replied: "Some of these victims can be helped if they get to a doctor on time, before the pressure chokes the heart. In France, a country of much duelling, a Doctor Dupuytren has reported successful treatment of pistol shot injuries to the heart by *pericardiocentesis*, that is, making one or several stabs through the chest wall into the pericardium and draining the blood." Anticipating the next question, the doctor was quick to add: "At the time of this shooting, Your Honour, I was in my office at Fort Hope, five hours away by canoe. The victim lived for only a few minutes."

The coroner's jury rendered a verdict of "wilful murder".

Reverend Crickmer brought me this clipping—the obituary for Dr. Fifer from the *Victoria Colonist*. It states that he was a native of Germany, a widower, aged about 40 years, leaving a child in San Francisco to mourn his loss. That he was a long-time resident of San Francisco, where he practiced medicine, although it was charged that he was not a regularly educated physician. He had resided at Yale since early 1858 and was much beloved by his friends. On several occasions, the paper pointed out, it was asserted that the deceased mal-treated patients who came under his care, and about a year ago a violent assault was made upon him by a woman at Yale, who alleged that he had mal-treated her child.

Ignorant scandal-mongers they are, never checking their facts, I thought, but I thanked the reverend politely. It is three years since Little Sara Allard died. Who does not know that many bereaved people strike out in anger, at the first person they can think of to blame for their loss? Dr. Fifer was right to threaten a libel suit and demand a retraction when, last year, Thomas Yorke instigated a rumour that the doctor had participated in a duel with a Mr. McSerley on Hill's Bar. Everyone knows Yorke's politics. And who does not know that many physicians and surgeons become doctors through an apprenticeship, especially in California which has retained the Mexican tradition?

The paper's innuendo, hinting that apprenticeship training is inadequate and results in mistreatment of patients, appeared to add credibility to Wall's story. In a statement made to the officers by whom he was taken into custody, the accused said his reason for killing Dr. Fifer was that the doctor had mal-treated him two years ago, causing his condition to worsen. Wall admitted that he had often said that he would some day kill Dr. Fifer.

Some attempted to defend the prisoner Wall by claiming that he was rendered insane by the maltreatment he had sustained at the hands of the deceased, and that this malpractice was a mitigating factor in his crime. However, every published account countered the "insanity plea" by highlighting how much "method in his madness" Wall's actions exhibited. Testimony at the coroner's investigation proved: that Wall had hung about Yale, hovering for two hours, before killing Dr. Fifer; that the large number of patients and friends of the deceased in and around the doctor's drug store had deterred Wall from committing the deed in the presence of witnesses; that Wall's canoe ready manned and waiting at the beach all the time was evidence of pre-meditation and a well-executed escape plan. Wall had confronted his victim, handing Dr. Fifer a newspaper to read, and, while his victim was in the act of reading, coolly shot him down. The Crown stressed that the well-thought-out plan and subsequent flight of the murderer demonstrated the utter absurdity of the claim that Wall was insane.

The Victoria *Colonist* commented: "If this man Wall is allowed, through the influence of false sympathy, to escape a well-merited punishment, no physician who practises in the two colonies will in future be worth a straw. The murder appears to us to have been one of the most deliberately planned and coolly executed tragedies that it has ever become our painful duty to record".

Sheriff Commeline himself gave me this paper: SUBPOENA. "It says that you, Ah Chung, will be required to testify as a witness in court. Come to the courthouse first thing in the morning." As requested, I had permission to attend the trial in the Yale Courthouse for the murder of Dr. Fifer. Judge Matthew Baillie Begbie was presiding, Mr.

Allard was chairman of the jury.

The day was August 2, 1861, the fourth Friday after the day the doctor died,

Judge Begbie, a giant of a man, strode into the courtroom, dressed in a fancy fur-trimmed robe with a white wig on his head. Once he was seated, Sheriff John Evans called out: "In the name of Her Majesty Our Queen, to aid in the discovery and prosecution of crime, Court is now declared open."

Judge Begbie asked that the indictments be read aloud before he asked the four men how they pleaded. The accused, Robert Wall, for murder, McHagan for accessory before and after the murder, Sha-en-Khmethen Uslick for accessory after the fact, and Indian Jim for accessory after the fact, all pleaded Not Guilty. The judge acknowledged that the witnesses were present; then he called for them to come forward, be sworn in, and give evidence.

Mr. John Davis: "I remember the fifth of July. I was at Dr. Fifer's store in the evening, it was, I think, about 7 p.m. Dr. Fifer and his Chinaman, his boy servant, were there. The doctor was in his usual state of health."

"Did you see the prisoner, Robert Wall, that evening?" the judge asked.

"Yes, Your Honour. The prisoner Wall entered and walked towards the inner room. He asked if the doctor was in. The boy said, 'Here is Doctor Fifer'; the doctor was just at the entrance to the inner room when the boy said it. I also pointed out the doctor as the prisoner moved to the door; I thought the prisoner was about to consult the doctor."

"What made you think that, Mr. Davis?"

"The prisoner had his hand in the breast of his coat. I thought it was perhaps cut; I went out the faster, returning to the bench. I stood for an instant on the threshold. As soon as I reached it, I heard the word 'Fifer!' mentioned, and repeated by the boy. Immediately afterwards, I heard a shot. It was not very loud; I thought it might have been a firecracker. I did not turn round at first, but immediately afterwards I heard the cry of Dr. Fifer, and of the Chinaman. It was a wild cry-out."

"What did you do, Mr. Davis?"

"I turned around towards the second room when the prisoner twisted behind my back at the moment I turned, and skipped out into the street. When I reached the inner room, the deceased was leaning against the wall. I gave the alarm, running, shouting 'Murder! Murder! Dr. Fifer is shot!' with all my might.

"The prisoner ran very fast to the canoe which was waiting for him, Your Honour. I saw him; he stumbled in very quick and they took off immediately. I was very near when he reached the canoe, ten or twenty feet off. I cried 'Murder!'; I never stopped until the canoe was out of sight. 'Dr. Fifer is shot; this man has shot Dr. Fifer!' I saw the prisoner McHagan in the canoe and called out to him to stop. McHagan looked at me in such a way as to cause me to draw back. The prisoner McHagan and the two Indians were waiting, ready to set to work immediately. They went off instantly as far as they could go; they were all four at work paddling. I saw no pistol in Wall's hands. If he had pointed the pistol at anybody, I must have seen it, but they were all at work with their paddles."

"So, you are saying, Mr. Davis, that no one was being coerced to assist with Mr. Wall's flight?"

"That is correct, Your Honour. The bow of the canoe was turned down the stream. I can swear to McHagan. His face was at first turned away but he turned fully around when I kept on calling out; he looked so fiercely that I did not advance further. The prisoner Wall was too quick for me; I never reached him."

"You say you recognized Mr. McHagan as being one of the men waiting in the canoe? Do you recognize either of the other two defendants, Mr. Davis?"

"No, Your Honour. I cannot say that I recognize either of the Indians. I just know they were Indians."

"Once the canoe had departed, what did you do next, Mr. Davis?"

"I returned to the shop in two or three minutes, perhaps four. Dr. Fifer was quite dead, at least he appeared to be so; he did not speak."

Benjamin Bailey was called to testify. "I remember the fifth of July. I was standing in my house when I heard a shot. It had a dull sound. I said 'that is a murderous-sounding shot,' having heard such in California. I looked out and at first saw nothing, but presently saw a man run across the street at the same time I heard the shot. I heard Davis and Ah Chung shouting. I started in pursuit assuming that the doctor had been shot at; I was only five or six feet behind the man when he jumped down the perpendicular bank. I did not see his face and could not swear to him. I stood at the edge of the bank and saw the man making for the canoe some twenty-five feet off, perhaps a little further. There were two Indians and a white man; I cannot swear to the Indians."

"But you recognize one of the white men?" Judge Begbie asked.

"The prisoner McHagan is the other man. I can swear to him. I did not call out in English. I called to the Indians not to go. I said 'Halo clatawa ict bosston mamaloose, halo, halo.' I saw that Davis went close down and then backed off from them a little. I have seen such rows elsewhere, and I know it is not safe to venture too far if one is unarmed. I heard Davis call 'Murder!' very loud. Everybody must have heard."

John Evans testified: "I know the prisoner McHagan. He was at Fort Hope on the Fourth of July. I was there also; he said he was going to Yale. The next time I saw him was on the sixth of July. He said nothing at first, as to where he had been. He came towards me out of the woods, about one half mile below Hope. He asked me what was going on there. I said there was a great excitement about the murder of Dr. Fifer. He then asked if they were out on the hunt. I think he then asked me what he had best do now; no, I'm wrong;

he thought he had best go and work on the roads, and perhaps it might blow over. I said he had best give himself up now, for after what he had said, he might get me into a mess. He said he hated to do it. He went, however. I showed him the courthouse of Mr. O'Reilly, and I was present when he gave himself up. Some time before this I had asked him where the other man was. He said he did not know; he had not seen him since two shots were fired the previous night."

This witness then spoke directly to the accused, Mr. McHagan: "I saw you on the morning of the sixth of July. You said you wished to give yourself up and asked me to show you the way. You said you believed you had got yourself into trouble about going up to Yale the day before. You said you had only got $3 for the job. I don't recollect your stating that you had no previous knowledge of Wall's intention."

Edward Coffey was called to testify and sworn: "I am constable here. The two Indian prisoners have been in my custody on this charge. I received them from Mr. O'Reilly at Fort Hope. They told me that they were in the canoe which brought Wall to Fort Yale."

George Dietz was called and sworn: "I knew the late Dr. Fifer. I saw his body after death. I was present and assisted at the post-mortem examination. His death was caused by a musket gunshot wound in the left breast. The bullet went through the left lung, the heart, and into the stomach."

Then it was my turn. I was called to the witness' chair. "State your name and occupation," Judge Begbie ordered.

"I am Ah Chung, manservant; Dr. Fifer was my employer."

"Tell us what you witnessed, Ah Chung."

"On the evening Dr. Fifer was shot, I saw the prisoner Wall come in with a paper. He said 'I have something here for the doctor.' I stayed outside the door and heard something crack. I ran in and said 'Who fired a cracker?' I saw the doctor holding up his hands; then he backed into a corner and sank down against the wall. I then ran outside and screamed." But repeating to a room full of white men the details of the worst day of my life, I got confused. All I could see was the doctor, in the corner, on the floor, his spectacles down his nose. The judge continued to speak to me but I could not follow his questions. Finally, Judge Begbie said, "Step down, Ah Chung." I left the room, so as not to disturb the proceedings. So what happened after I testified, I heard later from Mr. Allard.

Ovid Allard: "When I was called on for his defence, the prisoner Wall said that Dr. Crane had told him that Dr. Fifer had poisoned him and that he would never be well again. 'I went from one place to another with everyone looking at me in contempt. Finally, I shot the man,' he said. He sounded mentally deranged, although he did not say in court that he heard the voice of God telling him to do it. He fired a single shot from a derringer pistol which killed Dr. Fifer.

"The prisoner McHagan put in a long written statement: he was born in Ireland; he joined the U.S. Army; he deserted to British Columbia; he had known the prisoner Wall previously, but only slightly; he knew Uslick, Sha-en-Khmethen Uslick, well; he met Wall again recently; he vehemently asserted that he had no previous knowledge of Wall's intention nor, indeed, any clear knowledge of what had taken place.

"Both Indians alleged complete ignorance, saying that they only acted in compliance with orders from their employers, the White men who had hired them to paddle to Yale. They thought the great hurry of the departure was due to the need to be on time to catch the steamboat on its return trip. They had left it at Emory's Bar that morning; it had not come further owing to the high water.

"In his charge to the jury, Judge Begbie explained the insanity defence, that we could only find Wall 'Not Guilty by Reason of Insanity' if we were convinced that he could not distinguish right from wrong. If he knew what he planned to do was wrong, he is Guilty. The judge left it up to us to decide whether we believed the prisoner McHagan had or had not any previous knowledge of Wall's intention. If he knew, we should convict him as a principal to the murder; if he did not know until after it happened, we should convict him as an accessory after the fact. If he knew nothing, we should acquit him. The same would apply to the Indians. The judge concluded his charge to the jury by saying, 'In case of doubt, lean on mercy.'"

It did not take the jury long, Mr. Allard told me. They returned after a short deliberation. As foreman, he announced: "We the jury find the accused, Robert Wall, guilty of murdering Doctor Fifer. For the prisoner Mac McHagan, on the charge of Murder, Not Guilty; on the charge of accomplice to murder, Not Guilty; on the charge of accomplice after the fact, Guilty. For the prisoner Uslick, on the charge of accessory after the fact, we find Guilty. For the prisoner Indian Jim, on the charge of accessory after the fact, we find him Guilty."

Then, it was Judge Begbie's bitter task to mete out the appropriate penalty. Although Dr. Fifer was American, Judge Begbie knew how much the community respected him, not only for his work as a physician, but as mayor of their town, for his selfless devotion to the needs of the people. The judge recognized the anger of the townspeople at having their doctor taken from them. He also recognized their underlying fear, that this murder somehow represented the triumph of evil, a finger in the face of British justice, because Wall had often said he was going to kill Dr. Fifer but the law could not prevent it.

Judge Begbie sentenced the Indian paddlers first, giving them both one year of penal servitude. To McHagan, he awarded seven years penal servitude. Then he reached into a satchel beside his booted feet on the floor, positioned a black cap over top of his wig, and intoned: "Robert Wall, for the murder of Doctor Max Fifer of Yale, in the Colony of British Columbia, I sentence you to be hanged by the neck until dead. Furthermore, the sentence of hanging shall be carried out in full view of the public, at the location designated by me—namely, over the grave of the victim, Doctor Fifer. May God have mercy on your soul."

13

KNOCK. KNOCK. KNOCK.

Not again! Do they not have better things to do on this black day than bother me again?

Knock. Knock. Knock.

It sounds too gentle for Mr. Tennent. I wait. I listen. I do not wish to see anyone.

Knock. Knock. "Ah Chung?"

It is Reverend Crickmer's voice. I cannot be discourteous. I slide the bolt open. "Reverend Crickmer!" He is standing there, alone, his shoulders drooping, prayer book in his hand still kept open with one finger between the pages, his face grey, telling of his last duty that is now completed. "Come in, come in, sir!" I motion to him. "I make tea."

The reverend removes his hat, follows me past the empty pantry shelves, and sags on to the bench in the kitchen, his chin resting on his chest.

I still have a small fire in which riffles of dry newspaper are slumping into ash. This kettle, along with the teapot, will come with me on the steamer, to prepare my own meals on the journey. Everything else is packed and waiting.

"You were right, Ah Chung. You were so right not to attend. It was ghastly, putting a young life to death."

"I am glad I told you last night, Reverend Crickmer, that I did not intend to go. I did not want to see another man die before my eyes." To watch his neck stretch, his body jerk and dance above my master's grave.

"Max would have been appalled, Ah Chung. He would have been horrified at what went on today."

"Yes. That too is why I did not wish to go." Dr. Fifer would have been dismayed. At such a display, at such a symbolic act, an act which stood for everything he was trying to forget, to escape. For everything for which he was trying to make amends, to find alternative punishments for men who harm, who kill their fellow man.

"I'm sure that Judge Begbie meant well in selecting the location," Reverend Crickmer continues, "and I'm sure he felt the need for a very public declaration that murder will not be condoned. But homicide is never pretty, whether there appears to be a justification or not, whether it is authorized by law or not."

It's just ice. Absurdly, I can only think of one of the reverend's oft-repeated jokes. Question: How is a hanging like a winter-frozen pond? Answer. Both are just ice. Just ice.

"Did you hear from Governor Douglas?" I ask, remembering that the reverend had been awaiting a reply to his objection to hanging a mad man, to his request for mercy, for commutation.

"Ay, Ah Chung. I did. The execution was set for eight o'clock this morning. I had a sleepless night, awake at the slightest noise, hoping to hear the steamer's whistle. Finally I dressed and went to see the magistrate who was also up early, talking to eight men in his office on the occasion of the day. Maybe you did not hear—Martin Gallagher from New York Bar is reported to have said that, although McGowan has left Hill's Bar, Wall does have friends who might raise a posse and spring him. As a result, the execution had to be carried out under heavy guard, with elaborate security preparations being taken against an attempt to free the prisoner."

"I interrupted the magistrate's swearing-in ceremony: 'Allow me. Captain, to speak in confidence; my visit concerns the execution. I have sent an appeal to the Governor to spare Wall's life and I expect a reply to arrive by this morning's boat. Would you use your good offices to postpone the execution by one hour, to nine o'clock, so as to give a chance for a reply?'

He listened to my plea and replied: 'Of course, Reverend. It is my duty to see that justice is carried out; we would not want to learn of a death sentence commuted to life after the horse is out of the barn and the man suspended by his neck!' He called to his clerk: 'Mr Tennent, see to it immediately that the execution is put off until nine o'clock!' and resumed the swearing-in of extra constables.

"At about eight thirty, we heard the echo of the steamer as the sound of its whistle bounced off the quiet mountains. I rushed to the landing. The first thing I saw was the ominous large brown package from the Governor in Victoria, bearing the great red seal and the Royal Arms. How intense life can be at certain points, Ah Chung. I opened the official letter and read what Governor Douglas' secretary had written: 'His Excellency the Governor acknowledges the receipt of your letter and has asked me to convey my thanks to you for your benevolent attention to the convict, R. Wall. The circumstances of the case are not such as would justify His Excellency to extend royal clemency.'

"Then, by separate mail, Ah Chung, I received a personal letter; my very kind hearted old friend Governor Douglas replied in the feeling and Christian way in which I knew he would. He agreed with me that Dr. Fifer's murderer was not fully responsible morally; however, he proceeded to say that the act had been so brazenly public and daringly lawless, perpetrated on a prominent American in the presence of Americans and other foreigners, that he dare not take upon himself the responsibility of staying the execution. In the present atmosphere of instability in the gold fields, he had to set an example to others. There had to be a solemn judicial warning.

"This was the final decision, Wall's fate was sealed; he was doomed."

I signalled Magistrate Sanders by shaking my head at him, to proceed with the original preparation. I walked home quickly to share the distressing news with Mrs. Crickmer who, like yourself, has chosen not to attend. Then, I went back to the jail to perform my duties.

"How appalling it is to look at the countenance of one in the prime of his life, perfectly hale and well, who is face to face with an absolutely inevitable, ignominious and violent death. As the prisoner Wall did not know of my letter, I said nothing to him about the reply. He offered me, half-smoked, his short cutty pipe, carved with a shamrock and harp, which I accepted from him as the smithy came to strike off his irons. Wall complained of a very dry throat and begged for something with which to lubricate it. There was nothing at hand, so we waited while he hastily ate some cold soup. Then he went quiet, seeming to reconcile himself to die.

"I walked by his side, across the flat, about a quarter of a mile, where you and I walked together last night, Ah Chung. Picking our way around boulders and through barren stumps of fir and pine, we approached the cemetery and the gallows over the grave. Little did the condemned man seem to care that the derrick was directly above a fresh grave mound and, as the verdict stipulated, above the doctor's resting place, on the river's edge, beneath a pretty hill."

"A beautiful and peaceful spot," I agree. Reverend Crickmer goes on as if I am not here.

"I attempted words of comfort and strength as we strode along toward that terribly visible trysting place. I know many of the authorities had not believed Wall's repentance and suspected he was 'gulling the parson,' yet what worldly good did that do him? Soon all were convinced that no rescue was planned, and that there was a genuine reason for the murderer keeping so close to me, both in life and at the time of his death.

"On our way up the platform, the constables left us, staying behind as we mounted the steps. The magistrate and attendants too remained at a distance of some forty feet. Wall sat on a block and was pinioned by the wizened little old man we met in that very place last night. Today, this man had covered his face, and his gestures and the grotesque dress he wore by way of remaining anonymous were weird and revolting, like something one reads about in a Sir Walter Scott romance. I was not surprised that Wall shuddered when this apparition touched him at such a time and for such a purpose. My own voice faltered when I read God's word and the words of comfort in the Book of Common Prayer.

"I knelt down and prayed with Wall. Side by side on the drop, we prayed for all those present. I offered him one final opportunity to speak a word to God, but he made no sign. He stood so silent that I feared it was as it had been at his trial in court—that he was in shock from over-excitement. Then, all of a sudden, he seemed strangely sobered and wonderfully strengthened. He advanced in a slow shuffle to the front of the platform and began to speak so calmly that the crowd at first scarcely realized that so ferocious a murderer could be the person who was uttering such calm, warning words.

"Better than any mere hysterical rhapsody, better than any sensational pietistic religious sentiment, the drift of Wall's concise address, from such a preacher, from such a pulpit, is a sermon not likely to be forgotten. 'Gentlemen,' he said, 'Gentlemen, I now can feel, and do acknowledge, that my sentence is just; and God has been merciful to me. I cannot comment on the treatment that Doctor Fifer used towards me. The medicine he gave me at times entirely ruined my brain. I gave my victim no time to repent; but God has been more merciful to me for He has given me space for repentance. Oh, Gentlemen, if I only had read my Bible, I should not be standing here before you now, in this ignominious and awful situation. I have no more to say, Good bye.'

"Then he shuffled back to where he had been standing, pinioned on the drop, beside the hangman who was holding the rope in one hand and the white hood in the other. The death tree formed the frame of the picture. To hear a man speak thus visibly moved some of the thick-skinned four hundred present. My own thoughts were in turmoil. In the 'day of visitation', I speculated, that homily will have had its own value, as a preparative dispensation. Then I bid my brother a bitter, affectionate farewell.

"Wall had concluded his address; the hangman took the rope and slipped the noose over; Wall offered his head, bending it. He swallowed frequently; I watched his Adam's apple moving and his chest heaving. He moved his neck around, as one would with a collar too tight. I thought of a chicken's gizzard, Ah Chung, how my mind wished to escape this reality. Then the executioner pulled the fatal bag of oiled silk over his face and adjusted the hemp collar.

"Suddenly, the boards on which Wall stood gave way. The fall downward was stopped by a jerk, with an acute snapping sound at the neck."

Reverend Crickmer continues, as if he has to speak the words to expel the vision from his head. "There was a concussion, as though the whole structure was coming down in a dreadful shudder. Wall writhed and struggled for some minutes, in a horrible *danse macabre*, appearing as if his neck were not broken, but then the body became quiet. The hangman got me off the drop. I rushed to the back of the scaffold and threw myself down in prayer. Suspended between heaven and earth, Robert Wall, the man I have counselled for weeks, is now a dull, distorted mass, his hooded head facing the day's grey sun.

"In the hour between ten and eleven o'clock this morning, Robert Wall joined our Saviour in paradise.

"I waited there, as did many of the crowd. The body was left hanging for half an hour before being cut down and its skeleton manipulated into the pine coffin which had been waiting for it, and buried by the authorities in a grave that had already been dug, a little ways off, so as not to be a final insult to the doctor. As I was repeating hasty prayers over the new grave, I saw a canoe leaving, taking the hangman to Hope."

Reverend Crickmer sits quietly, his story finished, his need to talk sated. Question: What bone is funnier than the funny bone? Answer: The humerus. My own brain too is crowded, and wishes to escape this place. My tree has fallen, and this monkey must scatter.

The tea has steeped and the cups are waiting. I lift the pot to pour.

Knock. Knock. Knock.

I nod to excuse myself, leave my guest, and approach the door gingerly, still expecting the worst with every new arrival.

As the latch lifts and the hinges creak open, I see Indian Charlie. He nods and almost smiles as he hands me a small woven basket filled with tiny packets, large golden leaves, folded, and tied with strips of reed. Emanating from the basket I can smell the wood-fire aroma of salmon, dried on their racks by the river, and smoked in the smokehouses in their village. Wrapped, packed to carry on a journey.

Food for my passage.

"Um goy," I say, forgetting myself. "Um goy. Thank you." I am not ashamed to let him see the tears on my face.

EPILOGUE

Max William Fifer, newly arrived in New York from Germany in 1846, volunteer in the American army during the Mexican War, trained as a hospital steward in California. When he demobilized, he took with him a military-issue apothecary's mortar and pestle which he used for ten years in his medical practice in San Francisco. Fifer brought the mortar with him to Yale, British Columbia, in 1858, and, after his need for it diminished, passed it on to his assistant, Ah Chung.

After Fifer's murder in Yale in 1861, Ah Chung took the mortar back with him to San Francisco and used it in his own natural medicine and drug store in Chinatown. Twenty-five years later, he was visited by a Canadian policeman inquiring about a burned human skull found in the ruins of Dr. Fifer's old building. The inquiry triggered in Ah Chung a desire to return to pay his respects to his deceased mentor.

In 1886, Ah Chung travelled back to Yale by boat and train. He carried the mortar with him, perhaps as part of a plan to honour Dr. Fifer in his final resting place. Sadly, Ah Chung could find no remnants of his former·life in Yale—the house had burned down, no faces were recognizable, and the doctor's grave had been obliterated by the Canadian Pacific Railway tracks. Ah Chung abandoned his pilgrimage and turned to go back to San Francisco.

In conversation at the closest international border crossing at Huntingdon on Sumas Prairie, Ah Chung discovered a mutual connection. Customs Officer Thomas Fraser Yorke identified himself as the first immigrant child born in the Colony of British Columbia. He had been born in Yale, on October 21, 1858, and Dr. Fifer had attended his birth. Ah Chung presented the mortar to Yorke, explaining its provenance—that they had used it in the drug store, in the doctor's office, and in the kitchen; that he had carried it with him, secreting precious grave dirt, when he left Yale; and that he had returned, hoping to burn an offering of food for Dr. Fifer, but because the grave had been desecrated, he was unable to do so.

In 1945, Thomas Yorke's widow donated the mortar to the Vancouver Museum and Archives where it remains in storage.

(Another relic, Royal Engineers' pick axe #791, abandoned by Sapper Colston after his injury in September of 1860, was recovered recently and is kept in the Yale Museum.)